Malai'ka

Angels in Islam

Stephen J. Vicchio, Ph.D.

Wisdom
Editions
Minneapolis, Minnesota

Minneapolis
FIRST EDITION APRIL 2020
Malai'ka: Angels in Islam

Printed in the United States of America.
10 9 8 7 6 5 4 3 2 1

Cover and interior design: Gary Lindberg

ISBN: 978-1-950743-22-3

For Grace Alsawi

Contents

Malai'ka

Angels in Islam

Stephen J. Vicchio, Ph.D.

Introduction

For each person there are angels in succession, before and behind him. They guard him by the commands of Allah. Verily, Allah will not change the good conditions of a people as long as they do not change their state of goodness themselves (by committing sins and being ungrateful and disobedient to Allah.) But when Allah wills a people's punishment, there can be no turning back of it, and they will find besides it no protector.

—The Holy Qur'an, 13:11

The Prophet said, "When Allah ordains something in Heaven, the angels beat their wings in obedience to His statement which sounds like that of a chain being dragged across a rock." His statement, "Until when the fear is banished from their hearts, the angels say, 'What was it that your Lord said?' And the reply, 'He has said the Truth. And He is the most high, the greatest.'"

—Sahih Bukhari, *Hadith* (Volume three, no. 573)

You will see the angels circling around the Throne, glorifying their Lord in praise. It will be decided between them with Truth. And it will be said, "Praise be to Allah, the Lord of all Worlds."

—The Holy Qur'an, 39:75

The work that follows is a study of the many views of the Mala'ika, or "angels," in the Islamic faith. This study consists of ten chapters, all of which explore some particular aspect of the angels in Islam. The major goal of the first chapter is to present a comprehensive introduction to the understanding of the Mala'ika.

After exploring some etymological roots and cognates of the word, we will enumerate and discuss the major places in Al-Qur'an, and in traditional Hadith literature, where angels are found to be prominent.

From this material, we shall arrive at several conclusions about the nature and functions of angels in Islam, including that Allah created the angels before human beings; that the angels were made from light, as opposed to the clay from which humans were made; and that there are several different kinds of angels in the Islamic faith, including guardian angels, recording angels, archangel, and angels assigned by Allah to more specific tasks.

We also explore in Chapter One a figure known as the *Ruh-al-Qudus*, or "Holy Spirit," which sometimes is seen as a synonym for the angel Jibril, or Gabriel, and by some seen as a figure quite like the Holy Spirit in the New Testament. Finally, we will show in the first chapter that belief in angels is among the six principal "Articles of Faith" in the Islamic religion, or *Diyana* in Arabic.

In Chapter Two, we explore the central role of the most important *Malak*, or angel, the singular form, in the Islamic faith—that is, the angel Jibril. He has this lofty status in Islam because he is the messenger who was chosen by Allah to bring the revelation of Al-Qur'an to the Prophet Muhammad in a series of revelations that lasted twenty-three years. Although Jibril is only mentioned by name two times in the Holy Book, he nevertheless shows up in a variety of other names, including the *Ruh al-Qudus*, the *Ruh al-Amin*, and the *Rasul Karim*. We also introduce in Chapter Two and explore more fully in Chapter Seven, the role of Jibril in the history of Islamic art.

The principal aim of Chapter Three is to explore the other archangels in Islam in addition to Jibril. These include: *Mika'il* (Michael), *Israfil* (Raphael) and *Azrael*, or the Angel of Death. After exploring the places in the Qur'an and in traditional Hadith literature where these angels appear, we then go on to explore other prominent angels in the Muslim faith. Among these are: Ridwan, the Keeper of Paradise; Malik, the Keeper of Hell; and the *Qariyyabim* (Cherubim), the Keepers of the Throne of Allah.

The chief goal of Chapter Four is to present a variety of *Mala'ika* who, in one way or another, are associated with death in the Islamic faith. In addition to Azrael, the Angel of Death, we will also explore the angel Malik who rules Hell; Ridwan, or Rizwan, the angel responsible for Paradise; and Munqar and Naqir, a pair of angels who interrogate the dead in their graves. Chapter Four, then, is about Muslim eschatology.

The main aim of Chapter Five is to explore and discuss the nature and roles of a group of beings known as the *Houris* in the Islamic faith. Traditionally, they are seen as comely, buxom maidens who greet believers on entering Paradise. In Chapter Five, however, we reject this traditional view in favor of a more recent suggestion by German Philologist Christoph Luxenberg who says the Houris are "pieces of succulent fruit."[1] In Chapter Five, in addition to the roles that the Houris have played in Islam, we will also explore the roles that angels played in the earliest battles in the Islamic faith.

Above all, we will attempt to show in Chapter Five that the Houris are to be understood in a metaphorical way as representatives of good deeds in the Muslim faith. If a Muslim leads an exemplary life, then these good deeds ascend to Paradise and are transformed into the comely, buxom maidens who will greet believers of the Faith. We also will deal in Chapter Five with the claim that Martyrs in Islam are thought to be greeted by seventy-two of these Houris, or "Virgins," a common belief among some Muslims in contemporary life.

The roles of guardian and recording angels are discussed in Chapter Six. After exploring a number of passages in the Bible where recording and guardian angels are mentioned, we then enumerate the places in Al-Qur'an and Hadith literature where these celestial beings have some prominence in the Muslim faith. Following this, we then discuss the relative value of good deeds versus bad deeds in Islam, arguing that the former is far loftier and weightier in Islam than bad deeds. In fact, we also will show in Chapter Six that intentions play a central role in Islamic moral discourse.

In Chapter Seven, we will examine the development of Islamic art from the Abbasid Empire in the seventh and eighth centuries to the Persian and Turkish empires from the fourteenth to the nineteenth centuries. Along the way in Chapter Seven, we also will show that the *Mala'ika* have maintained a central place in Muslim art from its inception in the seventh century to the present.

More specifically, in Chapter Seven we examine the many ways angels have been depicted in Islamic art, particularly in relation to the birth of the Prophet Muhammad; the bringing of Al-Qu'an by the angel Jibril to Muhammad, the Night Journey; and the role of angels in the earliest of Islamic battles. We also will pay considerable attention in Chapter Seven to the depictions of the *Mala'ika* in particular classical texts in Islam. Among these are Rashid al-Din's *Jami'al-Tawarikh*, and the fourteenth-century Turkish *Siyer-i-Nebi*.[2]

Our main goal in Chapter Eight of this study is to explore the nature and roles of another category of celestial beings in the Islamic faith—entities called the *Jinn* (singular, *Jinni*). There, as we shall see, we show that the Jinn possess free will, make moral decisions, and are capable of Salvation and Damnation. We will also explore in Chapter Eight the relationship King Sulayman (Solomon) is said to have had with the Jinn, including recruiting them to help in the construction of the temple in Jerusalem, as well as other building projects in ancient Israel.

In Chapter Eight, we also explore the roles that the Jinn play in relation to human beings. Indeed, the bad Jinn are thought constantly to be at work corrupting the morals of people, or the causing of injury to humans in various ways. In fact, in Chapter Eight, we introduce a range of stories and tales told about the Jinn in Islam, and how they are believed to trick people in various ways to turn toward Evil.

The subject of Chapter Nine is the ontological status of the Mala'ika in relation to the Jinn, to human beings, and to the Houris. We will compare and contrast these various classes of beings. Along the way, we specifically raise the question of what is the nature of the figure of *Iblis*, or *Shaytan*, the two most common words for the Demonic in Islam. Is Jibril a *Jinni*, or is he one of the *Mala'ika*? Although there have been various answers to these questions, we ultimately conclude, as many Muslim scholars do, that *Iblis* is to be understood as one of the *Jinn*, as well as the leader of the *Jinn*. We will concentrate on the figures of *Iblis, Shaytan,* and the *Shayatin*, in Al-Qur'an, in Hadith literature, as well as in the History of Islamic Philosophy.

Finally, in Chapter Ten, we will make some general observations about the major conclusions to which we have come to in this study of angels in Islam. The most important of these is that angels always have had a central role in the development and the history of the Islamic faith. Above all, the most important role of angels in the Muslim faith is to worship Allah and to follow His Will, no matter what. To worship Allah is to follow His commands, to know Him, to obey Him, and to enforce His laws in every aspect of the believer's life. In fact, as we shall see later in this study, angels do not have free will. Thus, it is impossible for them not to follow the will of Allah.

As the Holy Book of Islam, the Qur'an, tells us at Surah 16:49–50:

> Everything in the Heavens and every creature on the
> Earth prostrates to Allah, as do the angels. They are not
> puffed up with pride. They fear their Lord, above all,
> and they do everything they have been ordered to do.[3]

This notion that the *Mala'ika* only do what Allah has ordered them to do is the most fundamental conclusion that Muslims can make about the nature and functions of the angels in Islam. Since they do not possess free will, it is impossible in the Islamic faith for angels to disobey Allah. The primary functions of the angels in Islam, then, is to worship Allah and to do His will, no matter what.

We will now proceed to the first chapter of this study and the etymological roots of the Arabic terms *Malak* and *Mala'ika*. This will be followed by a kind of primer on the idea of angels in the Islamic faith—these beings who are made from light who existed before the creation of Jinn and humans, and who are the primary messengers that Allah sends to human beings.

Chapter One:
The Nature of Angels in the Islamic Faith

Angels serve as a link between God and human beings. Created out of Light, immortal and sexless, they function as guardians, recorders, and messengers from God. They are transmitters of God's message, communicating divine revelation to the prophets.

—John Esposito, *Islam: The Straight Path*

Angel:a divine figure that is able to cross the luminal zone between the sacred and the profane.

—Scott Noegel, *Historical Dictionary of Prophets in Islam and Judaism*

He sends the angels with revelation by His command to any and all of His creatures as He pleases, saying, "Warn that there is no God but I, so fear me."

—The Holy Qur'an, 16:2

Introduction to Angels in Islam

In the Islamic tradition, angels are unseen beings of a luminous and sacred substance that act as intermediaries between Allah and the world of sensible reality. The belief in the existence of angels has been one of the most central beliefs in the Islamic faith since its beginning in the 7th century.

The Arabic words for "angel" and "angels" are "*malak*" and "*mala'ika.*" These words have earlier Semitic cognates related to the Ugaritic and Hebrew root, MLK, from which we get the Arabic for "king" (*Malak*), as well as the Hebrew for "angel" and "angels" (*malak* and *malakim*). In Arabic, the singular *malak* is usually written without the Hamza. In the Islamic Holy Book, Al-Qur'an , the word appears in both the singular and the plural. It also appears twice as the dual form, or *malakayn*, at Surah 2:96 and 7:19. In those two instances, the word is employed to designates two angels, specifically *Jibril* and *Mika'il*.

The plural form, or the word *mala'ika,* occurs many times in the Qur'an, but the singular occurs only about a dozen times in the Holy Book. Altogether, the words "angel" and "angels" occur about ninety times in the Qur'an. Of these, it is in the plural form in over eighty cases. In addition, the Arabic word, *Rasul,* usually translated as "Messenger" is sometimes employed specifically to talk about angels. This is a practice that occurs throughout the Holy Book.

The word *Rasul*, and its plural form, *Rusul,* come from the Arabic verb *rasala*, which means "to send a message." These words are employed at the Holy Book's 2:213, 4:69 and 165, 3:144, 33:40, and 57:25, in addition to a variety of other passages in the Qur'an. In several places in the Holy Book, the Arabic *Malak*, when it is not rendered as "angel," is translated as "Messenger," and sometimes as "King," when the Arabic word *Malik* is employed.

The use of the Arabic words *malak* and *malik* have changed considerably over time in the history of the Islamic faith. Bernard Lewis discusses this development in his book, *Islam and the West*. He informs us:

> Any Arabic-English dictionary will tell us that *malik* equals king and king equals *malik*—almost like a mathematical equation. But the word *malik* in Arabic has been used at different times with many different meanings. In the Qur'an it appears as a divine epithet, and yet, at about the same time, it also appears as a term that describes a Tyrant, a bad Ruler, an autocratic

Ruler, and a non-religious Ruler. In the period of the early caliphate, it seems to have gone out of use for human monarchs, except as an occasional term of abuse. It was later revived by Iranian dynasties, the Samanids and Buyids, apparently as an Arabic cover for the Persian term, *Shah*, and was used as a sub-royal rather than a royal title...[4]

What was true of the word *Malik* in Arabic was also true for the words *malak* and *mala'ika*. Indeed, the meanings of these words have changed radically over time until they received their present meanings of "angel" and "angels." Belief in angels is one of the five principal "Articles of Faith" in the Muslim tradition. The Holy Book's 2:177 alludes to that fact when it tells us:

Piety does not lie in turning your face to East or West. Piety lies in a belief in Allah, the Last Day, and the angels, and the Scriptures, and the Prophets, and the disbursing of your wealth out of love for Allah, among your kin and the orphans, the wayfarers, and the mendicants, the freeing of your slaves, the observing of your devotional obligations, and in praying the *Zakat*, and fulfilling any pledge you may have been given; and being patient in hardship, adversity, and times of peril. These are the men who affirm the truth, and the ones who follow the straight path.[5]

The Arabic word *Zakat* literally means "that which is purified." It refers to an obligation that all believing Muslims contribute two and a half percent of their income to charity. The word *Zakat* is mentioned in the Holy Book at 7:156, 19:34 and 55, 23:4, 27:3, 30:39, 31:4, and Surah 41:7.

The same judgment about the importance of angels in the Muslim faith is also expressed at the Holy Book's 2:185. There the text relates:

Each one who believes in Allah, and His angels, His books, and the Prophets, and We make no distinction between the apostles, for they say, "We hear and obey,

and we seek your forgiveness, Oh Lord, for to You we
shall journey to the end.[6]

A Hadith from Sahih Muslim confirms this central role of the belief in angels in the Muslim faith. The ninth-century Persian collector of Hadith tells us:

You want to know about the meaning of faith? It is that you believe in Allah, His angels, His Books, His Messengers, and the Last Day, and that you believe in the Decree, both the good and the bad of it.[7]

Indeed, the belief in angels is so central to the Muslim faith that the Qur'an's 4:136 says:

Oh believers, believe in Allah and His Messengers, and the Books He has revealed to His apostles, and the books revealed before. But he who believes not in Allah and His angels and the Books of the Prophets, and the Last Day, has wandered too far away.[8]

In the Islamic tradition, only Allah knows the number of angels. The Qur'an 74:31 informs us, "and their number (angels) we have fixed."[9] The Holy Book also tells us that there are different ranks of angels, as well as divisions of the work that they do. Again, as the Qur'an 74:31 relates:

There is not among us, except those who have a known position; and we indeed are the ones who glorify Allah.[10]

In Islam, angels are said to have been created from Light (*Nur*), but not a light that is visible to humans. Another Hadith from Sahih Muslim says:

The angels are created from Light, just as the *Jinn* are created from smokeless fire, and mankind is created from what you have been told about (i.e., Clay).[11]

The same judgment was made by Baghdad-born collector of Hadith, Ahmed Ibn Hanbal (780–855), theologian, Jurist, and Martyr for his Faith, when he wrote:

Angels are created from light, the Jinn from fire
containing smoke, and Adam from that already told to
you (from black, white, and red sand.)[12]

In Islam, this explains how the human race became various colors.
Jabir Ibin Abdullah, one of the seventeenth-century Companions, or
Sahaba, of the Prophet Muhammad, gives us a more detailed Hadith
about Light and Creation. He informs us:

Almighty Allah created the *Nur* (Light) of your Prophets
before anything else. Then, when He decided to create
the World, He divided the Light into four portions.

From the first part, He created the Pen (*Qalam*) of Destiny. From
the second, the Divine Tablet (*Lawh-e-Mahfooz*). From the third, the
Divine Throne (*Arsh*). The fourth part was then divided into another
four (portions). From the first part, He

created the angels who are the bearers of the Divine
Throne, from the second, the Divine Chair, and from
the third, the remainder of the angels.[13]

In some traditions in Hadith literature, Allah Himself is referred
to in relationship with the Light, like this comment from Alama
Fassi, "The Almighty Allah is an incomprehensible Light. He is the
splendid glow of that Light, while the angels are the sparks that come
from that resplendent Light."[14] Abu Sheikh (955–1018), a prominent
Shiite, Persian scholar, also concludes that "angels are created from the
Nur (Light) of Allah.[15] The image of Light is used many times in the
Qur'an, where most often it is employed as a metaphor for Allah. That
the angels are made from Light, the first thing created by Allah, may
imply that the *Mala'ika* are the beings closest to Allah.

Surah five gives us one example of the use of Light in
the Holy Book. It tells us: To you has come Light and a
clear book of Allah. Through which Allah will lead those
who follow His pleasure to the path of peace, and Who
guides them out of darkness into the light by His will
and to the path that is straight.[16]

The Arabic word *Nur* is a cognate of the Hebrew *Aor*. The word *Nur*, and its derivatives, are employed forty-nine times in the Qur'an. In fact, one of the Holy Book's Surahs, Surah 24, is called *An-Nur*, or "The Light." It consists of sixty-four ayats, or verses, and it gets its name from Ayats 35 and 36. The word *Nur* is often contrasted with the Arabic word *Zulamat* or "Darkness."

Surah 24:35–36 also makes a connection between Allah and Light. Those verses inform us:

> Allah is the light of the Heavens and the Earth. The semblance of His Light is that of a niche in which is a lamp; the flame within the glass is a glittering star, as it were, lit with oil of a blessed tree, the olive; neither of the East nor the West, whose oil appears to light up even though fire does not touch it. Light upon Light, Allah gives it to those whom He wills. So does Allah advance precepts of wisdom for men, for Allah has knowledge of everything. The Light is lit in houses of worship, which Allah has allowed to be raised, and His name is remembered in them. His praises are sung morning and evening.[17]

The Light of Allah and its relationship to both believers and hypocrites is discussed at the Holy Book's 57:12–14:

> The day you see believers, men and women, with their light advancing ahead and to the right of them, they will be told, "There is good news for you this day of gardens flowing with rivers, and where you can live forever." This will be the great attainment.

> On the day of the hypocrites, men and women, will say to believers, "Wait for us that we may borrow a little light from your Light." And they will be told, "Go back and search for your light." And a wall shall be raised between them in which there will be a door. Within it will be benevolence and retribution throughout. They will call to them, "Were we not with You!" They

will answer, "Certainly." But then you let yourself be
tempted, and waited in expectation but were suspicious
and were deceived by vain desires until the Decree of
Allah came to pass, and the deceiver duped you in
respect to Allah.[18]

Frequently in the Holy Book, the image of *Nur*, or Light, is
employed as in this passage. Believers in Allah will bask in Allah's
Light, while the hypocrites will have little access to it.

The image of "Allah's Light" occurs over a dozen times in the
Qur'an. Most all of them refer to believers in a positive light in relation
to it and to the hypocrites in a negative fashion. Indeed, the hypocrites
usually are identified with the *zulamat*, or "darkness" in Islam. In fact,
the word *zulamat* is used a number of times in Al-Qur'an. At Surah 6:1
and 59, and 57:9 and 13, for examples. The hypocrites, at Surah 57:13,
ask of Allah to "borrow a little light of Your Light."[19] But they are not
given it. Rather, they are given *zulamat*.

It is not clear in the Islamic tradition when Allah created the
Mala'ika, but we know it must have been before Adam and Eve, for
the angels were asked to bow down before Adam, suggesting the angels
were around before the creation of people. The Holy Book's 2:30 tells us:

Behold, your Lord said to the angels, "I will create a
representative (Adam) on Earth.[20]

Tenth-century Arab interpreter, Imam Baihaqi, reports the
following speech that the angels were said to make after the creation
of Adam:

Oh Allah, You have created a being that eats and drinks,
cohabits, and travels. Make the world a place for their
dwelling, and let us be inhabitants of the Hereafter.[21]

The angels bowing down to Adam after the latter's creation
is discussed in a number of places in the Holy Book. The principal
reference comes at Surah 2:30–34. The text informs us:

Remember when you said to the angels, "I have placed
a trustee on the Earth, and They said, "Would you place

one there who would create disorder and shed blood, while we intone your litanies and sanction Your name?" And Allah said, "I know what you do not know." Then He gave Adam the knowledge of the nature and reality of all things, and then set before the angels and said, "Tell me the names of these if you are truthful." And they said, "Glory to You, oh Lord. Of this knowledge, we have none, except what You have given us, for You are All-Knowing and All Wise."[22]

Then He said to Adam, "Convey to them their names," and when he had told them, Allah said, "Did I not tell you that I know the unknown of the Heavens and the Earth, and I know what you disclose and what you hide. Remember when We ask the angels to bow down in homage to Adam, and they all bowed, except Iblis, who disdained and turned insolent and so became a disbeliever."[23]

This reference to knowing the names of the animals is something not granted earlier to the angels. Thus, humans have knowledge not possessed by the *Mala'ika*. This may well be the origin of the view that humans have a higher ontological status than do the angels.

This above passage, and others like it in the Holy Book, point out that an animosity sometimes exists between Shaytan, or Iblis, and human beings. The Qur'an suggests that the primary source of this animosity is that Shaytan is made from Fire, while humans are made from clay.[24] Thus, in Iblis' view, his ontological status is higher than that of Adam's.

In Islam, angels are very powerful creatures whose natural form includes wings, which are not necessarily like the wings of birds or flying animals like bats. The Holy Book's Surah 35:1 tells us:

Praise be to Allah, Who created out of nothing the Heavens and the Earth. Who made the angels messengers with wings, two, three, or four pairs, and adds to creation as He pleases. For Allah has power over all things.[25]

In Islam, angels do not have a gender, but they can, nevertheless, appear in the form of a man, as one *Malak* did at the time that Prophet Muhammad received his first revelation from the angel Jibril. Indeed, Muhammad thought the angel was a man. Throughout the Qur'an, individual angels appear to many of the Islamic Prophets in the form of men, including Ibrahim (Abraham), Maryam (Mary), Zechariah, Lut (Lot), Musa (Moses), and many other figures in the Old and New Testaments.

The Holy Book tells us that angels have two, three or four pair of wings (35:1), that they do not consume food (25:7 and 25:20), that there are angels that record the deeds of people on Earth (50:17–19), that sometimes angels protect people on Earth (86:4), that there are angels that accompany souls (*Nafs*) of the dead to Heaven and Hell (32:11 and 43:77), that on Judgement Day, Allah's throne (*Arsh*) will be carried by angels (60:17), there are angels that guard human beings (13:11 and 50:17–21), and that all that angels may do is perform the Will of Allah for them. In fact, angels are so obedient in the Islamic faith it is believed that the *Mala'ika* do not possess Free Will and cannot disobey.

A clear division of the labor of angels can be seen in Islam. Some are given the task of bearing the Throne of Allah (Qur'an 69:17).[26] A Hadith from ninth-century collector of Ahadith, Abu Daud, speaks of the majestic *mala'ika* carrying the Throne of Allah. He informs us:

> I have been given permission to speak about one of the angels of Allah who is carrying the Throne. The distance between his earlobes and his shoulders is equivalent to a seven hundred year journey.[27]

There are angels in charge of Revelation, natural places and events, the weather, the pure worship of Allah, and anything else that the Omnipotent One Wills. Another angel is responsible for blowing the trumpet, or *Sur*, that will usher in the Last Days. His name is *Israfil* (Raphael). More will be said about this *Malak* later in this study. The Islamic faith also posits a belief in guardian angels that also record the good and bad deeds of human beings. The Holy Book's 82:10–11 speaks of these particular *Mala'ika*:

Surely, there are Guardians over you, illustrious Scribes, who know all that you do.[28]

Islam believes in one angel that is responsible for bringing death to human beings, as well as others whose job is seeing that souls arrive in Heaven or Hell. A Hadith from Abu Al-Bukhari suggests that there are angels entrusted with the development of fetuses in the womb. He observes:

> The way that each of you is created is that you are gathered in your mother's womb for forty days as a sperm drop and then for a similar length of time as a lump of flesh. Then an angel is sent, and he breathes the spirit into you and is charged with four commands: to write down your provision, your life-span, your actions, and whether you will be happy or wretched.[29]

Another Hadith from Abu Bukhari makes the same point. He relates:

> Allah has put an angel in charge of the womb. He says, "Oh Lord, a drop, Oh Lord a clot. Oh Lord, a morsel. When Allah desires to complete the creation of the fetus, he says, "Oh Lord, male or female? Wretched or happy? How much provision? How long a life?"[30]

Abu Bukhari also writes about angels who visit people in the grave when he relates:

> When someone is placed in his grave and his companions turn and go, and he can still hear the tread of their sandals, two angels come to him and make him sit up and say to him, "What do you say about this man, Muhammad? May Allah bless him and grant him peace?" Then He will say, "I testify that he is a slave of Allah and His Messenger." It will be said, "Look at your place in the Fire. Allah has given you in exchange for it, a place in the Garden."[31]

In a variety of places in the Holy Book, believers in Allah mistake human beings for angels. The Qur'an's 6:8–9 and 50, 11:15 and 33, and 17:97 are good examples, as is 12:31, where women believe that Yusuf (Joseph) is an angel because he is so handsome. Indeed, the text tells us of the women seeing Yusuf, "When they saw him they were so wonderstruck, they cut their hands, and they exclaimed, 'Oh Lord, preserve us! He is no mortal but an honorable angel.'"[32]

Sometimes the angels are called the "Heavenly Hosts" or "Multitudes" (*al mala'al-a-la*). The Holy Book's 37:6–8, for example, tells us:

> He decked the nearest heavens with ornaments of stars, so that they are not able to listen to the angels of the higher orders, and are pelted from all sides.[33]

Surah 38:69 speaks of "no knowledge of the higher assembly," presumably another reference to the higher assembly of the *Mala'ika*.[34] Surah 89:22 speaks of "The coming of the Lord, along with rows and rows of angels. Angels are sometimes sent by Allah to assist believers in times of war, as Surah 8:9–10 tell us:

> Remember when you prayed to your Lord for help. He hears you and said, "I shall send a thousand angels, following behind you at your side."[35]

A few verses later, the Holy Book speaks about what the angels did. The text informs us:

> It was not you who killed them (the enemy), but Allah that did so. You did not throw what you threw (sand into the eyes of the enemy at Badr), but Allah to bring out the best in the faithful by doing them a favor of His own. Allah is All-Hearing and All-Knowing.[36]

A Hadith from Sa'd Ibn Abi Waqqas, the Prophet Muhammad's maternal uncle and companion, speaks of the role of angels at the Battle of Uhud. He tells us:

> I saw the Prophet on the day of the Battle of Uhud. With him were two men fighting with him, dressed all in white, who fought as fiercely as they could. I had never seen them before, nor did I see them after that.[37]

This is a reference to the Battle of Uhud, which was fought on March 17, 624. It was a key battle in the earliest days of Islam, as well as having been a turning point in Muhammad's struggle against his opponents, the Quraish Tribe of Arabia. The Prophet Muhammad was born into the Banu Hashim Clan of the Quraish Tribe. He was expelled, however, when he began to preach Monotheism, and the Quraishi became angry about it.

The Battle of Badr has been passed down in Islamic History as a decisive fight attributed to Divine intervention. The Holy Book's 3:123–125 provides another account of the Battle of Badr. It reveals:

> For Allah helped you during the Battle of Badr at a time when you were helpless. So act in accordance with the Laws of Allah, and you may well be grateful. Remember when you said to the faithful, "It is not sufficient that your Lord should send for your help three thousand angels from Heaven? Indeed, you are patient and take heed for yourselves; and the enemy comes rushing at you suddenly, and your Lord will send you even five thousand angels on charges sweeping down.[38]

In another Hadith narrated by Mu'aadh ibn Rifaa'ah al-Zuraaqi that came from his father who was present at the Battle of Badr, he informs us, Jibril came to the Prophet and asked, "How do you rate the people who were present at Badr?" He said, "They are the best of the Muslims" or something similar to this.[39] Then the angel Jibril said, "So it is with the angels who were present at Badr."[40]

This notion that the angels of Allah assisted the nascent Muslims in battle is also a central belief in regard to the Battle of Uhud, which was fought on March 23, 625, at Mount Uhud in northwest Arabia. This battle preceded the Battle of Badr. The Holy Book's Surah 3:152 tells us about the Battle of Uhud:

> The promise made to you by Allah was verified when you destroyed the foe by His leave, until you were unmanned and disputed the order, and then disobeyed the Apostle, even after He brought you in the sight of the victory that you longed for.[41]

The Qur'an also speaks of ranks of angels that will be present at the End of Time. Surah 77:38 suggests:

> On the day when the Spirit and the angels stand in ranks, no one will speak, except for him who is authorized by the All-Merciful and who proclaims what is right.[42]

Surah 25:25–26 of the Holy Book proclaims:

> The day when the Heavens are split in the clouds, and the angels are sent down in rank after rank, the Kingdom that day will belong in truth to the All-Merciful. It will surely be a hard day for the disbelievers.[43]

The Qur'an also tells us that on that day, "Eight angels will bear the Throne of the Lord above their heads."[44] It also tells us that the Ark of the Covenant also will be borne by the *Mala'ika*, as well. The Holy text tells us:

> The sign of His Kingship is that the Ark will come to you. It will contain Serenity from your Lord and certain relics left by the families of Musa and Haran (Moses and Aaron). It will be borne by angels. There is no sign for you in that you truly are Believers.[45]

The Holy Book also indicates that the *Mala'ika* do not eat (Qur'an 51:26–28), they do not get bored or weary (21:20), they never get tired of "worshipping Allah Night and Day," nor do they feel themselves above it (41:38). In the Muslim faith, angels are neither Divine nor semi-Divine beings. They are intermediaries between Allah the Merciful and human beings. Angels in Islam are not objects to be worshipped or prayed to, for they do not deliver our prayers to Allah. Their job is simply to submit to Allah, and above all, to carry out His Will.

In the Islamic faith, there are no fallen angels, and humans do not become angels after death. Iblis is not one of the fallen angels, but rather he is numbered among the Jinn, as we shall see in a later chapter of this study. The Jinn, of course, is another race of beings created by the Will of Allah.

A Hadith recorded by both Sahih Bukhari and Sahih Muslim suggest an analogy that speaks of the nature of the *Mala'ika*. They say, "angels are to the House of Heaven as humans are to the Kaaba and the city of Mecca. This tradition explains:

> *Al-BaitAl-Ma'amur* (the House of Heaven) is always inhabited like the Kaaba for the people of Earth. Each day seventy thousand angels pray in this House, and when they exit from it, they will never get back into it. This shows how numerous are the angels.[46]

Another Hadith from ninth-century collector Al-Hakim At-Tabarani also speaks of the relations of angels to humans. Abu Tabarani observes:

> When Adam died, his children did not know what to do with the body, so the angels taught them. The angels washed his body an odd number of times, then they buried him in a grave with a niche of land and said, "This is the way that Allah wishes the sons of Adam to treat the dead."[47]

One final Hadith about the nature of angels in Islam comes from the authentic collection of ninth-century scholar Sahih Bukhari. He observes, "angels of mercy do not enter a house where there is a dog or a picture of a living thing (a human being or an animal).[48] Some interpreters suggest that this is the origins of the prohibition against displaying Allah, His angels or the Prophet Muhammad in any physical representations, but the issue of angels and their relationship to dogs is a much more complicated matter that we will discuss later in this study.

Scholars Kecia Ali and Oliver Leaman, in their book *Islam: Key Concepts*, give us a summary of much of what we have said so far in this first chapter. They observe:

> Angels are very active in the Qur'an and are described in a variety of ways. They may have two, three, or four pairs of wings (35:1); they do not need to eat (25:7 and 20); and they are said to be very beautiful. Sometimes they fight on the side of the righteous (3:124). They

note our actions (50:18), and take the souls of the dead and guard over Hell (32:11 and 43:77). The angelic guards are said to be nineteen in number (74:30). On the Day of Judgment, God's throne will be carried by angels (69:17). The Ark of the Covenant holding the *sakinah* (the inspired peace) will also be borne by the angels (2:248). There is a High Council of angels (37:8 and 38:69) who repel eaves-dropping demons with bolts of fire. Some angels are described by name, such as the "two angels of Babylon, Harut and Marut, who teach people white magic. There is also Gabriel and Michael (2:98). The former is associated bringing down Revelation (26:193), and is called the "Faithful Spirit." And in the Hadith accounts he accompanies Muhammad on his heavenly ascension or *Miraj*. The Qur'an calls Azrael the Angel of Death and names Israfil as the angel whose trumpet blast will mark the Day of Judgment (69:1).[49]

This passage mentions a number of the most important features of Islamic views of the *Mala'ika*, many of which will be discussed in this and the following chapters. The Holy Book's 6:8–9 asks why Allah did not send an angel to accompany the Prophet Muhammad in his task, but the Holy Book tells us that would have made it too easy for the audience to accept the message. "The only miracle in the Qur'an," Ali and Leaman suggest, "is taken to be the Qur'an itself, and its unique and perfect style and composition."[50] Nevertheless, in the next section of this first chapter, we shall speak of those places in the Muslim Holy Book where angels are mentioned by name, or where they are to be identified by their job descriptions, at some length in the following chapter.

Angels Mentioned in Al-Qur'an

There are a number of angels mentioned directly in the Holy Book, Al-Qur'an. By far, the most important of these is the angel Jibril (Gabriel). We will explore the role of Jibril in the Islamic faith. It is enough now, however, to say that the angel Jibril is the principal conduit by which divine messengers are sent from Allah to all of the prophets in Islam. Jibril was the conveyor that brought Muhammad the Qur'an, as well as the Gospels to Isa (Jesus), and the Tawrah (Torah) to Musa (Moses). The angel Jibril also was the origin of the inspiration of Ibrahim (Abraham), the father of the three religions, or Peoples of the Book, Judaism, Christianity, and Islam.

The Arabic expression, *Ahl al-Kitab*, or "Peoples of the Book," refers to religious traditions with a scripture such as Judaism, Christianity and Islam. It is also sometimes applied to other religious traditions like the Zoroastrian faith in ancient Persia. The ancient Jews had a similar expression in Hebrew, *Am Ha-Sefer*. The Arabic expression is employed at Surah nine, ayat 29 that instructs believers to:

> Fight those People of the Book who do not believe in Allah and the Last Day, who do not prohibit what Allah and His Apostle have forbidden, nor to accept Divine Law, until all of them pay a protective tax in submission.[51]

The figure of the angel Mika'il (Michael) in Islam is called the "Angel of Justice." Some Muslim sources say that Allah commanded Mika'il to look all over the universe and to command the movements of the stars and planets, all the galaxies, and the forces of nature.

Some other traditions suggest that Mika'il is responsible for the growing of crops, as well as the bringing of food and rain. More will be said of *Malak Mika'il* in a later chapter on archangels in Islam, as well.

Other angels mentioned specifically in the Holy Book include: Azrael, Malik and Israfil, the Arabic name for Raphael. Azrael is the Angel of Death. His job is to order the assigned angels to take an individual's soul at a time specified by Allah. Azrael has countless other angels under his command. The angel Malik is another *Malak* associated with death. He is responsible in Islam for guarding the Gates of Hell, or *Jahannam* in Arabic.

Israfil is the angel responsible for signaling the coming of Judgment Day by blowing his horn, or *Sur*, and sending out what is called the "Blast of Truth" in the Muslim faith. In Islamic iconography,

Israfil is usually depicted as having a large, hairy body that is covered with mouths and tongues, and that reach from the Seventh Heaven to the Throne, or *Arsh*, of Allah.

Again, more is said of these archangels—Azrael, Malik and Israfi—in Chapter Three.

In the meantime, a Hadith recorded by Sahih Muslim mentions these three archangels in a prayer from the Prophet Muhammad. The Prophet is said to have called on, "Oh Allah, Lord of Jibril, Mika'il, and Israfil, Creator of the Heavens and the Earth, Knower of the unseen and the Seen, You are the Judge of matters when Your slaves differ with each other."[52] Other of the *Mala'ika* mentioned in the Qur'an are the guarding angels. Each human being is assigned two of these guardians, one on the right and the other on the left. They are called *Hafizin*, or "Guardians" over mankind. They are cognizant of what people do and they write it down. In a few places in the Holy Book, it suggests that Allah is ascribed the writing of these deeds at Surah 107:4 and 70:4, for example. In other passages, the recording is delegated to the guardians, as at Surah 82:10–12. These verses report:

> Surely there are Guardians over you, illustrious Scribes
> who know what you do, and write it down.[53]

The Arabic names for these guardian angels are *Qiramun* and *Qatibin*. The former, who sits on the right of a person, records the good deeds. The latter angel, on the left, records the evil deeds. The value of these acts, however, are quite different. One good deed in Islam is considered as valuable as ten evil acts, at least in regard to the human's quest for salvation.

Four other angels are mentioned by name in the Holy Book, as well as the chief collectors of Hadith in the Islamic faith. The names of these angels are *Munkar* and *Nakir*, and *Harut* and *Marut*. The former pair are angels who are said to interrogate human beings in the grave about their good and bad deeds. The latter pair, Harut and Marut, are angels who were sent as a test to the ancient Israeli tribe of Babylon. *Munkar* and *Nakir* only are discussed in Hadith literature, while *Harut* and *Marut* appear at Surah two, ayat 102 of the Holy Book that tells us:

> And they follow what devilish beings used to chant

against the authority of Sulayman, though Sulayman never disbelieved; and only the Devils denied, who taught sorcery to men, which they said had been revealed. To the angels of Babylon, Harut and Marut, who, however, never taught it without saying, "We have been sent to deceive you, so do not renounce your faith."[54]

A Hadith from Abu Hurayra speaks of the roles of Munkar and Nakir. Hurayra informs us:

When the deceased is buried, there comes to him two blue-black angels, one of whom is called Munkar and the other Nakir. They ask him, "What did you used to say about this man?" And they answer, "He is a slave and messenger of Allah." Then the others say, "We knew before then that you used to say this." Then his grave will be widened to a size of seventy cubits. And it will be illuminated for him. Then they tell him, "Sleep." Then the dead man says, "Go back and tell my family. Tell them that I sleep like a bridegroom whom no one shall awaken except my most beloved," until Allah raises him up.[55]

There are a number of traditions on Harut and Marut that do not appear in the Holy Book. One of these says that the pair is said to have yielded to sexual temptation and that they now are consigned to a pit near Babel where they teach white magic to human beings. This may be the source of the narrative at Surah two, ayat 102.

On the other hand, if the deceased was a hypocrite, the angels say they knew beforehand that the Earth was told to squeeze him so that he would be crushed until his ribs interlock, and he will remain that way until Allah raises him up. There are several Hadith concerning the guardian angels. One tradition from Abu Dawud comes in the context of Surah 13, verse eleven. Abu Dawud, who died in 889 in Basra, was a Persian-born scholar who traveled extensively in Iraq, Egypt and Syria, among many other Islamic locations. In the Hadith in question, Abu

Dawud remarked about the Qur'an's 13:11:

> These angels guard people from falling into potholes,
> those who slip off the top of a wall, or try to avoid falling
> objects...Life would be impossible if Allah removed
> these angels.[56]

Great Syrian Sunni scholar Ibn Kathir (1300–1373) also comments on the guardian angels in his Hadith. He informs us:

> These angels are with us all the time, except when we
> have sexual intercourse or are in the bathroom.[57]

Earlier in this first chapter, we mentioned a section of the Qur'an that implies that an angel named Malik is the Keeper of the Gates of *Jahannam*, or Hell (see Surah 43:77). The Holy Book also tells us that Malik has assistants. The Qur'an's 74:30–31 speak specifically of these Keepers of Hell. The Text reveals:

> Over it (Hell) are nineteen guards. We have not
> appointed anyone but angels as Keepers of Hell. And
> their numbers that we have fixed is to make it a means
> of contention for non-believers.[58]

Some Muslim scholars have pointed out that since there are only nineteen "Keepers" of Hell, the inhabitants of Hell should be able to overwhelm them, but some collectors of Ahadith point out that each of the nineteen has the strength to control all of humanity by himself alone.

The Holy Book's 40:49–50 mentions these Keepers of *Jahannam*, or Hell. The Text tells us:

> Those in the fire will say to the Keepers of Hell, "Ask
> your Lord to reduce the punishment by one day for us."
> Then, they will say, "Did not your Apostles come to you
> with clear proof?" They will answer, "Indeed, they did."
> Then "Pray," the Keepers will say, but the prayers of
> unbelievers will be in vain.[59]

In a later chapter entitled "Angels Associated with Death in Islam," we speak at length about these Keepers of Hell, as well as their master, Malik. Not surprisingly, the Muslim tradition also believes in angels who are the Keepers of Heaven, or *Jannah* in Arabic. They also have a leader. His name is Ridwan, or Rizwan. Ridwan does not appear in the Holy Book, but there are several descriptions of his minions, like these verses in Surah thirteen:

> Perpetual Gardens which will enter with those of their fathers, spouses and children who were virtuous and at peace, with angels coming in from every door, saying, "Welcome, peace be on you for you have persevered. How excellent is the recompense of Paradise (*Jannah*).[60]

Surah 39:73 also speaks specifically about the Keepers of Paradise, when it tells us:

> Those who were mindful of their duty to the Lord will be driven in groups to Paradise until they reach it and its gates are open, and its Keepers will say to them, "Peace be on you; you are of the joyous, so enter here so that you will live forever.[61]

The Holy Book is very clear that both Malik and Ridwan, as well as their followers, submit to the Will of Allah. Indeed, of all that is said about the *Mala'ika* in the Qur'an, the most important thing is that all of the angels, being the creatures of Allah, in the final analysis can do nothing but follow the Will of Allah. Even the Keepers of Hell, in the exercising of their duties, are doing nothing more than following the Will of the Almighty Allah. This judgment is made quite clear at the Qur'an's 21:27–28, where it tells us of the angels: They do not precede Him in their speech, and they act on His command. He knows what was there before them, and what is to come in the time after them.[62]

The Holy Spirit in Islam

In addition to the heavenly beings discussed so far in this first chapter, the Muslim Holy Book also speaks of a figure it calls *Ruh al-Amin*, or "Faithful Spirit." Sometimes this figure is simply called *Ruhana*, or "Our Spirit" (see Qur'an 19:7), or *Ruhina*, also "Our Spirit" at 21:91.

At still other places in the Holy Book, this same figure is known as the *Ruh al-Qudus*, or the "Holy Spirit." The expression of the *Ruh al-Qudus* appears four times in the Muslim Holy Book.

These come at Surah 2:87, 2:253, 5:110 and 16:102. At times, the Qur'an uses the term *Ruh*, or "The Spirit," such at the Holy Book's 78:38 and 97:4. There is even the employment in the Holy Book of the Arabic expression, *Ruhul Amin*, or the "Honest Spirit." Two examples of the use of this expression come at the Qur'an 16:102 and 26:192–193. Thus, there are a variety of uses in the Qur'an of the Arabic word *Ruh* and its many derivatives.

At the Holy Book's 19:17, for example, the text tells us:

> And We took cover from them, and We sent Our Spirit (*Ruhana*) to her who appeared to her in the concrete form of a man.[63]

This verse appears in connection with the angel Jibril appearing to Maryam, the mother of Isa (Jesus). At other times, the Qur'an simply speaks of Allah's *Ruh*, or "Spirit," as in this description of Allah bringing life to the body of Adam:

> Then proportioned and breathed into him His Spirit, and as well he gave him the sense of hearing, sight and feeling. And yet, how little is the gratitude that you offer.[64]

This same wording about breathing life into the body of Adam can also be seen in the Qur'an's 38:72, 15:29, 21:95, and 66:12. In this latter passage, the text refers to breathing life into Maryam. It tells us:

> And of Maryam, daughter of Imran, who guarded her chastity, so that We breathed into her a new life from Us. And she believed the words of her Lord, and His Books, and she was counted among the obedient.[65]

The Arabic expression the *Ruh al-Qudus*, or "Holy Spirit," is used throughout the Qur'an. It is employed at 15:40, 16:102, 26:191–195, 2:87, 2:253 and 5:110. A good English translation of the Holy Book's 26:191 goes something like this:

> Your Lord is mighty and merciful, and this Qur'an is a revelation from the Lord of all the worlds when

the trusted Holy Spirit (*Ruh al-Qudus*) descended to communicate with your heart that you may be a warner in elegant Arabic. This is indicated in the Books of earlier People.[66]

The *Ruh al-Qudus*, or "Holy Spirit," is mentioned in a variety of other passages in the Holy Book of Islam, including 2:87, 97–98, 2:253, and 16:102. In the first of these, the Holy Spirit visited Maryam, the mother of Jesus, as was the verse from Surah two, verse 253. *Al-Nahl*, 16:102 tells us that Allah uses the Holy Spirit to bring revelations to His Prophets, while 2:97–98 indicates that it is the angel Jibril who brings those revelations.

A number of the major collectors of Hadith also write about the *Ruh al-Qudus*, like this tradition from Sahih Bukhari, when speaking of sending strength to the poet Hassan Ibn Thabit (563–674), one of the *Sahaba*, or "Companions" of the Prophet Muhammad. Abu Bukhari has Muhammad pray, "Oh Allah, give him strength with the Holy Spirit (*Ruh al-Qudus*)."[67] Similar Ahadith from At-Tirmidhi and Abu Dawud agree. They tell us that "Allah, the Glorious and the Mighty, as strengthened Hassan with the Holy Spirit (*Ruh al-Qudus*); and the Holy Spirit is with Hassan in his work."[68]

Two major interpretations of these terms have arisen among scholars of Islam, both historically and among contemporary thinkers. The first view, which is the more traditional one, says that references to the Holy Spirit in Islam are nothing more than to act as a synonym for the angel Jibril, the high-ranking *Malak* who was assigned by Allah the job of bringing His Revelations to the Apostles and Prophets of Islam. Thus, in this first view, the Qur'an refers to Jibril both by name and by using the designation the *Ruh al-Qudus*, or "Holy Spirit."

The way in which this conclusion is arrived at goes something like this. The Holy Book's 2:97–98 tell us that the angel Jibril brings down Divine Revelation from Allah into the heart of the Prophet Muhammad, but the Qur'an's 16:102 informs us that it is the *Ruh al-Qudus* that brings Divine Revelations to Earth. From these two premises, we arrive at the conclusion that the Holy Spirit and the angel Jibril must be one and the same thing. Thus, in some instances, the figure is called Jibril, and in others, he is called the *Ruh al-Qudus*, or "Holy Spirit."

The second interpretation of the identity of the *Ruh al-Qudus* suggests that the term is employed in much the same way as it is used in the New Testament. One piece of evidence for this view is that at Surah 26:191–195, the Holy Book mentions the Holy Spirit and that he inspired the "Books of earlier Peoples, as well."[69] Presumably, the Qur'an speaks here of the Old and the New Testaments.

Passages like Luke 1:26–35 is an illustrative example of the New Testament's view of the Holy Spirit. The NRSV translation of this passage says this:

> In the sixth month, the angel Gabriel was sent by God to the town of Galilee called Nazareth, to a virgin engaged to a man whose name was Joseph, of the house of David. The virgin's name was Mary, and he came to her and said, "Greetings, o favored one, the Lord is with you." But she was much perplexed by his words and pondered what sort of greeting this might be. The angel said to her, "Do not be afraid, Mary, for you have found favor with God. And now you will conceive in your womb and will bear a son, and you will name him Jesus. He will be great and shall be called the Son of the Most High. The Lord God will give to him the throne of his ancestor David. He will reign over the House of Jacob forever, and of his kingdom there shall be no end." Then Mary said to the angel, "How can this be since I am a virgin?" And the angel said to her, "The Holy Spirit shall come upon you, and the power of the Most High will overshadow you; therefore, the child to be born shall be holy, and he shall be called the Son of God."[70]

Those who hold this second perspective that the Holy Spirit in Islam is similar to the idea of the Holy Spirit in the New Testament point to other New Testament passages to bolster their argument. Among these are Matthew 1:20 that tells us, "But just when he had resolved to do this, an angel of the Lord appeared to him (Joseph) and said, 'Son of David, do not be afraid to take Mary as your wife, for the child conceived in her is from the Holy Spirit.'"[71]

The Gospel of Matthew's 3:16 is also given as evidence that the *Ruh al-Qudus* in Islam is similar, or identical, to the role or place of the Holy Spirit in the New Testament. This verse in Matthew tells us:

> And when Jesus had been baptized, just as he came up from the water, suddenly the heavens were opened up to him, and he saw the Spirit of God descending like a dove and alighted on him. And a voice from heaven said, "This is My Son in whom I am well pleased."[72]

A number of passages in the Old Testament, as well, also may establish the connection between the "Spirit of God" and the Muslim *Ruh al-Qudus*. The Book of the Prophet Isaiah 11:2 tells us that "The Spirit of the Lord inspired Isaiah to prophecy. Psalm 104:29–30 declares that the Spirit of the Lord "brings life to humanity," much like the Gospel of Matthew and the *Ruh al-Qudus* in Islam. The Spirit of the Lord also brings courage to a number of patriarchs in the Old Testament, such as Joshua, at Numbers 27:18; Saul, at First Samuel 10:9–10; Othniel, in Judges 3:10; and Gideon, at Judges 6:34.

From this analysis, we may conclude that the "Spirit of the Lord" in the Old Testament and the Holy Spirit in the New Testament, both appear to be precursors to the idea of the *Ruh al-Qudus*, or Holy Spirit, in the Qur'an and traditional Hadith literature. But when we say that the concept of the Holy Spirit in Islam has a similar role to that figure in the New Testament, we do not mean that Muslims are taught to believe in the Trinity of Father, Son and Holy Spirit.

Indeed, the Holy Book of Islam quite explicitly rejects the Trinity at Surah 4:171, 5:73 and 5:116. The first of these tells us, "…So believe in Allah and His Apostles and do not call Him Trinity. Abstain from that for your own good."[73] The Qur'an's Surah 5:73 is even more explicit about the Trinity. The Holy Book tells us:

> Disbelievers are those who surely say, "God is the third of the trinity." But there is no God other than Allah, the One, and if you do not desist from saying what they say, then indeed those among them who persist in disbelief will suffer painful punishment. Why do you not turn

toward Allah, Who is both Forgiving and Kind?[74]

From Surah four, verse 177, we are given some rules of inheritance, as well as a belief that there is only one God Who Knows All Things. The other passage in the Holy Book mentioned above seems to imply that Maryam, the mother of Isa, is part of the Trinity in the Christian tradition. But the Qur'an's 5:116 rejects this view, as well. Thus, when we say that the *Ruh al-Qudus* in Islam has a similar role to the "Spirit of the Lord" in the Old Testament, and to the Holy Spirit in the New Testament, we do no mean in reference to a belief in the Christian Trinity. So what do Muslim scholars mean when they make this claim about those similarities?

The Arabic word *Ruh* is a cognate of the Hebrew term, *Ruah*, which gives us a hint about the role of the Holy Spirit in Islam. In ancient Judaism, the word *Ruah* was employed to express both "spirit" and "breath." These are the two principal uses of the word *Ruh* in Arabic, as well.

The first sense of the word in the Holy Book is that it creates human spirits and places them into the bodies of fetuses. Allah uses the Holy Spirit in this sense to blow into the mother's womb the human *Ruh*, or Spirit.

The Islamic faith, for the most part, is against the practice of abortion because it is believed that the human fetus is given its soul (Nafs in Arabic) shortly after conception.

This notion that the Holy Spirit in Islam creates life in the womb is supported by a variety of passages in the Holy Book, such as 15:29, 19:17–19 and 66:12. The Qur'an's 19:16–19 speaks explicitly of this function of the *Ruh al-Qudus*. The text reveals:

> Commemorate Maryam in the Book. When she withdrew from her family to a place in the East, and took cover for them. We sent a Spirit of Ours to her who appeared before her in the concrete form of a man. "I seek refuge in the Merciful from you, if you fear Him," she said. He replied, "I am only a Messenger from your Lord sent to bestow a good son to you."[75]

In the same Surah of the Holy Book, at ayat twenty-two, it suggests that it is the angel Jibril who is responsible for bringing life to the womb (Surah 19:22). The other function of the *Ruh al-Qudus* in Islam is that the figure brings strength and courage to believing Muslims. This view is most exemplified at the Holy Book's 58:22. This text reveals that:

> You will find those who believe in Allah and the Day of the Resurrection loving those who oppose Allah and His Prophets, even though they be their father's sons, or brothers, or their kin. Allah has inscribed in their hearts belief and has supported them with His own Grace. He will admit them to the Gardens with rivers flowing by, where they will abide forever. Allah accepts them and they are happy in the pleasure of Allah. They are the Army of Allah. Will not that Army be the Victors?[76]

This second function of the Holy Spirit in Islam also is exemplified at Surah 40:15, 5:110 and 16:102. The latter passage tells us, "You say it has been sent by Divine Grace from your Lord with the truth to strengthen those who believe, and as a guide and good news for those who have submitted to Allah."[77] This second function of the *Ruh al-Qudus* in Islam can be seen at the Holy Book's 40:15 that gives us something like this:

> Most exulted of positions, Lord of Power. He directs inspiration by His command to any of His creatures, as He wills to warn men of the Day of Reckoning.[78]

From Surah five, ayat 110, we get:

> And when Allah will say, "Oh Jesus, son of Mary, remember the favors I bestowed upon you and on your mother, and I reinforced you with My Grace, that you spoke to men when you were in the cradle, and when in the prime of life; when I taught you the law and the judgment and the Torah, and the Gospel; when you formed the state of your people's destiny out of mire, and you breathed a new Spirit into it.[79]

This second function of the *Ruh al-Qudus* in Islam, then, is to breathe life into the bodies of certain Prophets or to supply strength or inspiration to them sometimes in the form of Grace. These passages discussed above also are connected to the idea in the Holy Book that Allah forms men from dust and then simply says, "Be!" or *"Kull!"* in Arabic, and He was. For example, consider Surah three, ayat 59 that reveals:

> The similitude of Isa before Allah is that of Adam. He created him from dust, then said to him, "Be! And he was." The Truth comes from the Lord alone; so be not of those who doubt it.[80]

Conclusions

The major goal of this chapter has been to give a comprehensive introduction to the understanding of *Malak* and the *Mala'ika* (or "angel" and "angels") in the Islamic faith. In the first section of this chapter, we have discussed the etymology of these Arabic terms, and we explored a variety of cognates in other Ancient-Near-Eastern languages, such as Hebrew and Ethiopic, a language from which many Arabic words likely arose.

In the second section of this chapter, our primary task was to enumerate the many places in Al-Qur'an where angels are mentioned or discussed. We also have explored in this chapter many of the places where angels can be found in the major collectors of Hadith in Islam, where angels are prominent. In the closing section, we have described and discussed at some length a figure called the *Ruh-Al*-Qudus, or "Holy Spirit," or sometimes the *Ruh al-Amin*, or the "Faithful Spirit."

Scholars of Islam have disagreed about the nature of this figure. Some thinkers suggest that the Holy Spirit in Islam is nothing more than a synonym of the activity of the angel Jibril in the Holy Book and beyond. Others think the *Ruh al-Qudus* is tied to how Biblical writers express the figures of the "Spirit of the Lord" in the Old Testament and the Holy Spirit in the New Testament. Those who hold this second perspective often point to many Biblical passages as precursors to the idea of the Holy Spirit in Islam.

Among these passages in the Old Testament, we have mentioned verses from the Prophet Isaiah, the Book of Psalms, and the Books of First Samuel, Numbers and Judges. Among these precursors to the idea of the *Ruh al-Qudus* in the New Testament are the Gospel of Luke 1:26–35 and the Gospel of Matthew 1:20 and 3:16. At the very end of this first chapter, we have suggested that the Holy Spirit in Islam has had at least two primary functions; those are, creating life into the wombs of human beings, and secondly, to bring Grace and Strength in support of all true believers in the Faith. More specifically, the Islamic Holy Book reveals that Allah strengthens the hearts of the faithful, such as at Surah 58:22.

In the second chapter of this study to follow, we shall explore the unique and lofty roles of the angel Jibril in the Muslim tradition. As we shall see, the *Malak Jibril* has a place that is unparalleled among the *Mala'ika* in the Islamic faith, both in Al-Qur'an and beyond.

Chapter Two:
The Angel Jibril (Gabriel) in the Islamic Faith

The words recited by Gabriel to Muhammad in the cave are the first verses of the Qur'an revealed to Muhammad.

—Ingrid Mattson, *The Story of the Qur'an*

On the night the angel Gabriel conducted the Prophet, mounted on a winged-horse called Buraq, through the seven Heavens, where he spoke with God and prayed with other Prophets.

—Akbar Ahmed, *Islam Today*

…If you assist one another against him, then surely his helper is God, and Jbril and the righteous believers, and besides him, the angels are his helpers.

—The Holy Qur'an, 66:4

Introduction

The Arabic name for the angel Gabriel, or *Gavriel* in Hebrew, is the word Jibril. The Hebrew *Gavriel* comes from the noun *Geber*, which means "a valiant man" or "a valiant warrior."

The Hebrew name is used in several places in the Hebrew Bible, or Old Testament. The name Jibril in Arabic is sometimes used as both a first and family name, though famous Arabic scholar Imam Malik (711–795) was against that practice of using it as a family name.

The name *Gavriel*, or Gabriel, is employed at the Book of Daniel 8:16 and 9:21 in the Hebrew Bible. The figure also received considerable attention in the pseudepigraphical literature where his title and position become more explicit. He is one of the four presences in First Enoch 40:3 who gaze down from Heaven (9:1). He is called one of God's "Glorious ones" in Second Enoch 21:3. Gabriel sits "at the left hand of God at Second Enoch 24:1; and he is said to "set over all powers" at First Enoch 40:5. In the ancient Jewish tradition, the angel Gabriel was one of the seven principal archangels.

It is most likely that the Arabic form of the name was derived from the ancient Hebrew meaning. In fact, in modern Arabic, the name Jibril is employed as a synonym for "archangel."

In fact, our principal aim in this second chapter is to describe and to discuss the figure of Jibril in the historical and contemporary contexts of the Faith. In a later chapter of this study, we shall describe and discuss the other archangels in the Islamic faith, Chapter Three.

The *Malak Jibril*, or "angel Jibril," is only mentioned by name in two passages of the Muslim Holy Book. These come at Surah 66:4, which is used as an epigram for this chapter, and at Surah 2:98 where Jibril is mentioned along with *Mika'il*, or Michael. The angel Jibril does appear, however, quite frequently in Hadith literature.

The tri-consonant root of the name *Jibril* is JBL or Jim-Ba-lam. This root is employed forty-one times in the Muslim Holy Book Al-Qur'an. In thirty-nine of those, it uses the word *Jabal*, which means "mountain" or "hill." The other two uses of the JBL root come in connection to the use of the angel Jibril at the Holy Book's 66:4 and Surah two, ayat 98. Our first tasks in this second chapter are to discuss the precursors to the angel Jibril, as well as an analysis of where the figure appears in Islamic history.

Precursors to the Angel Jibril

The most important source for the idea and function of the angel Jibril in Islam is the Biblical tradition. The Aramaic name *Gavri'el*, from the same Semitic Root JBS, means "God is my strong man" or "God is my hero." The angel Gabriel is used in a variety of non-canonical works, including several references in the Books of Enoch. Gabriel is mentioned, for example, at First Enoch 9:1–2, along with the angels, Michael, Raphael, Uriel, and Suriel, as being present at the destruction of the *Nephilim*, in chapter six of the Book of Genesis.[81] At Enoch 10:13, Gabriel was commanded to go to "the biters, the reprobate, to the children of fornication, to the sons of the Watchers from among men; and to bring them forth and incite them against each other." The text continues:

> Let them perish under their mutual slaughter, for a great length of days surely will not be theirs.[82]

At the Book of Enoch 20:7, we are told that Gabriel "presides over fiery serpents," and 40:9 informs us that the angel "presides over all that is powerful."[83] The angel Gabriel also appears four times in Canonical literature.

In chapter eight of the Book of Daniel, he explains the vision of a horned ram as portending the destruction of the Persian Empire. In chapter nine, Daniel reports Gabriel "touching" him as he flew by. Chapter ten contains another vision of an angel that is also most likely Gabriel. Finally, in the New Testament, it is the angel Gabriel that foretells to Zachary the birth of John the Baptist, or *Yahya* in Arabic, as well as to Maryam (Mary), the birth of Isa, or Jesus. It is the final of these Biblical sources, at the Gospel of Luke 1:10–20, that is the most important precursor to the Muslim idea of the angel Jibril in that Gabriel reveals to Zachary the news about John, and to Maryam, or Mary, about Isa (Jesus). In this passage, Zachary complains that he is an old man and is no longer capable of producing a child. But the angel assures him that the birth of John will follow anyway. There is also an account in the Gospel of Luke, at 1:26–37, that contains an account of the foretelling of the birth of Isa, or Jesus, to his mother Maryam, or Mary. Gabriel only appears in these two passages in the Gospel and nowhere else in the New Testament. These two passages from the Gospel of Luke are important for our purposes, for they contain a number of features of the view of Jibril in the Islamic faith. Among these features are the reticence of Zachary/Zacharias and the announcements of the births of Yahya and Isa to their father and mother.

We also will show in this second chapter that the *Malak Jibril*, in Islam, has at least two other major roles in the Muslim religion. First, he is responsible for bringing *Al-Qur'an* to the Prophet Muhammad, so that he could promulgate the Faith. And secondly, he is the principal agent to brings Revelation to all of the other major prophets in Islam. This brings us to a discussion of the places in Islam where the *Malak Jibril* appears, the topic of the next section of this chapter.

The Figure of Jibril in Al-Qur'an

As we have suggested above, the Arabic name Jibril only appears twice in the Islamic Holy Book. These come at 2:98 and 66:4. We have used the latter passage as an epigram for this chapter. At Surah two, ayats 97 and 98, the text employs the name Jibril twice. The text tells us:

> Say, "Whoever is the enemy of Jibril who revealed the word of Allah to you, by the dispensation of Allah, reaffirming what has been revealed before, and is a guidance and a good news for those who believe. Whoever is the enemy of Allah and His angels and Apostles, and of Jibril and Mika'il, then Allah is an enemy of such believers."[84]

Surah two, verse 97 implies that it was the angel Jibril who brought the Qur'an to Prophet Muhammad. Surah 16:102, however, at least at first blush, seems to contradict this claim, when it says:

> Say, the *Ruh al-Qudus*, the Holy Spirit, has brought it [the Qur'an] down from your Lord with truth, that it may make firm and strengthen the Faith of those who believe; and as a guidance and glad tidings to those who have submitted.[85]

This verse suggests it is the Holy Spirit that brought Prophet Muhammad *Al-Qur'an* and not the *Malak Jibril*, but this is no real contradiction if the angel Jibril and the "Holy Spirit" in Islam are one and the same thing. In the history of Islamic philosophy, many of the earliest and most important Islamic scholars make this identification of the Holy Spirit, or the *Ruh al-Qudus*, with the angel Jibril. Among these scholars are Ibn Kathir, Ibn Abi Hatim, Ibn Abbas, and Arabi Ibn Abbas.

Even though this identification is the majority opinion, there is still some evidence that contradicts that identification. At the Holy Book's 78:38, for example, tells us about the Day of Reckoning:

> The Day that the Spirit and the angels will stand forth in ranks, and none shall speak except any who is permitted by Allah, Most Gracious, and He will say what is right.[86]

This verse from Surah 78 seems to suggest that the Spirit (*Ruh*) and the angels (*mala'ika*) are separate things. If Jibril is an angel, then he could not be the Spirit. A Hadith from Sahih Muslim also makes the same point. The Hadith collector says:

> Aisha said, "The Messenger of Allah used to pronounce while bowing and prostrating Himself: all Glorious, All Holy, Lord of the angels and the Spirit."

Again, these quotations seem to imply that the Spirit and the angel Jibril are distinct. Therefore, the *Ruh al-Qudus* cannot be an angel. In another Hadith from Sahih Muslim, from Volume I, number 6550, he quotes from poet Hasan Ibn Thabit. In two lines of a poem, Ibn Thabit says: "Whether anyone among you [the Quraysh] chooses to satirize the Messenger of Allah, or praise him, or help him, it is all the same. And Jibril is the Emissary of Allah, is with us, and indeed, the *Ruh al-Qudus* has no match.

Again, the second line in this poem seems to differentiate between the angel Jibril and the Holy Spirit, but that could only be true if the *Malak Jibril* and the *Ruh al-Qudus* are not the same thing. It may well be, however, that the conjunction *wa*, or "and," may be employed in the sentence to identify two nouns with each other, and that is the major point of view—the Holy Spirit and the angel Jibril are one and the same thing.

More will be said about this later in this section. Nevertheless, although these are the only three direct references to the *Malak Jibril* in *Al-Qur'an,* earlier, in Chapter One we have alluded to the fact that a number of Islamic scholars believe that the angel Jibril is being referred to when the Holy Book uses the Arabic expressions *Ruh al-Qudus* or "Holy Spirit," the *Ruh al-Amin* or "Faithful Spirit," and even the *Rasul Karim* or the "Noble Messenger."

Four good examples of the use of the *Ruh al-Qudus* in the Holy Book can be found at 2:81; 2:254; 5:110 and 6:104. The "Faithful Spirit" is employed at Al-Qur'an's 26:193. The "Noble Messenger" at 81:19, and the Arabic expression *Shadid-al-Quwwah* or the "Terrible Power" is also used to express the actions of the angel Jibril. Indeed, the "Terrible Power" is employed at Surah 53:5.[87]

According to twelfth-century scholar Al-Baydawi, the name "Jibril" signifies a "Servant of Allah."[88] Since Jibril revealed Al-Qur'an to the Prophet Muhammad, the figure was viewed by Jews in Arabia at the time as their enemy. This explanation, Baydawi and others suggest, is the key to understanding the Holy Books Surah two, ayats 97 and 98. Thus, Jibril's enemies are Allah's enemies. Muhammad's cousin and one of his first converts to Islam, Abdullah Ibn Abbas,

> who lived in the late seventh century, points out that most of the Surahs of Al-Qur'an begin with the three letters, ALM, or *alef, lam*, and *min* in Arabic. Ibn Abbas tells us that, "The A stands for Allah, the L for Jibril, and the M for Muhammad. Thus, Jibril is a central figure in the Muslim faith.[89]

It was *Malak Jibril* that brought the command to *Iqra!*, or "Recite!" as recorded in Surah 96:1–5 of the Islamic Holy Book. The Qur'an tells us:

> Recite in the name of your Lord, Who created Man from an embryo. Recite, for you Lord is Most Beneficent, Who taught by the pen, taught Man what he did not know.[90]

Scholar Ingrid Mattson speaks of the meaning of this central passage when she writes:

> The words recited by Gabriel to Muhammad in the cave are the first verses of the Qur'an revealed to Muhammad. The first word, *Iqra!*, that means read

or recite, indicates both what is to be the continuous manner of revelation and the basis for naming the collected words. For the next 23 years, until his death, Muhammad will receive words from God. He will listen to these words and recite them to his community. The Prophet and then his followers will then recite these words back to his God in their prayers and devotion. Collectively and individually, these words are called Al-Qur'an, the Recitation.[91]

Dr. Mattson goes on to describe subsequent revelations from Allah to Muhammad, brought by *Malak Jibril*. She writes:

After his first few encounters with the angel, which the Prophet seems to have experienced as awesome, even frightening, Gabriel's presence became less unsettling to him and he describes their later encounters in a way that suggest an almost easy familiarity. Gabriel met me by the side of the road...The Prophet told his followers that God's words were revealed to him in other ways. In particular, he said that sometimes the revelation came to him "like the ringing of a bell," after which he grasped what was revealed to him. The strain placed on Muhammad as he received the revelation was sometimes evident to those who were present. Aisha, the wife of the Prophet, is reported to have said, "Sometimes the revelation would descend upon the Messenger of God, and, although it was a cool morning, his forehead would glisten with perspiration."[92]

It was *Malak Jibril* who brought to Muhammad the command to Recite!, as recorded in Surah 96 of the Muslim Holy Book. For this reason, the angel Jibril is regarded by Arabs as the "Keeper of the Heavenly Treasures [of revelation]." Jibril is described as being one of the *Muqaribin*, that is, the angels "Who approach Allah." With three other of the *Mala'ika*—those discussed at length in Chapter Three— Jibril will survive on the Last Day, when Death will overtake all of

Allah's other creatures. The Arabic word *Muqaribin* is applied to Isa, at Surah three, ayat 45. At 4:172 of the Muslim Holy Book, some angels are called *Muqaribin*; and at 56:10–26, the *Muqaribin* are identified as *Sabiqu*, or "foremost in Faith in the Hereafter." Presumably, the term applies to certain of the *Mala'ika*, as well as to the best of human beings.

Finally, the Qur'an's 53:4–6 give us a description of Jibril's beauty, or what some call his "innate traits." The text tells us, "It is nothing but Revelation revealed, taught him by one immensely strong, possessing great power and splendor. He stood there stationary."[93] Sahih Bukhari reports a Hadith from Muhammad's wife, Aisha, in which she says the Prophet related that:

> Sometimes the angel comes in the form of a man and talks to me, and I grasp Whatever he says.[94]

A variety of other Ahadith are extant about the appearance of the angel Gabriel. In Volume VI, chapter sixty, number 380, for example, Sahih Bukhari tell us, "Abdullah Ibn Ma'sud informed us that Muhammad had seen Jibril with six hundred wings."[95] Kecia Ali and Oliver Leaman give this description of *Malak Jibril*, bringing his first Revelation to the Prophet Muhammad:

> From its inception, the Qur'an has been an aural and an oral text. Muslim tradition holds that in the first instance of revelation the angel Jibril appeared to Muhammad as he was meditating in a cave on Mount Hira, on the outskirts of the City of Mecca. The angel commanded him, "*Iqra,*" a word that means both read and recite. Muhammad's repeated denials that he did not know how to read or what to recite were to no avail, and he did eventually repeat the first verses of the Qur'an's 96:1–5. "Recite in the name of your Lord who created, created the human being from a clot. Recite and your Lord is most Generous, the One who taught by the pen, taught the human being what he did not know.[96]

Thus, the primary role for the angel Jibril was to bring the Revelation of Allah to the Prophet Muhammad, and this message was to be the Holy Qur'an. For the next twenty-three years, the angel Jibril continued to bring these Revelations to the Prophet until his death in 632. Most interpreters also believe that it is the *Malak Jibril* who is being referred to at the Holy Book's Surah 58:8–12, that informs us:

> Then he drew near and closer until a space of two bow lengths or even less remained, when he revealed to his votary what he revealed. And his head did not falsify what he perceived. Will you dispute with Him what he saw?[97]

The Arabic expression *qaba qawayini* or "two bow lengths" occurs several times in the Qur'an including this ayat at 53:9. The expression is employed in the Muslim Holy Book to indicate nearness in space, the distance of putting two bows, length to length, or about five feet or so Ibn Kathir, Ibn Arabi, and others maintain. Other thinkers, like Ibn Masud, for example, interpret the *qaus* to be a "cubit," or the length from a man's elbow to the tip of his middle finger. Both of these interpretations suggest closeness.

Many Islamic interpreters believe this episode in Surah 53 is the Prophet Muhammad seeing the *Malak Jibril* in his natural form. The same Surah goes on to speak of another time when Muhammad appears to see the angel the same way. The text announces:

> He saw him indeed another time, by the Lote Tree, beyond which none can pass, closer to what is the Garden of Tranquility.[98]

The Arabic expression, *Sidrat al-muntaha*, or the "Lote Tree" in Surah 53 marks the border of the Seventh Heaven in Islam, a point past which none of Allah's creatures may travel. During the *Isra* and *Mi'raq*, only Muhammad accompanied by *Malak Jibril*, are allowed beyond that point. The Lote Tree also appears elsewhere in the Muslim Holy Book, at Surah 34:16 and 56:28, for example.

Finally, some Muslim interpreters suggest that Jibril and Mika'il, Gabriel and Michael were two of the three *mala'ika* that visited Ibrahim (Abraham) in Surah 11:69 that revealed:

> Our angels came to Ibrahim with Good News and said, "Peace be on you."[99]

There is some disagreement about how many *Mala'ika* come to visit Prophet Ibrahim in this episode; some say two, others three or more. Nearly all interpreters agree, however, that these angels came to Ibrahim in the form of human beings, and they did not discuss their identities. Therefore, Ibrahim took them for strangers and brought a roasted calf for their entertainment. We cannot be certain, therefore, that *Malak Jibril* was one of the angel strangers.

In addition to these references to the *Malak Jibril* in the Muslim Holy Book, *Al-Qur'an*, there are also a number of references to the figure in classical Hadith literature. In the next section of this second chapter, we shall explore some of these references to the angel Gabriel.

Jibril in Classical Ahadith

The *Malak Jibril*, or angel Jibril, appears in a variety of classical Hadith in the Islamic tradition. By far, the most important of these comes from Umar Ibn Al-Khattab (583–644), powerful and influential Muslim Caliph and companion to the Prophet Muhammad. Murata and Chittick introduce this Hadith that is sometimes called the "Jibril Hadith," or the "Gabriel Hadith" in some circles. They tell us this about the tradition in question:

> Any explanation of the beliefs, practices and institutions that make Islam a major religion can benefit from a model that makes sense in terms of modern scholarship and has a basis in traditional Islamic learning. When we began teaching introductory courses on Islam several years ago, we chose as our model a famous and authentic Hadith that Muslim thinkers have often employed for similar purposes in classical texts. Typically, we ask our students to memorize the Hadith in the fashion on traditional learning. Even if they do not memorize it, by the end of the course, they will find it hard to forget, since it contains in capsule form everything they have learned in the semester.[100]

Murata and Chittick go on to give a version of the Gabriel Hadith. They observe:

Umar Ibn Al-Khattab said: one day, when we were with God's messenger, a man with very white clothing and very black hair came to us. No mark of travel was visible on him, and none of us recognized him. Sitting down before the Prophet, leaning his knees against his, and placing his hands on his thighs, he said, "Tell me Muhamad about submission."

He replied, "Submission means that you should bear witness that there is no God but Allah and that Muhammad is God's messenger; that you should perform the ritual prayers, pay the alms tax, fast during Ramadan, and make pilgrimage to the House if you are able to go there."

The man said, "You have spoken the truth." We were surprised at this questioning of him and then declaring that he had spoken the truth. He said, "Now tell me about Faith. He replied, "Faith means that you have faith in God, His angels, His books, His messengers, and the Last Day; and that you have faith in the measuring out, both its good and its evil.

Remarking that he had spoken the truth, he then said, "Now tell me about doing what is beautiful. He replied, "Doing what is beautiful means that you should worship God as if you see Him, for He sees you. Then the man said, "Tell me about the Hour?"

It will come at the very end, and the relationship of the question is far more important than the relation of the questioner. Then the man said, "Then tell me about its marks." He said, "The slave girl will give birth to her mistress, and you will see the barefoot and the naked, the destitute, and the shepherds vying for each other in buildings." Then the man went away. After I waited a long time, the Prophet said to me, "Do you know who the questioner was, Umar?" I replied, "God and His

Messenger know best." Then the Prophet said, "That was Jibril. He came to teach you your religion."[101]

This particular Hadith is ingenious because it is an important teaching tool that spells out the basic beliefs of the Islamic faith. The Gabriel Hadith essentially teaches us four separate things. Each of these things is central for understanding the Muslim faith. The first of these is that there are three essential aspects of Islam: *Islam, imam,* and *ihsan,* or "Submission, Faith, and Virtue."

The second part that the Gabriel Hadith teaches us is the importance of what has come to be called the "Five Pillars of Faith," or in Arabic the *Arqan ad-din*, which forms the principal ritualistic requirement of Islam and which define the believer's relationship to Allah. The first of the Five Pillars is the *Shahadah* or the "Confession of Faith." It says, "There is no God but Allah and Muhammad is His Prophet." The *Shahadah* is the first thing spoken to a newborn Muslim, and the last thing whispered into the ear of the dead.

The second of the Five Pillars of Islam is known as *Salat,* or ritual prayer. It requires the believer to pray five times a day. These prayers must be performed in the direction of the City of Mecca and involve first standing, then inclining, prostrating oneself, and finally, sitting. These prayers are read or chanted from the Holy Book, and if chanted, they must be done from memory in the Classical Arabic of *Al-Qur'an.* It is not allowed to have a book in one's hand when saying the *Salat,* nor can these prayers be done in any other language than Classical Arabic.

The third of the Five Pillars of Islam is called *Sawm Ramadan*, or the fasting during the month of Ramadan every year. During this month, all believers must refrain from food, drink and sexual relations from dawn to dusk. Ramadan occurs at different times of the year. The Muslim calendar beings lunar rather than solar, so the severity of the fast differs from year to year. The fast is intended to purify the believer as a renunciation of the world.

Zaqat, or "Almsgiving" is the fourth of the Five Pillars. It is a ritual requirement to distribute a portion of one's wealth to the poor. This requirement was instituted in Islamic Law, or *Shariah*, that constrains every Muslim to give two and a half percent of his or her wealth to the poor.

The *Hajj*, or the final of the Five Pillars of Islam, is the requirement to make a pilgrimage to the Holy City of Mecca at least once in his or her lifetime. The requirement is actually to make the pilgrimage to the city, as well as the *Kaaba*, a sacred shrine in the center of the city. By recreating many of the events of the lives of the prophets Ibrahim and Ismail, who are in the Muslim faith, the founders and the makers of the Kaaba, one injects oneself into the core of Islamic history, as well as also reevaluating one's life and society of that history.

The third thing that the Gabriel Hadith teaches us is that all Muslims are required to believe in six propositions called the "Six Articles of Faith." These are beliefs in Allah, His angels, the Revealed Books, the Bible and Al-Qur'an, the Prophets, the Day of Judgment, and finally, Allah's Decree regarding the ultimate destiny of each individual. These six beliefs, as we have indicated in Chapter One, are known as the "Six Articles of Faith," or in Arabic *Masjid Al-Muslimin*. The Six Articles of Faith in Islam are listed three times in the Muslim Holy Book. They come at Surah 3:84, 4:163–165, and at 6:84–87.

In addition to the Gabriel Hadith, there are also a number of other Ahadith about the *Malak Jibril*. One tradition from Ibn Abbas tells us this:

> Allah's Apostle was the most generous of all the People, and he used to reach the peak of generosity in the month of Ramadan when Jibril met him. Jibril used to meet him every night during Ramadan to teach him Al-Qur'an. Allah's Apostle was the most generous person, even more generous than the strong, uncontrollable wind in the haste to do works of Charity.[102]

The Prophet Muhammad's wife, Aisha, also provides us with a Hadith about her husband and the *Malak Jibril*. She says:

> Jibril made a promise with Allah's messenger to come at a definite hour; that hour came, but he did not visit him. And there was in his hand (in the hand of Allah's Apostle) a staff. He threw it from his hand and said, "Never has Allah or his messengers (angels) ever broken His promises." Then he cast a glance and, by chance, found a puppy under his cot and said, "Aisha,

when did the dog enter here?" She said, "By Allah, I do not know." He then commanded, and it was turned out. Then Jibril came, and Allah's messenger said to him, "You promised me, and I waited for you, but you did not come." Whereupon, he said, "It was the dog in your house that prevented me to come, for we angels do not enter a house in which there is a dog or a picture.[103]

Sometimes the major Ahadith on *Malak Jibril* do nothing more than speak of the angel's physical appearance, like this tradition from Abu Ishaq ash-Shabani (1290–1346), the prominent architect of the Mali Empire under the rule of Mansa Musa. Shabani observes:

I asked Zir Ibin Husbaish regarding the statement of Allah, "And was at a distance of but two bow lengths or even nearer; so did Allah convey the inspiration to His Slave (Jibril)." And then he (Jibril) conveyed to Muhammad on that, and Zir said, "Ibn Mau'ud informed that the Prophet he had seen that Jibril has six hundred wings."[104]

Al-Qur'an, as well, speaks of *Malak Jibril* splendid beauty when it says, "It is nothing but Revelation revealed, taught to him by one immensely strong, possessing power and great beauty. He stood there stationary." (Qur'an, 53:4–6.) Perhaps the most important appearance of the angel Jibril in Islam comes in the episode known as Muhammad's Night Journey, or his *Isna wa Mi'raj*. This episode is taken up in another section of this chapter.

In some traditions, Jibril is called the "Trusted Guide of the Prophets." In fact, in his *Qisas al-Anbiyah*, or the "Stories of the Prophets," Al-Kisai says that Jibril was the messenger to all of the prophets.[105] This work of Ali Al-Kisa'I, who died in 804, first appeared in English in the 1898 edition of I. Eisenberg in his thesis on Muhammad Ibn Abd Allah Al-Kisa'i. A complete English edition was later produced in 1922.[106]

Some translations say that *Malak Jibril* first appeared to Muhammad when the prophet was a child. The only other prophet in

Islam where this is said to be true is Isa (Jesus), where Jibril is said to have given Isa the power to speak to his mother, Maryam, when he still was in the womb. In fact, at Surah three, ayat forty-six, the Holy Qur'an tells us that Prophet Isa also will "speak to people while in the cradle."[107] This brings us to an analysis of the appearances of angel Jabril in his created, or natural state, the topic of the next section of this second chapter.

Appearances of Jibril in His Natural State

Several Ahadith in the major collectors refer to Muhammad's wife, Aisha, suggesting that her husband saw the angel Jibril when he was in the form he was created, or *fi surati hi* in Arabic. These episodes occur at Surah 81:23, where Jibril was seen "on the horizon," and at *Al-Sidra*, or "Lote Tree," that appears in the Muslim Holy Book at Surah 34:16, 53:14 and 16, and 56:28. The first of these passages, the one at Surah 34:16, tells us this:

> But they turned away, so We let loose on them with the inundation of a dyke, and replacing their garden with two other gardens which bore only bitter gourds, and tamarisks, and a few sparse Lote Trees.[108]

It does not appear that this is the reference that Aisha makes to Muhammad seeing in his *Fi surati hi*, or natural state. The two mentions of a Lote Tree at Surah 53:14 and 16 may be more helpful. The text tells us:

> By the Lote Tree beyond which none can pass, close to which is the Garden of Tranquility, when the Lote Tree was covered over with what it was covered over.[109]

Although this tree appears to have had some sacred function, it is not entirely clear what that function is. This brings us to the reference to the Lote Tree at Surah 56:28. This verse speaks of people in Paradise "reclining under the shade of a thornless Lote Tree." Aisha says that Muhammad saw the angel Jibril in his natural form that most likely refers to a vision of the Prophet in Paradise, perhaps on the *Mi'raj*, in which Prophet Muhammad stood under the shade of the Lote Tree.

The importance of these passages on the Lote Tree most likely refer to a certain tree at the edge of Paradise, where no one but Muhammad and Jibril could go—a view we have described earlier in this second chapter. This is the major interpretation in most of the references to the Lote Tree in the major collectors in Hadith literature, or the *Al-Sidiq* in Arabic. Abu Hurayra, for example, tells us this about the tree in question, "The Apostle of Allah said, 'In Paradise, there is a tree under the shade of which a rider cannot travel across its shade in seven hundred years.'"[110]

George Sale, one of the first modern English translations of *Al-Qur'an,* suggests that the "Lote Tree," or *Sidrah* in Arabic, is a tree "beyond which the angels themselves cannot pass," or, as others imagine it, "beyond which no creature's knowledge can extend."[111] Sale also points out that other commentators believe verse 6 refers to "A Host of angels worshipping around the tree,"[112] and he says another tradition speaks of "The birds that perch on the branches of the Sidrah."[113]

Other Ahadith on the Lote Tree concentrate on the enormous size of the *Sidrah*, or the nature of the tree. About the former, Ibn Abbas speaks of the tree's great height, while Sahih Wawud relates the *Sidrah* to the Ziziphus species, a prickly or piny shrub.[114] Still other exegetes, like Hisham Ibin Urwah, tells us that those who cut down the Lote Tree will enter Hell with their heads down.[115] A similar tradition can be found in the Hadith of Abd Allah Ibn Habashi.[116]

Many other Hadith describe what the Prophet Muhammad saw in his "Natural State." Many say *Malak Jibril* has six hundred wings in which every pair fills up all the space from East to West. Another account says that when Muhammad saw the Lote Tree, the prophet was seated on a *Qursi*, a venerable name for a "chair," that sits between Heaven and Earth, as revealed in Surah 74.[117]

Another tradition from Sahih Bukhari, says that the Prophet Muhammad saw *Malak Jibril* in his natural state, while the angel was in a cloud, which may refer to Aisha's comment.[118]

In many depictions of the *Malak Jibril* in Islamic iconography, he is often shown wearing two green garments and a silk turban, while seated on a white horse, presumably *Buraq*. A number of Shiite and Sufi interpreters, like Ibn Al-Farid, for example, the thirteenth-century mystical Arab poet, sees the vision of the Lote Tree as a kind of mystical experience in which the prophet sees angel Jibril in his natural state while the prophet's companions see an ordinary man. More is said about these images in Chapter Seven on angels in Islamic art.

These traditions point to the fact that the *Mala'ika*, and particularly *Malak Jibril*, have the power to change their shapes, sometimes appearing in the form of a human.

In a number of other Ahadith, the *Mala'ika* are shown as enormous creatures. Indeed, one ordinary Arabic word for "throne" is *Takhat*, but Allah's Throne is always called *Al-Arsh*. The Semitic root RSH, from which the Arabic word *Arsh* comes, is often used to designate "sacred places," as in the "Throne of Allah."

Another Hadith from Sahih Bukhari speaks of the appearance by Jibril, in his natural state, in the cave on Mount Hira:

> While I was walking, I heard a voice from Heaven, I raised my head and saw the angel who had come to me in the cave at Hira. He was sitting on a Throne between the Heavens and the Earth. I was very scared of him, and I went back home and I said to my wife, "Cover me!"[119]

In another tradition from Abu Bukhari, he speaks of the mission of the *Malak Jibril*. Sahih Bukhari observes:

> The mission of Jibril is not restricted only to conveying revelation from Almighty Allah. He used to come to the Prophet Muhammad every night in the month of Ramadan, to teach him the Qur'an. According to Ibn Abbas, "The Messenger of Allah was the most generous of people, and he was at his most generous time during Ramadan, when he used to meet Jibril; and he used to meet him every night during Ramadan, to study the Qur'an with him. The angel was more generous with him in doing the Good than the strong wind when it blows.[120]

A number of Ahadith also describe the role that *Malak Jibril* played in the building of the Kaaba and the establishment of the *Hajj*.

Ali and Leaman describe something of these functions of the angel Jibril. They observe:

> The angel Gabriel revealed its site [of the Kaaba] to Ibrahim and Ismail, and they were instructed to build it on this original site. The *Maqaam Ibrahim*, the "Place of Abraham" (Qur'an 2:125), is still today indicated there, together with the footprints of Abraham. The area one mile around the Kaaba was sacred and no warfare was to take place there, nor was any blood spilled. Abraham and Ishmael were also instructed in the ceremonies of the Pilgrimage [*Al-Hajj*.], which now included not only circumambulation of the Kaaba (2:125), but also the ritual of the *Sa'*, the movement back and forth seven times between *Al-Marwa and Al-Safa*, in reenactment of Hagar's movement as she reached for water in the Valley of Bakkah.[121]

Scholars Ali and Leaman continue their analysis:

> When Pilgrims today drink from the spring of Zam Zam, which is located in the sacred precincts, they are celebrating the miraculous appearance of the angel Gabriel who brought forth water for the thirsty Hagar and her son.[122]

Several other Ahadith are extant that discuss the role of the angel Jibril in the bringing of the waters to the Zam Zam. One Hadith tells us:

> Jibril made Zam Zam flow by the command of Allah, the Almighty, as an honor to Ismail and his mother after the Prophet Ibrahim had left them in a deserted valley near the present day site of the Holy Kaaba. She panicked because of the desolation of the place and asked her husband, "To whom are you going to leave us?" He said, "To Allah, the Almighty." She said in turn, "In Him, I trust." "Did He order you to do that?" "Yes," he answered. And as he left, he prayed to Allah, the Almighty, to provide them with company and means of

subsistence. In return for her deep faith, Allah told Jibril
to bring forth the Zam Zam.[123]

Several other Ahadith tell the same tale, where the well of the
Zam Zam is brought by the actions of the angel Jibril, on the order of
the Will of Allah. Traditions from Abu Bukhari, Sahih Muslim, and Ibn
Tabarani, all tell similar tales.[124] In another Hadith from Al-Bukhari,
the Hadith scholar speaks of Messenger Muhammad, so that he could
learn to pray as Allah wanted it to be performed. According to Abu
Masud, the messenger said, "Jibril came down and led me in prayer, so
I prayed with him, then I prayed with him, and then I prayed with him.
He counted off on his fingers five times."[125]

When the prophet saw Jibril the first time in his *fi surati hi*, or
"Natural Form," Muhammad is said to have fainted. He fainted, not
out of fear, or from what he was seeing, and it was not because he
believed Jibril would harm him. Rather, he thought he was seeing a
very great thing, and he was so fascinated by the aura of it, that he
fainted. There are also a number of "Pseudo Prophets," pretending to
be inspired by a vision of the *Malak Jibril*. In many of these, the angel
is said to have appeared in his natural and created form, as in the two
times he appeared that way to the Prophet Muhammad. A Hadith from
al-Tabari speaks specifically of false prophets.[126]

Kidhb Anibiya, or "False Prophets," are also discussed in a
number of passages of the Muslim Holy Book, including Surah 33:36
that reveals, "If anyone disobeys Allah and His Messenger, he is indeed
on a wrong path," as well as this line from the same Surah, ayat 73 that
tells us, "He that obeys Allah and His messenger already has attained a
great Victory."[127]

In some Muslim traditions, the *Malak Jibril* assigns the soul, or
nafs, to its place after death. Nerina Rustomji, in her book *The Garden
and the Fire*, tells us:

> When the soul arrives in the grave, it is greeted by
> two angels who conduct the Torment in the Grave, to
> determine where the soul will travel just after the Day
> of Judgment.[128]

The expression "torment of the grave," or *Adhab al-Qabir* in Arabic, in the above quotation is an Islamic concept pertaining to the period following death but prior to the Day of Judgment when the souls of the unrighteous are punished in the grave. Hadith literature contains numerous pieces of evidence and descriptions of the punishment in the grave, including Ahadiths from Ibn Abbas, Abu Hurayra, Ibn Annas and Umm Salama.[129]

The Prophet Muhammad's first wife, Khadijah, is afforded a special place in Paradise. Nerina Rustomji discusses that place and the angel Jibril's role in assigning that place. Rustomji observes:

> According to Hadith Collectors, Khadijah learned of her place from the angel Jibril.
>
> One day, Khadijah was bringing Muhammad some soup while he was in the presence of Jibril. Jibril instructed Muhammad that he should tell Khadijah that she has a palace in the Garden where there will be no noise and no fatigue.[130]

Professor Rustomji adds the comment, "Presumably, he was indicating that the palace would be a reward for the labor of her actions in this life. While in the Qur'an, this place is only designated as *Qasar*, in several Hadiths, it becomes identified as a palace.[131] In some Islamic traditions, the prophet asks the angel Gabriel from whence the rivers of water, milk, wine and honey flow, and emanate where they flow (Q47:14.), Jibril tells him that they go to the basis of *Kawthar*, an Arabic term to indicate "abundance." Indeed, the 108th Surah of Al-Qur'an is called *Al-Hawthar*. The word comes from an Arabic verb that means "to have plenty," which is odd given the fact that *Al-Kawthar* is the shortest of the chapters of the Holy Book, with only three verses.[132]

The *Malak Jibril* also plays a central role in most Islamic treatises on Eschatology or the Study of Last Things. Rustomji speaks of Al-Qazwini's thirteenth-century, *The Wonders of Creatures and Marvels of Creation*, when she writes:

> The text is part of the genre of wonders that describe the fantastic creations of the World. These wonders

begin with the first elements of creation and end with an explanation of the various climes of the World and their odd characteristics.[133]

Ms. Rustomji continues by describing the particular roles of *Malak Mika'il* and *Malak Jibril*:

> The opening Sections are devoted to eschatological narratives which include angels that will bring about the Day of Resurrection, and angel Isra'fil blowing the horn, angels of the dead recording their deeds, and angels Mika'il and Jibril.[134]

The *Malak Jibril* is also said to have visited the Prophet Idris, a figure who is thought to be the Hebrew Bible's Enoch. In Islam, Idris lived during a period of drought, inflicted by Allah to punish the people of the world who have forgotten Allah. Idris prayed for the salvation of his people and for the end of their suffering. This occurs by the receiving of rain, through the intercession of *Malak Jibril*. The Arabic word for rain is usually, *Matir*, or *Jaww Matir*, "it is raining." Another word, *dharba*, is usually employed for a "storm."

The principal reason that Prophet Idis is associated with Enoch of the Old Testament is that in Genesis 5:21, as well as passages in the Qur'an and Hadith, Enoch/Idris said that "God took him up."[135] Prophet Idris is mentioned in two places in Al-Qur'an, at 19:56–57 and 21:85. In the latter passage, Idris and other prophets are called "men of fortitude." At Surah 19:56–57, Idris is called "A truthful person and a Prophet," and "He was raised to an exalted station."[136]

In some Muslim traditions, it is said that when Idris left the Earth, the *Malak Jibril* was the first figure he sees when entering Paradise."[137]

One final Prophet in Islam to whom the angel Jibril is said to have appeared is Zakarias, or Zechariah, who is the guardian of Maryam, or Mary, the Mother of Isa. The Holy Book of Islam, at Surah three, verses 33 to 37, tell us this about Maryam and Zakarias:

> Remember when the wife of Imran prayed, "Oh Lord, I offer what I carry in my womb in dedication to your service, accept it, for you hear everything and know

everything. And when she had given birth to the child, she said, "Oh Lord, I have been given birth to a girl. But Allah knew better what she delivered. A boy could not be as that girl was. "I have named her Mary," she said, "And I give her into your keeping. Preserve her and her children from Shaytan, the ostracized." The Lord accepted her graciously and she grew up with excellency, and was given up into the care of Zakarias. Whenever he came to see her in her chamber, he found her provided with food, and he asked, "Where has this come from?" "From Allah," she said, "Who brings food in abundance to whomever He wills."[138]

This passage from Surah three of Al-Qur'an continues:

Then Zakarias prayed to the Lord, "Oh Lord, bestow me no offspring, virtuous and good. You answer all prayers." Then angels appeared to him in his chambers when he was in prayer. "Allah sends you good tidings of Yahya (John) who will confirm a thing from Allah, and be a noble, and continent, and a prophet and one of those who are upright and good.[139]

Then Zakarias asks, "How can I have a son. I am old and my wife is barren."[140] Then came the answer: "Allah does as He Wills."[141] Then Zakarias said, "Give me a sign [ayat], Lord." Then Allah replied, "The token will be that you will speak to no one for three days, except by signs; remember your Lord much, and pray at evening and at sunrise."[142]

Two other traditions in Islam that sometimes are ascribed to the *Malak Jibril* are the building and establishing of the Zam Zam, the sacred stream in Mecca that came forth when the angel Jibril instructed Ismail and his mother to kick the soil, whereupon the Zam Zam began to flow.

The other tradition is the establishment of *Al-Aqsa*, or what the Jews call "The Dome of the Rock," a temple built on the spot where Muhammad ascended to Heaven during the Mi'raj. This mosque complex reminds all Muslims of that blessed night when the prophet was taken miraculously by the *Malak Jibril*. Indeed, *Al-Aqsa* was the first holy place to which all Muslims, including Muhammad, should direct their prayers. Later, Allah ordered the prophet to turn toward the Kaaba and Mecca instead.

Other Hadith on *Malak Jibril* in traditional Sunni literature include an account of the angel Jibril and Prophet Ibrahim, "the father of hospitality," who is said to have been visited by the angel with various revelations, including the view that it was Jibril that halted the sacrifice of Ibrahim's son, and that Jibril provided the animal for sacrifice in this instance. Passages of the Holy Book at 21:91 and 66:12 refer to an angel appearing to Maryam, the Mother of Isa. Later exegetes have assumed the angel to have been Jibril. At Al-Qur'an's 19:17, an angel appears to Maryam in the form of a man, but it may be that it was the angel Jibril in his "Natural State," for she comments about the angel's beauty. There are also many representations of Muhammad and Jibril on their trip on the Mi'raj in much of Islamic iconography, to which we will turn in the next section of this second chapter.

Finally, there is a Hadith provided by At-Tirmidhi in which Allah sends Jibril to Paradise and says, "Take a look at it, see what I have prepared for its inhabitants." When the angel returns, He tells all that all will want to enter it. Then Allah sent Jibril to Hell to look around. The angel found that Hell was in layers, one above the other. When the angel returns to Allah, he tells the Almighty that no one will want to enter it. So Allah declares that Hell will be ruled by lusts. Then Allah sends Jibril back to Hell, and then the angel returns and pronounces, "No one will ever escape from it."[143] This brings us to some comments on Jibril in Muslim art.

Jibril in Muslim Art

Most of the artistic representations of the *Malak Jibril* in Islamic art are related to the angel bringing revelations to various prophets in the Muslim faith, including Ayyub, Yunus, Maryam, Isa, Muhammad, and many others. One of the most richly illustrated Persian manuscripts of the sixteenth century is the *Zubdat-Al-Tawarikh*, which is owned by the Museum of Turkish and Islamic Arts in Istanbul.[144]

The museum was built in 1583 during the reign of Sultan Murad III. Another copy is at the Chester Beatty Library (Ms. 414) in Dublin, Ireland. All three versions of this text are illuminated. Each has ninety-one folios and forty miniatures. The *Malak Jibril* appears in many of them, usually bringing revelations to various of the Muslim prophets.[145]

The angel Jibril frequently is shown, for example, in scenes related to Prophet Isa's Ascension into Paradise. In one image of the *Zubdat al-Tawrikh*, the Prophet Muhammad is shown sitting in a Mosque, along with several of his companions. A flaming halo crowns the prophet. A descending Jibril has come to deliver a revelation to the Prophet Muhammad.[146]

Other artistic depictions from the same text show Jonah escaping from the fish; Joseph, or *Yusuf*, from his well; and *Ayyub*, or Job being healed from the sores on his body. This brings us to the major conclusions of this second chapter. In the third chapter we will describe and discuss the roles of the other archangels in the Islamic faith.

Conclusions

In this chapter, we have attempted to explore the figure of the *Malak Jibril*, or the "angel Gabriel" in the Islamic faith. As we have shown, Jibril occupies the loftiest place among all the *Mala'ika*, or angels, in Islam. Among other reasons for this conclusion is the fact that he was the angel that brought the Revelations of *Al-Qur'an* to Prophet Muhammad, in a series of revelations that began in 610 and lasted twenty-three years. The figure of Jibril, however, is only mentioned by name on two occasions in the Holy Book, at 2:97–98 and 66:4. We also have suggested that when *Al-Qur'an* uses the expression *Ruh al-Qudus*, or "Holy Spirit," and the *Ruh Allah*, or "Spirit of God," many Islamic interpreters believe that these are none other than Malak Jibril, as well.

In the next section of this chapter, we described and discussed a Hadith from Muhammad's wife, Aisha, where the angel Jibril appears. The principal document we explored in this part of the chapter has come to be known as the Jibril or Gabriel Hadith. We have pointed out that this traditional Hadith acts as a compendium of the central beliefs of the faith of the Muslims, including the six Articles of Faith, and the five moral requirements of the faith.

In another section of this chapter, we explored the places among the traditional collectors of Hadith literature where the *Malak Jibril* appears. In this discussion we mentioned the two places where Aisha describes when the Prophet Muhammad saw the angel Jibril in his *fi Suruti hi* or in his "Natural State." In one of these, Muhammad saw the angel on the horizon, and the other is related to the incident at the Lote Tree.

In the next section, we described and discussed the role that the angel Jibril has played and what came to be known as "The Night Journey," or *Mi'raj*, in which *Malak Jibril* guided the prophet from Mecca to the city of Jerusalem, and then on to meet many other prophets on a journey to Paradise. In the final section, we discussed the role that the Malak Jibril played in bringing revelations to other prophets in the Islamic tradition. Among these prophets we explored were Adam, Lut (Lot), Musa (Moses), Yusuf (Joseph), Yunus (Jonah), Idris (Enoch), Maryam (Mary), and Zakarias or Zechariah. In each of these examples, the angel Jibril appears to the prophet announcing a revelation.

In Chapter Three, we shall explore the many roles of other archangels besides Jibril in the Islamic faith. Among these figures, as we shall see, are Mika'il (Michael), Isra'fil (Raphael) and Azrael, the Angel of Death in Islam. We introduce this latter *Malak* in Chapter Three, but he will be discussed at more length in Chapter Four.

Chapter Three:
The Other Archangels in Islam

Here, in epitome, are the great themes of the Qur'anic religion and its authentic atmosphere, urgent, forceful, and confident, and decisive, 'a book in which there is no doubt,' holding in its reach time and eternity, angels and men, truth and error, nature and signs, the piety of the good, and the doom is evil, and all within the immediacy of a strenuous prophetic encounter with a vexing and recalcitrant people.

—Kenneth Cragg, *The Religious Life of Man: The House of Islam*

The number of angels and their identities are unknown. Certain angels are identified in the Qur'an and in Islamic tradition: Jibril, the carrier of messages, Mika'il who guards places of worship; Izrael, the bringer of death; Israfil who will sound the trumpet to mark the Day of the Resurrection.

—C. T. R. Hewer, *Understanding Islam*

Allah and His angels shower their blessings on the Prophet. Oh believers, you should also send your blessings on him, and you should salute him with a worthy greeting.

—The Holy Qur'an, 33:56 (Author's translation)

Introduction

The general conclusion among Islamic scholars is that archangels are the highest order of angels, and those are the angels most often mentioned in the Muslim Holy Book Al-Qur'an as well as in the principal collectors of Hadith in both Sunni and Shiites Islam. The archangels are those who are considered closest to Allah in terms of their servitude. Indeed, their meaning and purposes are more detailed in Islam than any other of the angels.[147] Ibn Arabi, the thirteenth-century Spanish scholar, says that at the Resurrection, Hell (*Jahannam*) will be drawn along by 70,000 angels and that the width between these guardian angels is the distance of a seventy-year march.[148]

Ibn Arabi's comment seems to imply that there are many more archangels in Islam beyond the *Malak Jibril* or angel Gabriel. Similar traditions are told by Al-Sharani (1614–1690), a Kurdish scholar who taught in Medina in the mid-seventeenth century. His principal work is *Al-Mukhtassar*. This tome contains a commentary, or *Tafsir*, on Al-Qur'an. Another work on archangels in Islam are some comments written by seventeenth-century Indian mystic Fadl Allah Al-Hindi al-Burhanpuri.[149]

American scholar John Kalter in his book *Islam:What Non-Muslims Should Know* makes a number of general comments in introducing the category of archangels in Islam. Kalter writes:

> Angels often play a role in Islam similar to what is found in Judaism and Christianity, where they function primarily as messengers for Allah. A prime example of this is Gabriel, who Muslims believe to be an intermediary through whom Allah revealed the Qur'an to Muhammad.[150]

Professor Kalter goes on to explore the roles of the other archangels in Islam, pointing out that each *Malak* has a role in Islam that is unique. Ziauddin Sardar, in his book, *What Muslims Believe*, also writes of the special power and the unique place of each of the Muslim archangels. Mr. Sardar writes:

> The archangels were created with different forms and with different powers. Each is charged with a certain

duty. The three main archangels are: Jibril [Gabriel], the angel of Revelation; Israfil, the angel who will announce the advent of the Day of Judgment; and Azrael, the Angel of Death. Angels in the Muslim tradition do not make themselves known to ordinary men—only to Prophets.[151]

Our main task in this third chapter is to describe and to discuss the chief archangels in the Islamic faith, to explore where they appear in Al-Qur'an, as well as in traditional Hadith literature. This, in turn, will be followed by separate sections in this chapter on the other archangels, besides *Malak Jibril.*

In some Muslim traditions, there is a belief that the archangels and the regular angels were created from the body of Allah. Israfil is made from His heart; Jibril is made from Allah's Intelligence; Azrael, the Angel of Death, or *Malak al-Mawt* in Arabic, comes from His judgment; and Mika'il, the patron of Israel, comes from Allah's spiritual desire and ambition.

There are four archangels whom all Muslims are required to acknowledge. In addition to the angel Jibril (Gabriel), who we examined in Chapter Two, the Muslim faith also recognizes three other archangels. Their Arabic names are: *Mika'il* (Michael), *Isra'fil* or Raphael, and *Azrael*, which is the name of the *Malak Al-Mawt*, "Angel of Death," in Islam. Our principal aim in this third chapter is to describe and to discuss the roles of these three angels, in the Qur'an, in Hadith literature, and elsewhere in Islam.[152]

Although there are no explicit references to archangels in the canonical texts of the Hebrew Bible, there are a variety of ancient Hebrew terms that began to be employed in regard to special angels in the Old Testament, or angels with a higher status. Among these ancient Hebrew terms are the *Melek Elohim*, or the "Messenger of God;" the *Melak Adonai*, or the "Messenger of the Lord;" The *Bene ha Elohim*, or the "Sons of God;" and the *ha Qodesim*, or the "Holy Ones."[153]

References to special or higher angels are uncommon in the Hebrew Bible, except in later works like the Book of Daniel, for example. But special angels are mentioned briefly in the stories of

Jacob who wrestled with an angel, and Lot who was warned by two special angels of the impending destruction of Sodom and Gomorrah in chapter nineteen of the Book of Genesis. The Book of Daniel is the first Hebrew Bible text to mention these special angels by name. It is, therefore, widely speculated that Jewish scholars came upon the names of these angels during the Babylonian Captivity. In fact, Rabbi Simeon ben Lakish of Tiberius, in the third century CE, tells us that the specific names for the angels "were brought back by the Jews from Babylon.[154]

Another goal of this third chapter is to explore a number of other of the *Mala'ika* that are mentioned by name in the Qur'an or the writings of the major collectors of Ahadith in the Religion of Islam. To that end, we shall begin Chapter Three with a treatment of *Malak Mika'il*, or "angel Michael," among believers in Islam. We will then proceed to Isra'fil, and then on to Azrael.

Sources for Islamic Archangels

The most important source for the Islamic idea of archangels is to be found in the Hebrew Bible or Old Testament, as well as ancient Hebraic apocryphal literature. The four principal archangels in Islam, Jibril, Mika'il, Isra'fil, and Azrael or Izrail, all have a prominent place in ancient Judaism. The angel Michael, whose Hebrew name means "one who is like God," is the most prominent of the angels in the Hebrew Bible. He is considered to be the leader of the "Host of Heaven." He is believed to have appeared to Moses as the fire of the burning bush, at the third chapter of Exodus, as well as having rescued Daniel from the Lion's Den in the sixth chapter of the Book of Daniel. Michael is also believed by the ancient Jews to be an angel of mercy, repentance, and righteousness in the faith of the ancient Hebrews.

The name Isra'fil is the Arabic equivalent of Raphael. In Hebrew, this angel's name means "God has healed" or "God Heals." He was given this name in the Old Testament because it is said that he "healed the Earth" after it was defiled by the fallen angels. In fact, Raphael heals the figure of Tobit from blindness in the Book of Tobit at chapters two and three of that work.[155]

The angel Azrael, or Izra'il in Islam, is the *Malak Al-Mawt*, or the "Angel of Death." In Jewish mysticism, in the *Kaballah*, Azrael is a personification of evil. Scholar J. E. Hanauer, in chapter five of his *Folklore of the Holyland*, speaks of Azrael as "subordinate to the Will of Allah, with the most profound reverence."[156]

In both Jewish and Muslim sources, Azrael will be the final creature to die, and in the meantime, he records, and sometimes erases, the deeds of people on Earth. In Morocco, there is a custom of shaving the head but leaving a single tuft of hair on either side of the crown, so that at death it may act as a handle by which the soul is pulled from the body. Other Moroccans suggest the purpose of the "handle" is to pull the believer to Paradise (*Jannah*) on the Day of the Resurrection. In Islam, the *Malak Azrael* is said to reside in the Third Heaven.

As we shall see later in this chapter, the angel Azrael is sometimes depicted as an angel of destruction. In more contemporary terms, the angel in question appears as the central character in Anne Rice's 1996 novel *Servant of Bones*.[157] He is also a character in Arthur Miller's 1972 play *The Creation of the World and Other Business*.[158]

One other archangel mentioned in ancient Jewish literature is the figure of *Uriel*, whose name means "Fire of God," "Flame of God," "Light of God," or even "Sun of God." Uriel is sometimes referred to as the "Great Archangel of the Earth." It is said his influence is mostly felt in the summer months when the Sun is strongest. Angel Uriel is said to have warned Noah of the impending flood, to have aided in the burial of Adam, and to have led Abraham from the Ur of the Chaldeans. Some ancient Jewish texts suggest that Uriel stands at "The Gate of Paradise, holding a flaming sword." Uriel is said to be the Ruler of Magic, devotion, astrology, enlightenment, special insight, and sudden changes in the affairs of people. For this reason, Uriel is sometimes referred to as the "Winds of Change." In this sense, he frequently turns the worst of circumstances into great blessings. This brings us to an examination of the angel Mika'il in Islam.

The angel Mika'il in Islam, The *Malak Mika'il*, or "angel Michael," is mentioned only once by name in the Holy Book of Islam. This comes at Surah two, ayat 98. The text tells us, "Whoever is the enemy of Allah and His angels and Apostles, and of Jibril and Mika'il, then Allah is the enemy of such disbelievers." Rather than the conjunction *wa*, or "and,"

George Sale prefers *aw*, or "or," in his translation of 2:98. Thus, the eighteenth-century British translator of Al-Qur'an gives us this for 2:98:

> Whosoever is an enemy to God, **or** His angels, **or** Apostles, **or** to Gabriel **or** Michael. Verily, God is the enemy to the unbelievers.[159]

Muhammad Asad prefers this rendering of 2:98:

> Whosoever is an enemy to God **and** His angels **and** His Message-bearers, including Gabriel **and** Michael [should know that], verily, God is the enemy of all who deny the Truth.[160]

Asad calls the angels "Message-bearers," and he closes the line with, "God is the enemy of all who deny the Truth," which is a far cry from the literal Arabic of the verse:

> Who was the enemy of Allah and His angels and Messengers, and Gabriel and Michael, so then to Allah (is) an enemy to disbelievers.[161]

The Arabic noun used at the end of 2:98 is the word *Kafirin*, the plural form of *Kafir*, the common expression for one who does not follow the precepts of Allah. The word is employed a number of times in the Muslim Holy Book, including at 2:108; 3:52, 80, 167, and 177; 61:9, 12, 17, 23, 37, and 74; 16:106; and 49:7. The Arabic word *Kafir* is an active participle of the Semitic Root KFR, which most often means "to cover" or "to hide." By Muhammad's time, as well as to the present day, the word *Kafir* designates one who does not believe in Allah or His Prophet Muhammad,, or one who hides the truth about God.

What all commentators of Surah 2:98 have in common is the view that Jibril and Mika'il hold a special place among the *Mala'ika*, or angels of the Islamic faith. Indeed, for most Muslim Exegetes, the angel Michael is given a status among the angels above all but those at the very top of the angel Hierarchy that includes the *Malak Jibril*, or "angel Jibril."

Two different stories are told in the history of Isam to explain the Qur'an's 2:98. The first narrative says that the Jews, wishing to test the veracity of the revelation to Muhammad, asked the Prophet several questions, receiving truthful answers in each case. Finally, the Jews asked him, "Who brought you your revelation?" When Muhammad answered, "The angel Jibril," the Jews declared that this angel is their enemy, the angel of destruction. He is opposed by Mika'il who is said to be their angel protector, as well as the bringer of fertility and salvation.

In the second explanation of the Qur'an's 2:98, Umar, one of Muhammad's *Sahaba,* or companions, once entered a synagogue in Medina and asked the Jews questions concerning the angel Jibril. In response, they gave an account of *Malak Jibril,* like the first narrative outlined in the above analysis. Then Umar asked, in this second version, "What are the positions of these two angels with Allah?" The Jews replied, "Gabriel is on the right, and Michael is on His left, and there is enmity between them." Then Umar asked, "If they are that close to Allah, then why is there enmity between them?" Then he added, "But you are unbelievers more than asses are, and whoever is an enemy to these two angels is an enemy to Allah."[162]

Then Umar is said to have visited Muhammad, who received him with the words, "Jibril has anticipated you by a revelation. Whoever is the enemy of Jibril and Mika'il, is an enemy of Allah."[163] We are not aware of any Jewish tradition that suggests that the angel Gabriel is an enemy of the Jews, but the Hebrew Bible does contain a copious amount of information about the great attributes of the angel Michael. In the Book of Daniel 12:1, for example, Michael is called, "The Protector of your people," meaning the Israelites. In chapter 10:13–14 and 21 of the same book, the angel Michael again is said to be the "Protector of the Jews."[164] And in First Enoch 20:5, the angel Michael is referred to as "The best protected of the best of humankind."[165]

Some Muslim Exegetes suggest this second explanation of the Qur'an's 2:98 is connected to a tale that says that Mika'il has not laughed since the creation of *Jahannam,* or Hell. The origin of this view is not clear, but it does appear in several Ahadith, including one from Sahih Al-Bukhari's *Bad' al-khalk bab.*[166] Another account can be found in Al-Nasa'I's *Iftitah,* where the *Malak Mika'il* also incites Muhammad to recite Al-Qur'an, according to seven *Ahruf.*[167] The Arabic word, *haruf* is the plural form of *harf,* a term used to designate the seven principal stages in which Al-Qur'an was revealed to the Prophet Muhammad. The words *harf* and *haruf* do not appear in Al-Qur'an. Ibn Abbas, however, mentions seven *Haruf* in the following Hadith in which Muhammad says:

> Jibril recited the Qur'an to me in one *Harf*, and I recited it back to him. But I asked him to increase the number of *Haruf*, and he continued to increase them for me until we stopped at seven *Haruf*.[168]

Many other traditions from traditional Hadith literature confirm that the major times the Qur'an was revealed to Prophet Muhammad was seven, including Hadith from Ibn Shihab az-Zuhree, eighth-century Arab scholar, Ubay ibn Ka'ab, and Umar ibn Khattab, two seventh-century companions, or *Sahaba*, of the Prophet Muhammad.[169]

In Islam, the angel Mika'il is often depicted as the archangels of mercy who is responsible for bringing rain, thunder and snow to Earth. He is also said to be responsible for the rewards doled out to morally good people in this life. Thus, *Malak Mika'il* is said to provide nourishment for both bodies as well as knowledge to souls—a knowledge that they will need in the next life.

Some Muslim traditions suggest that Mika'il was the angel who taught Adam the universal greeting of peace with the words, "*Wa rahmatu Allahi was barakatahul*," or "Peace be on you and Allah's mercy and his blessings."

Malak Jibril wa Malak Mika'il, or angel Jibril and angel Michael are said to be the first of the *Mala'ika* to obey the orders of Allah and to bow down to Adam. The pair is also said to be the angels that purified Muhammad's heart during the Night Journey from Mecca to Jerusalem. Angel Mika'il is also remembered in Islamic history as one of the angels who aided

The Muslim Army in their first military skirmishes, beginning in the year 624. Indeed, he is thought of as the angel that led his cohorts into battle against the enemies of early Islam, the Qurashi Tribe. This brings us to a discussion of the angel Mika'il in Hadith literature, the topic of the next section.

The Angel Mika'il in Hadith Literature

In one tradition from the ninth-century collector of Hadith, Al-Tabarani, he tells us this about Malak Mika'il:

> Mika'il has assailants who follow his orders and makes the clouds and the winds move according to Allah's Will.[170]

In another Hadith from Ahmad, the Prophet Muhammad asks Jibril, "Why do I never see Mika'il laugh?" He replied, "Mika'il has not laughed since the Fire was created."[171] Again, it is not clear where this Hadith arose. There are no precedents to be found in the Hebrew Bible or Old Testament, nor in early Rabbinic sources. In a Hadith from Al-Bukhari, he has the prophet exclaim:

> Oh Allah, Lord of Jibril, Mika'il, and Israfil, Creator of the Heavens and the Earth, Knower of the unseen and the seen. You will judge between Your servants concerning where they differ. Guide me where there is a dispute concerning the truth by Your leave, for You guide whomever You will on the straight path.[172]

This Hadith is interesting because it seems to imply that the angel Israfil has a status that is comparable to Jibril and Mika'il. Although this judgment is made here by Sahih Bukhari, there is nothing in the other major collectors of Hadith that agrees with this claim. In several Ahadith, Mika'il's wings are said to be "the color of green emeralds," and he is covered with "Saffron hairs, each of them containing a million faces and mouths with as many tongues that speak a million dialects."[173] The archangels Mika'il is also said to have visited a number of other prophets in Islam, bringing various revelations to them. He is said to have appeared to Musa (Moses) as the fire in the burning bush, to have rescued Daniel from the Lion's Den, and to have told Maryam (Mary) of her approaching death. In a Hadith from Abu Hurayra, Jibril and Mika'il both visited the prophet Muhammad. The prophet had a toothpick in his hand that he immediately gave to Jibril, the angel who constantly gave him revelations. Then Jibril said, "Oh Muhammad, give it to the elder angel," and the prophet gave it to Mika'il. This

Hadith is most likely the source of the belief that the *Malak Mika'il* was created before the angel Jibril.[174]

In another Hadith from Sahih Muslim (821–875), Persian collector of Hadith, the prophet Muhammad says, "Allah gave me two celestial assistants to help me deliver my messages, Jibril and Mika'il."[175] This is another place where the Islamic tradition implies that the angel Israfil does not have the same status as the other two angels. Another way to see this fact is to point out that the dual form of the Arabic noun *Malak*, the word *Malakayn*, is only employed to refer to Jibril and Mika'il. Although Israfil appears to be an archangel, his status is lower than Gabriel and Michael in Islam.

The Arabic word *Malakayn* is also employed at Surah two, ayat 102, where it is used to designate the angels *Harut wa Marut*, or Harut and Marut. More will be said of these two angels later in this chapter. It is enough now, however, to say that some scholars believe these figures were two of the archangels in the Zoroastrian Faith.

In another Hadith by ninth-century collector Al-Tabuki, he tells us this about the *Malakayn*, Jibril and Mika'il, "One day, Allah announced to Jibril and Mika'il that one of them must die. Neither, however, was willing to sacrifice himself on behalf of his partner. Then Allah said to them, "Take Ali as an example, who was willing to give his life on behalf of Muhammad."[176]

In Ali Al-Kisa'I's *Tales of the Prophets*, he calls Mika'il "The Attendant of the Second Heaven," while he also says that Mika'il is "The Guardian of the Seas in the Seventh Heaven."[177] Sometimes Mika'il is mentioned as one of the pair of angels, along with *Malak Jibril*, who opened the breast of Muhammad to purify his heart during the Night Journey. This account is described at length by both Al-Tabari and Ibn Athir, as well as in Al-Qur'an.[178]

One final tradition about the angel Mika'il in Islamic history involves King Sulayman (Solomon) and his Vizier, who had noticed that jewelry began to go missing at the palace.

Sulayman assumed it was taken by evil Jinn, so he prayed to Allah to receive relief from the Jinn. In response to his prayer, Allah is said to have sent the *Malak Mika'il* to King Sulayman, bearing a gold ring. The angel tells the king if he wears the ring, its power will be at his disposal. Wearing the ring, Sulayman wished for his belongings to be returned to him, and in an instant, the lost jewelry appeared in the palace in its rightful place.

This Hadith shows that at times in Islam, when an angel is called to perform a particular job to help some human or to bring a special revelation to some prophet of Islam, that angel is not always Jibril, as in this case, it is *Malak Mika'il*. At times, the other archangels have been called by Allah to perform special tasks. In the next section of this chapter, we shall explore the image of the angel Israfil, the Arabic name for the angel Raphael. As we shall see, Muslim scholars both agree and disagree in places where the Judeo-Christian scriptures mention the angel Raphael.

The Angel Israfil in Islam

The Arabic name for the angel Raphael in Islam is *Israfil*, the third of the four archangels of Islam. A. J. Weinsinck, in his article on Israfil in the *Encyclopedia of Islam*, tells us that the word Israfil "is probably to be traced to the Hebrew *Serafin*, as a variant *Sarafil*." Weinsinck also suggests about Israfil:

> For three years he was a Companion to the Prophet Muhammad whom he initiated into the work of a Prophet. Gabriel took over this task and he began the communication of Al-Qur'an.[179]

Professor Weinsinck also tells us the following tale concerning Alexander the Great and the angel Israfil:

> Alexander is said to have met him [Israfil] before his arrival in the land of darkness. There he stood upon a hill and blew his trumpet, with tears in his eyes. If he is called the Lord of the Trumpet, it is most likely because he continually holds the trumpet in his mouth in order to be able to blow it at once as soon as God gives the order for the blast, which is supposed to arouse men from their graves. It is, however, also said that Israfil will be the first to be aroused on the Day of Resurrection. He will then take his stand upon the

Rock in Jerusalem and give the signal, which will bring
the dead back to life.[180]

In some Muslim traditions, it is said that the music of Israfil will
raise people from the dead, as well as refresh all those who already are
in paradise, or *Jannah*. It is also said in some traditions that three times
during the night, Israfil begins to weep. He sheds tears for those who do
not comply with their required *Salat*, or prayer.[181] In the Muslim faith,
the angel Israfil delivers commands from Allah to human beings; he
places spirits or souls in the bodies of humans, and, most importantly, he
is responsible for blowing his trumpet, or *Sur* in Arabic, at the coming
of the Last Days and the Resurrection of the Dead, at the End of Time.

Some Muslim traditions suggest that one of Israfil's four wings
"fills the West, the second fills the East, with the third he descends from
Heaven to Earth, and with the fourth wing, Israfil keeps himself veiled."
Israfil's two feet are said to be below the Seventh Earth, and his head
reaches the Throne, or *Arsh*, of Allah, in the Seventh Heaven. When
Allah wishes for something to happen, He causes a pen to write down
on a tablet that is situated between the eyes of Israfil. After receiving a
command from Allah about humans, it is sometimes said to travel from
Israfil to Mika'il or Jibril, and then on to the human to be visited. Many
Muslim accounts say that Israfil will blow his *Sur*, or horn, from the
Dome of the Rock in Jerusalem. There, he will announce the Day of
Resurrection, or the *Quimah* or *Qiamat* in Arabic. The trumpet is said
to be constantly poised, ready at the angel's lips, ready to blow when
Allah orders the angel to blow. In Islamic iconography, in a number
of Islamic traditions the angel Israfil is usually conceived as having
enormous wings and a huge, hairy body that is covered with mouths
and tongues. One wing protects his body, another shields him from
Allah, while the other two wings extend East and West. Irafil is said to
be overcome by sorrow three times a day and three times at night when
Muslims do not say their *Salat*, or required prayers.

It is said that Israfil tutored the Prophet Muhammad for three
years before he began to be visited by the *Malak Jibril*, beginning in
610. Israfil does not appear by name the Muslim Holy Book, but the
blowing of his trumpet is described in several places. It is said that in

the first blow, everything on Earth shall be destroyed. As the Qur'an's 27:87 tells us:

> When a single blast is sounded on the trumpet [*Sur*] and
> the earth and the mountains heave and are crushed to
> powder with one leveling blow, on that day will come
> what will come.[182]

On the second blow of Israfil's *Sur*, all human beings will be brought back to life again, or so the Holy Book's 36:51 tells us:

> When the second trumpet blast has sounded, they
> will come out of their graves and hasten to their Lord,
> saying, "Ah woe, who has roused us from our sleep?"[183]

Other references to angel Israfil blowing his *Sur* (or trumpet) are mentioned in the Muslim Holy Book at: 6:73, 18:99, 20:102, 23:101, 39:68, 50:20, 69:13, and 78:18–20. The final of these references reveals that:

> The day the trumpet blast is sounded, you will come
> in groups [or hordes]. The Heavens will open wide and
> turn into many doors; the mountains will be put into
> motion and turning into a mirage [or illusion].[184]

This is most likely an allusion to the fact that on the day of the Resurrection, people will travel in groups, and there will be many doors in Heaven (*Jannah*) through which people may enter Paradise. All of this will occur, Muslim history tells us, with three blasts from the *Sur*, or horn, of the angel Israfil.

These same judgments are also found at the Qur'an's 18:99 and 6:73. Contemporary Qur'anic translator Yusuf Ali gives us this for 18:99:

> On that day, We shall leave them to surge like waves on
> one another; the trumpet will be blown, and We shall
> collect them all together.[185]

Marmaduke Pickthal (1875–1936), in his 1930 English translation of Al-Qur'an, prefers this rendering of 18:99: And on that day, we will let some of them surge against others, and the trumpet shall be blown. Then we shall gather them all together in one gathering.[186]

The normal Arabic word for "horn" or "trumpet," is *buri*, or the plural, *Buriyat*. The noun employed at the Qur'an's 18:99, however, is the word *Sur*, which is only used in the context of Israfil signaling the End of Time with his three blasts. At the Holy Book's 6:73, the Arabic text gives us something like this:

> It is He Who created the Heavens and the Earth with Truth. The day He says, "Be!" It is, for His speech is the Truth. The kingdom will be His on the Day that the trumpet will be blown. The Knower of the unseen and the visible, He is the All-Knowing and the All-Wise.[187]

The Arabic verb "to be" that is employed at Surah 6:73 is the word *kun!* The inference is that all that it takes for Allah to bring something into being is simply the use of this Arabic verb.

This same verb, or the expression *kun fa-yakuna*, is employed a number of times in the Muslim Holy Book, including 2:117; 3:47; 16:40; 19:35; 36:82; and 40:68, in addition to surah 6:73 mentioned above. In each of these other passages of the Holy Book where the verb "to be" is employed in all of them, it refers to the fact that Allah brings something into existence simply by using that verb. Allah says, "Be!" and it is. This brings us to the places of traditional Hadith literature, where the angel Israfil is mentioned or discussed.

The Angel Israfil in Hadith

The figure of Israfil may be found in a number of entries of the traditional collectors of Hadith in the Islamic faith. In a Hadith from Sahih Muslim, for example, he relates the following story:

> Abu Salamah Ibn Abd Al-Rahman once said, "I asked Aisha, the Mother of Believers, about what Muhammad did to start his prayers at night [*quiyam al-layl*]. She said, "When he got up at night to pray, he would start his prayers with the words, "Oh Allah, Lord of Jibril, Mika'il, and Israfil, Creator of Heaven and Earth, Knower of the Unseen and the seen, You are the Judge in the matters in which Your slaves differ; guide me with regards to

disputed matters of Truth by Your permission, for You
guide whomever You will in the straight path.[188]

This Hadith seems to suggest that the angel Israfil has a status
in Islam that is comparable to that of Jibril and Mika'il. In a second
Hadith, from the collection of Abu Hurayra, he remarks that the Prophet
Muhammad said:

When Allah, the Most High created the Heavens and
the Earth, he made the *Sur* [the trumpet or horn] and
Allah gave it to the angel named Israfil; and the angel
placed it in his mouth, from that time until now, he is
holding the horn to his mouth and his eyes are fixed on
the Throne of Allah, the Most High; he is waiting for the
order from Allah to blow into his horn.[189]

The same tradition says that from that day, the angel Israfil has
never bowed down. He has never blinked, feeling that Allah the Most
High may order him to blow into the *Sur* before he is able to raise
his head, or before he is able to complete one blink of his eyes that
are fixed upon the Throne of Allah, waiting for the command to blow.
On that day, Allah will say, "Oh Israfil, blow your horn!" The same
tradition from Abu Hurayra continues:

The angel Israfil will blow into the horn and continue
to blow into it and he will not be getting tired or
require any rest. The sound from the horn will be so
terrifying that all those in Heaven and on the Earth will
be traumatized upon its sound, except for those whom
He, Allah, the Most High, wishes to be spared from the
terror of it all.[190]

It is said that the sound of the trumpet blasts at the End of Time will
send shock waves greater than atomic bombs throughout the universe,
causing the entire environment to rupture and to go into convulsions,
and chaos will reign everywhere. All the mountains will move from
their places, turning into fluffs of cotton and moving like clouds.
The Earth will begin to experience great earthquakes in every place,

splitting open and releasing hot lava and deadly gases. The oceans will boil and create great tidal waves. The sky, some traditions say, will turn black, and then the Heavens will be rolled back and will turn the color of copper-red with no clouds.

Then the Earth will be rolled back like a carpet or a scroll in the hands of the Almighty. On the day when the trumpet is sounded, young people who are strong and handsome will surely turn old in an instant, their hair turning white from the trauma, and their bones will begin to split and crack. Then, both the humans and the Jinn will experience a level of pain that is unimaginable. They will see the Heavens rupture, and all the stars will fall from the sky, and nothing will remain in their places, including the Earth itself.

In another Hadith on Israfil from Abdullah Ibn Abbas (619–687), uncle and companion of the Prophet Muhammad, he informs us:

> The archangel Jibril said to the Prophet, "This is the archangel Israfil. Allah, the Most High, created him standing at attention before Him. From the moment He created him standing at attention before Him. From the moment He created him, he never looks up. Between Israfil and Allah are seventy lights. There is not one of those lights he could approach, except to burn him.[191]

In the same tradition from Ibn Abbas, the seventh-century scholar relates about the angel Israfil:

> When the angels see Israfil descending towards the Earth with his trumpet, they will say, "Verily, Allah has ordered the inhabitants of the Earth to die, and the inhabitants of the Heavens to die.[192]

The Prophet Muhammad's uncle continues this Hadith when he writes:

> Then Israfil will bump into it, and the sound will come out of the horn which will be pointed toward the Earth. All living things on Earth will die, and then a sound will come out of the horn towards the Heavens, and all living beings there will, with the exception of Israfil.

Then, Allah will say to Israfil, "Oh Israfil, it is time for you to die." And then he will die.[193]

Some other collectors of Hadith, such as ninth-century Persian exegete Al-Tirmidhi, suggest that Israfil will make three blasts of his *Sur* at the End of Time. Abu Tirmidhi reports that Muhammad said of the *Malak Al-Mawt*, or Angel of Death, that he will blow his *Sur* only after the approval of Allah. Several other references to the Angel of Death appear in the Muslim Holy Book. These will be more fully explored in Chapter Four of this study.

It is enough now to say that Azrael, along with his minions or helpers, is responsible for the parting of the soul from the body at the death of every human being. The actual process of departing depends on the individual's personal history or record of good and bad deeds. The angel Azrael will look like a terrifying beast to the souls of evil humans, while the souls of good people will be separated from their bodies, like a drop of water leaving a glass. Indeed, Muslim history provides any number of metaphors for describing this event, like the tuft of hair handle among Moroccans described earlier in this chapter.

One narrative told about the *Malak Azrael* is that he brought Allah a handful of soil from which to create the first man, Adam, and this is how he earned the title, *Malak Al-Mawt*. Whether this is true or not, it is said that Azrael keeps a scroll of the deeds, both good and evil, of all humanity. On this scroll, traditions tell us, the names of the damned are circled in black, while the names of the saved are written in light. When the day of a person's death approaches, a leaf with that person's name on it falls from a tree beneath the Throne, or *Arsh*, of Allah. After forty days have passed, or so the tradition goes, the angel Azrael, or his helpers, severs the individual's soul from his or her body, sometimes by pulling on the lock of hair that attaches the soul to the body, or like a drop of water departing from the rim of a glass.

The angel Azrael is usually depicted in Islamic iconography as having gigantic proportions. One of his feet is said to rest in either the Fourth or the Seventh Heavens, while the other rests on a razor-sharp bridge that divides Paradise (*Jannah*) from Hell (*Jahannam*). The Arabic expression, "The wings of Azrael" is employed in Muslim traditions to refer to the *Malak Al-Mawt* approaching. Some Islamic traditions suggest there are several ways of forestalling the coming of Azrael, or his followers.

By reciting a *Dhikr*, a ritual prayer, a believing Muslim may prevent the Angel of Death from entering his throat. When a believer is in the process of distributing *Sadaqah*, or "Alms to the Poor," the angel cannot take him at that time. After all the protests that humans make to forestall the day of death, the Malak Azrael returns with an apple from Paradise inscribed with the *Bismillah*, "In the name of the Most Merciful and Compassionate," or the angel writes Allah's name on the palms of the believers before the souls leave their bodies. The souls of believers are gently drawn out and carried to the Heavens, while the souls of unbelievers are ripped out of their bodies and hurled down to Earth before they can reach the gates of Paradise (*Jannah*).

In addition to these archangels discussed earlier in this chapter, there are also a number of other *Mala'ika* or angels that are mentioned by name in the Muslim Holy Book. In the next section of this third chapter on angels in Islam, we shall explore and discuss some of these other celestial beings mentioned in the Holy Book, Al-Qur'an.

Other Angels Mentioned by Name in Al-Qur'an

In addition to the angels mentioned in the above analysis, there are at least ten other celestial beings mentioned by name in Al-Qur'an. Among these are: Malik, the angel who rules Hell; Ridwan, or Rizwan, the angel responsible for guarding Paradise; the *Qiramun wa Qatibin*, or the two angels who record the good and bad deeds of human beings while on Earth; Munkar and Naqir, a pair of angels who interrogate a person's soul while in the grave to determine its place in the afterlife; and Harut and Marut, a couple of angels, or *Malakayn*, who were sent by Allah as a test of ancient Israelites while in Babylon.

The Arabic expression *Qiramun wa Qatabin* comes from two different Semitic roots, KRM and KTB. The word *Qiramun* comes from the former root. It is related to the verb "to be honorable" or "to honor." The Arabic noun *Qatabin* comes from the root KTB, and is related to the verb, "to write," *keteb*, and to the noun *kataba* or "writing." Thus the expression, *Qiramun Qatabin* means "The honorable who write things down," in this case, the good and bad deeds of human beings. The Arabic expression is employed at the Qur'an's 6:61 and 82:10–11, among other places.

Some of these *Mala'ika* listed above are dealt with at length in the next chapter, for they are among the Muslim angels associated with Death (Malik, Munqar, Naqir, Qiramun and Qatabin.) Others are known by their jobs or roles in the history of Islam. Among these are the Keepers of Hell (39:71, 43:77, 66:6, 74:27–31, and 97:17–18), the Keepers of the Throne, or *Arsh* of Allah, at 40:7 and 69:15–17; and the guardian angels (6:61, 13:10–11, 43:80, 50:17–18, and 82:10–11). There are also angels who praise Allah night and day, described at the Qur'an's 21:20 and 41:38.

In addition to these celestial beings, there are also a number of angels with particular jobs that are only known from the principal collectors of Hadith, both Sunni and Shiite. There are different angels, for example, who are responsible for the Seven Heavens. Again, Abdullah Ibn Abbas, speaks of these *Mala'ika* in another Hadith. He observes:

The name of the angels in charge of Heaven are as follows, beginning with the sphere of the moon and in charge of cattle (*Isma'il*), eagles (*Mika'il*), vultures (*Sa'idya'il*), horses (*Salsa'il*), Houris (*Qalka'il*), heavenly youths (*Samkha'il*), and mankind (*Rufa'il*).[194]

Another of these special angels is discussed in several Ahadith from Abu Dhar and Abu Tirmidhi, for example, that refers to what they call the "angels of the Mountains." The overall authority for the Gates of Heaven is the angel Ridwan. The "Abu Dhar" mentioned above is Abu Dhar Al-Ghifari (590–652), a Medinan scholar who was the fourth or fifth person converted to the Faith of Islam. Abu Al-Bukhari also discusses this category of the *Mala'ika* in his Hadith. He observes:

> He has sent the Angel of the Mountains so that you might tell him to do to them whatever you want me to do. If you want, I can crush them between the mountains.[195]

Abu Tirmidhi also speaks of this angel in question. He reports:

> But there is an angel there, placing his forehead in prostration to Allah. By Allah, if you knew what I know,

you would laugh little and weep much. You would not enjoy your relationships with women, and you would go out into the street praying to Allah.[196]

Another classical Hadith also tells a tale related to the Angel of the Mountains. It comes from Prophet Muhammad's wife, Aisha, when she asked the prophet if he ever faced a day more severe that at the Battle of Uhud? The prophet is said to have answered:

Yes, I have experienced such things at the hands of your people and such a day was the day of Aqabah. On that day, I presented myself to Abdi Liah Ibin Abd Kulal and I offered him Islam, but he failed to respond to what I have offered. I, therefore, left with a heavy heart and was depressed. I felt some relief only when I reached Qarn Sa'alib. Here I looked up and saw a cloud over me; and inside the cloud, I saw the angel Jibril who called to me and said, "Allah, the Most High, has heard what your people have said to you and in your response to your offer. And now He will send you the Angel of the Mountains, and my Lord has sent me to you to carry out your orders. What should be done? Shall I crush them between two Mountains encircling the City of Mecca?" But the prophet responded and said, "I do not want their destruction. I am still hopeful that Allah will make some of their children good Muslims, who would worship Him, the One, without associating anyone with Him."[197]

Similar Ahadith about the "Angel of the Mountains," have been recorded by Abu Hurayra, Abu Bukhari and Sahih Muslim. In these, as well as the above examples, the Angel of the Mountains comes to the aid of the Prophet Muhammad, usually when he has had some sort of run-in of a moral character, where he successfully attempts to convert some humans to Islam.[198]

Another set of angels with a peculiar role in Islam is described in another Hadith from Abu Hurayra, who informs us:

The Messenger of Allah said, "Allah has angels who travel the highways seeking out the people of Dhikr [the worship of Allah]; when they find people remembering Allah, the Mighty and the Majestic, they call out to one another, "Come to what you hunger for! And they enfold them with their wings, stretching up to the lowest Heaven.[199]

The Holy Book of Islam, at Surah 21:20, also speaks of another peculiar set of angels. In Arabic, these *mala'ika* are called *Al-Qarraubiyyum*, or in English, "The Cherubim." The word only appears this one time in Al-Qur'an. The noun most likely comes from the Hebrew word, *Kruv*, or *Kruvim* (Cherubim), which in turn, if Roland De Vux is correct, is a cognate of the Assyrian term *Karabu* that means "to be near." The Muslim uses of the word *Al-Qarraubiyyum* are most likely related to the uses of the Cherubim in the Hebrew Bible and early Rabbinic materials such as the Book of Genesis 3:24, which speaks of *Cherubim* guarding the Garden of Eden after Adam and Eve had been expelled from it.

Another Hadith from Abu Hurayra tells us that the job of the Cherubim is to ask forgiveness for those who have passed wind. Abu Hurayra tells us that Muhammad said,

The angels keep on asking for Allah's forgiveness for anyone of you, as long as he is at his *Mu Sallat*, or "praying place," and does not pass wind.[200]

Another tradition, also from Abu Hurayra, makes the same point. He observed:

When he enters the Mosque, he is considered in prayer as long as he is waiting for the prayer and the angels keep asking for Allah's forgiveness for him and they keep saying, "Oh Allah, be merciful to him, oh Allah, forgive him, as long as he keeps sitting at his prayer place and does not pass wind."[201]

Two other Hadith about prayer and passing wind come from Sahih Muslim and Abu Al-Bukhari. In the first of these traditions, Sahih

Muslim says, "A person must make a *wudu* [ablution] if he hears a sound and perceives a smell of passing wind [or gas]."[202] In the Hadith from Al-Bukhari, he observes that "Allah would not hear the prayer," but he does not give a reason why this is the case.[203]

These four Ahadith about flatulence are part of a larger collection about angels passing wind in particular, or passing wind in general by Allah's creatures. What all of these traditions have in common is that the passing of wind in Islam is an act for which the believer must be forgiven for something that ordinarily is not thought of as a religious issue. Often in the history of Islam, flatulence is discussed in the context of prayer, and whether certain prayers, or ritual acts, annul the sin of passing gas.

A final class of angels in the Islamic tradition can only be found in the larger collectors of Hadith literature. These are the celestial beings, or *Mala'ika*, who are responsible for the conception of human beings in the womb. A Hadith from the collection of Abu Bukhari speaks explicitly about the role of these angels:

> The way that each of you is created is that an angel is gathered in his mother's womb for forty days as a sperm drop; and then for a similar length of time as a blood clot; and then for a similar length of time as a lump of flesh. Then another angel is sent and he breathes into the fetus, and is charged with four commands: to write down his provisions, his life span, his actions, and whether he will be wretched or happy.[204]

A Hadith from Sahih Muslim also speaks about the inter-uterine actions of these angels:

> The constituents of one of you are gathered in his mother's womb for forty days. Then it becomes a lump of chewed flesh, and, forty days later, Allah sends his angels to breathe in the spirit [or *Ruh*]. The angel comes with instructions concerning four things. The angel writes down his livelihood, his death, his deeds, and whether he will be doomed or blessed.[205]

This Hadith is different from the previous one because Al-Bukhari believes that an angel is responsible for conception and development of the fetus, while the tradition from Sahih Muslim thinks the angel in question is only responsible for the initial 120 days in the womb. Although these views appear to be different, the overall point is the same. Namely, that Allah is always responsible for the bringing of life, whether human or otherwise. This brings us to some observations about the angels and the roles in the Throne and Stool of Allah, or *Arsh* and *Qursi*.

The Mala'ika and the Arsh and Qursi of Allah (Throne and Foot Stool)

One final collection of archangels in the Islamic faith are those associated with Allah's *Arsh* and His *Qursi*, or His "Throne," and His "Foot Stool." The Throne of Allah is mentioned at a number of places in Al-Qur'an. Marmaduke Picktal gives us this English rendering for the Holy Book's 69:17:

> And the angels will be on all sides, and eight will that day bear the Throne of Thy Lord above them.[206]

At the Qur'an's 20:5, we see another mention of both Allah's *Arsh* and His *Qursi*. This text reveals:

> The Beneficient One, Who is established at the *Arsh* and the *Qursi*, and to Him belong all that is."[207]

From these and other passages in Al-Qur'an, we can glean three conclusions. First, Allah's Throne is carried by eight angels. Secondly, in addition to having a throne, the Almighty also has a *Qursi*, or "Foot-Stool." And finally, at the End of Time, Allah will appear to human beings, in the Highest Heaven, sitting on His *Arsh*, or Throne.

The Throne of Allah, and the angels who accompany it, are also discussed in a number of traditional Hadith in the Muslim faith. One tradition from Abu Al-Bukhari, indicates that:

> In Paradise there are one hundred levels that Allah has prepared for the Mujahadin who strive for the cause of Allah. The distance between each two levels is like

the distance between Heaven and Earth. When you ask
of Allah, ask Him for Al-*Firdaws*, for it is in the middle
of Paradise. Above it is the highest level of Paradise,
and above that is the Throne of the Most Merciful. And
from it, springs forth the rivers of Paradise.[208]

The Arabic term, *Al-Firdaws* literally means "Paradise." It is a
synonym for the word *Jannah*. Most scholars of Islam and the Arabic
language agree that it is a borrowed word from either Ethiopic or Syriac.

In another Hadith about the *Arsh* from Abu Bukhari, he tells us
that, "The *Arsh* is just above the Seventh Heaven."[209] This judgment is
confirmed by a Hadith from Sahih Muslim that says:

A man from among the Companions to Muhammad,
a man named Ansar, said that when Allah decrees
something, the angels surrounding the Throne Glorify
Him and sing His praises, both day and night.[210]

Exegete Ibn Kathir speaks of these same angels when he wrote:

The distance between the Seventh Heaven and the
Qursi is a distance of five hundred years. The Throne
is above the water and Allah is above the Throne, and
none of your deeds are concealed from Him.[211]

A number of other Hadith confirm the geography of the furniture
in the Great Beyond. Ibn Al-Qayyim (1292–1350), famous Hanbali,
Sunni scholar, for example, in his *zayad al-Ma'ad*, or "Provisions for
the Hereafter," tells us that, "The Throne of Allah is the roof of creation
and the greatest of created things."[212] This brings us to a discussion of
one final Muslim archangel, a celestial being known as *Seraphiel*.

The Archangels Seraphiel

In addition to the archangels of Islam discussed above in this
chapter, a fifth *Malak* known as *Seraphiel* also is sometimes mentioned
among the archangels in the Islamic faith.

Murata and Chittick give this description of how the human race
came to be, as well as the role of the angel Seraphiel. They write:

Some of the Prophet's Companions connected this diversity of colors among the peoples of the Earth in a suggestive way. They reported that when Allah wanted to create Adam, He sent the angel Seraphiel down to Earth to collect some soil. The Earth, however, protested. It did not want to give up anything of itself. Earthly creatures, especially humans, tend to be like that; they are very concerned about themselves and their integrity. The Earth begged and pleaded with Seraphiel who finally felt sorry for the Earth, and the angel went back to Allah and he asked Him what to do. Allah said it was not important, and that He decided to send another angel. So He sent Mika'il, but the same thing happened, and Michael came back empty-handed. Then Allah sent Jibril, but it was the same story. Then Allah sent Azrael, giving him special instructions. Azrael went down and explained to the Earth that he was merely going to borrow the soil for a short period of time, and that he would take personal responsibility for returning it. Having collected soil from the Earth's four corners, some red, some white, some black, and some yellow, Allah took the soil and mixed it together with water and molded the clay of Adam. This explains the diversity of human colors. And it also explains why Azrael is the Angel of Death. It is his responsibility to return the Earth to its proper place. Hence, he has to take away the human spirit and give the soil back to its rightful owner, the Earth.[213]

Not only do Murata and Chittick give an explanation for why there are different races of human beings on Earth, but they also, at the same time, introduce another of the Islamic guardian angels, this figure known as *Malak Seraphiel*. This angel is mentioned in the Third Book of Enoch and is the eponymously named Chief of the Seraphim, one of the orders of angels in ancient Judaism. In fact, in Hebrew Seraphiel's name means, "Prince of the Higher Order of Angels."[214]

In the Third Book of Enoch, the angel Seraphiel is described as being "An enormous, brilliant angel, as tall as the Seven Heavens." He has a face like an angel, but the body of an eagle. He is beautiful like lightning and the light of the morning star. Since he is the magic angel, Seraphiel is the Ruler of Tuesday and the planet Mercury. When Allah invokes him, it is always from the North, or so Gustav Davidson says in his 1967 work, *A Dictionary of Angels.*[215] Henry Corbin, in his *Man of Light in Iranian Sufism,* provides a poem on Seraphiel in which he suggests that the angel is one of the "Guardians of the Throne." The poem also mentions the *Houris of Paradise,* as well as the flowers that Seraphiel is said to deliver to each of the prophets.[216] It is likely that the name Seraphiel entered Judaism during the time of the Persian Empire and its occupation of Palestine. Henry Corbin suggests the Hebrew name comes from the Zoroastrian god *Sraosah.*[217]

In Muslim eschatology, the *Malak Seraphiel* is said to be the leader of the *Mala'ika* that carry the *Arsh*, or Throne of Allah. Other angels who also are sometimes mentioned as performing this task in Islam are *Kerubiel, Radweriel, Orphanniel* and *Chayyliel.*[218] This brings us to one final task in this chapter—the idea of whether there is an angel hierarchy in Islam.

Angel Hierarchy in Islam

One final question for this chapter on archangels in Islam is whether there is or is not an angel Hierarchy in the Muslim faith. By the time of Thomas Aquinas in the thirteenth century, the Christian tradition had settled on a hierarchy of angels, in which there were thought to be nine different kinds, or "choirs" of angels, with the Seraphiem at the top of this hierarchy. Thomas, who was known as the "angelic doctor," gives us this hierarchy in his *Summa Theologica*:

1. Seraphiem
2. Cherubim
3. Thrones
4. Dominations
5. Powers

6. Virtues
7. Principalities
8. Archangel
9. Angels[219]

There is no comparable hierarchy to be found in the history of Islam other than three observations that can be added about the matter. First, there is a general understanding that the archangels discussed in this chapter are the highest order of angels in Islam. Secondly, in Islam it appears that the *Qarriyahbim*, or "Cherubim," are another higher order of angels that quite possibly carry the *Arsh*, or Throne of Allah. And finally, there appears to be an order of *Mala'ika* in the Faith of Islam that is the ordinary, run of the mill category of celestial beings, so there appears to be at least three different kinds of angels in the Muslim faith.

Conclusions

Our principal aim in this third chapter has been a description and an explication of the archangels in the Faith of Islam. We have shown that in addition to the angel Jibril, there are at least three other archangels in the Muslim faith. Their names, as we have shown are Mika'il, Israfil and Azrael. Indeed, in three sections of this third chapter we explored the roles that these three *Mala'ika* play in the Islamic faith.

Additionally, in Chapter Three, we explored a range of other angels in Islam that appear to have had special roles in the Faith of Muhammad. Among these are: Ridwan, Malik, Munqir and Naqir, the *Qiramun wa Qatabin*, or "recording angels," and Harut and Marut, who were sent by Allah as a test of the ancient Israelites while in Babylon. We also described a final archangel whose name is *Seraphiel*. In that section of this chapter, we mentioned the role that Seraphiel may have played in the creation of the races of humankind, as well as the view that Seraphiel may be one of the eight angels who carry the *Arsh*, or Throne of Allah in the Islamic faith.

In the following chapter, we shall describe and discuss a range of angels in Islam associated, in one way or another, with the idea of *Mawt*, or "Death" in Islam.

Already in this study, we discussed a number of these angels, such as those responsible for parting the soul from the body, those responsible for Heaven and Hell, those who interrogate the dead in their graves, and those angels who record the good deeds and the bad deeds of humanity. We now turn to angels associated with death in Islam.

Chapter Four:
Angels Associated with Death in Islam

The Lord of inaccessibility created the Throne and placed it on the shoulders of the angels brought near. He created Heaven and gave it to Ridwan. He created Hell and gave it to Malik.

—Sachiko Murata, *The Tao of Islam*

The angel Malik is the guardian of Jahannam. His head is bowed and he recites, "Praise be to He Who commits no injustice.

—Sayed Nurjan Mirahmadi, "Angel Names and Their *Dhikr*"

If only you could see when the Angel of Death takes the souls of those who disbelieve, when the angels beat their faces and backs.

—The Holy Qur'an 18:50 (Author's translation)

Introduction

In the Islamic faith, there are a variety of angels associated with Death (*Maut* or *Mawt* in Arabic). In addition to Azrael, the Angel of Death or the *Malak Al*-Mawt, there are also a number of other celestial beings associated with death in one way or another. Among these other *Mala'ika* associated with death are Malik, the angel who rules *Jahannam*, or Hell, and his minions: Ridwan, the angel who is responsible for the Gates of *Jannah*, or Heaven; and Munqar and Naqir, the pair of angels, or *Malakayn*, who interrogate the dead in their graves.

Our main task in this fourth chapter is to describe and discuss, in turn, the roles that these angels mentioned above have played in Islamic eschatology. We begin this chapter by discussing the major precedents and sources of *Malak Azrael*, or angel Azrael, or the Angel of Death in Islam. This will be followed by a discussion of the *Malak Al-Mawt*, in the history of Muslim theology and philosophy. After these observations, Chapter Four also will contain subsequent sections on the other angels in Islam sometimes associated with death.

Sources for the Angel of Death in Islam

In Muslim theology, Azrael, the Angel of Death, is "forever writing in a large book and forever erasing what he has written." What he writes in the book is a person's birthday; what he erases is the name of that same person's death.

There are a number of precedents or precursors in ancient Near Eastern literature to the idea of an Angel of Death in Islam. In ancient Judaism, for example, Michael, Gabriel, and Sariel, all have been employed to designate the Angel of Death. In Zoroastrianism, the ancient Persian religion, the name of the Angel of Death was *Mairya*. Among the ancient Babylonians, he was called *Mot*. In early Rabbinic lore, there were fifteen angels of death. Their names were Yetzerhara, Adriel, Yehusiam, Abaddon, Sammael, Metatron, Gabriel, Mashhit, Hemah, Malach-ha-Mavet, Kafziel, Ksef, Leviathan, Rabhab, and, of course, Azrael.[220] In Falasha lore, the Angel of Death was called *Suriel*.[221]

Some accounts of Jewish folklore suggest that when the angel Rahab refused to part the Red Sea on the orders of God, the angel was assigned the task of taking souls at death. Another Angel of Death in Judaism became an angel known as *Yama* or the *Malach ha-Mavet*. The Babylonian Talmud in places associates the Angel of Death with *ha Satan* or the Satan. Thus, the legend says, he became evil rather than the good angel of which he was made. The ancient Hebrew term *Malach al-Mavet* is an obvious cognate of the Arabic *Malak al-Mawt*, or "Angel of Death."

Among other Semitic cognates to the words *Mavet* or *Mot* (Hebrew) and *Mawt* or *Maut* in Arabic are *Mauta* (Syriac), *Mewt*

(Maltese), *MWT* (Aramaic), and *Mutw* (Akadian). From all of this, it should be clear that the MWT root in Semitic languages is connected to various words for death in the ancient Near East.

Another commonality is the belief that one angel, or celestial being, has been given by God the job of separating the souls of humans from their bodies at death. The Semitic root MLK is usually the source for the word "angel" in these various languages, like *Malach* in Hebrew, and *Malak* in Arabic, for example.

This tradition of one angel being assigned the task of separating the soul from the body was adopted fairly early on in the Islamic tradition in the developments of eschatology, or the study of last things. Sometimes this angel is referred to as Azrael, or Is'rail in Islam, and sometimes as the *Malak Al-Mawt*, which may mean "Messenger of Death" or "Angel of Death" in Arabic. The Muslim Holy Book at Surah 32:11 is a good example of where the angel in question is called *Malak Al-Mawt*. This passage will be discussed in the next section.

A final source that may have influenced the Islamic view of the Angel of Death are certain passages from the New Testament. Among these is the Gospel of Luke 16:19–23, where the beggar Lazarus is the topic of conversation. The Gospel observes:

> Once there was a rich man who dressed in purple and linen and feasted splendidly every day. At his gate lay a beggar named Lazarus, who was covered with sores.
>
> Lazarus longed to eat the scraps that fell from the rich man's table. The dogs even came and licked his sores. Eventually, the beggar died. He was carried by angels to the bosom of Abraham. The rich man likewise died and was buried. From the abode of the dead where he was in torment, he raised his eyes and saw Abraham from afar off, and Lazarus resting in his bosom.[222]

The ancient Hebrew and Greek expression, "The Bosom of Abraham" was a New Testament and Jewish Apocryphal term signifying the abode of bliss in the life beyond the grave. The term is employed in the Fourth Book of Maccabees at chapter thirteen, verse seventeen. The

Hellenistic *Testament of Abraham* also uses the expression. The Greek word for "bosom" in the New Testament, at John 13:23, is employed to signify the "lap" of a person indicating "closeness" or proximity to someone or something. Thus, to be in Abraham's bosom meant to be in repose and happiness with the patriarch.[223]

This New Testament narrative of the angels carrying Lazarus off after death may well be another source for the Islamic perspectives of the Angel of Death. Many of the principal precursors to the idea of the Angel of Death in Islam can be found in earlier Biblical materials.

The angel of the Lord smites 185,000 men in an Assyrian camp at Second Kings 19:35. When the Angel of Death passes through to smite Egyptian first-born, God prevents the "Destroyer" from entering houses with blood on the lintel or doorposts (Exodus 12:23). At Second Samuel 24:16, the destroying angel rages among the people of Jerusalem, and King David sees the angel of the Lord "standing between the Earth and the Heavens, with a sword drawn and stretched out over Jerusalem."[224]

Both the Book of Job 33:22 and Proverbs 16:14 use the expression "Angel of Death," as does Psalm 89:45.[225] The targum of the latter passage translates the verse, "There is no man who lives and seeing the Angel of Death can deliver his soul from his hand."[226] The Midrash Rabba explains Ecclesiastes 8:4 as, "One may not escape the Angel of Death, nor say to him, 'Wait until I put my affairs in order,' or 'Take my son or my slave in my place.'"[227] As we shall see later in this chapter, it is common in the ancient or medieval Near East that when one encounters the Angel of Death, the human asks for a reprieve to put one's things in order or to asks if another can substitute in his or her place. The Babylonian Talmud tells us, "Where the Angel of Death appears, there is no remedy."[228]

The Midrash Tihuma says, "If one has sinned and confessed his fault, the Angel of Death may not touch him."[229] Other passages in the Talmud and Midrash suggest that God sometimes protects people from the Angel of Death. Other ancient Rabbinic texts suggest that certain acts of moral goodness can negate the anger and certitude of the Angel of Death.[230]

In the New Testament, Death or *Thanatos* is often seen as a metaphor or personification of death. One example can be found at

Acts of the Apostles 2:24, which tells us: But God raised him [Jesus] from the dead, freeing him from the agony of death because it was impossible for death to keep his grasp on him.[231]

Other New Testament passages are even more explicit, as in Romans 5, for example. The text speaks of Death having reigned "from the time of Adam to the time of Moses."[232]

Various passages in the Epistles also speaks of Christ's work on the Cross and at the Resurrection as a confrontation in which Death is defeated.

Another possible New Testament source for the Muslim Angel of Death is the fourth horseman in the Book of Revelation, chapter six, where he is pictured with Hades, the god of the underworld. The text says:

> When he broke open the fourth seal, I heard the voices of the four living creatures cry out, "Come forward." And I looked and there was a pale green horse. Its rider was named Death, and Hades accompanies him. They were given authority over a quarter of the Earth, to kill with the sword, famine, and plague, and by means of the beasts of the Earth.[233]

From Ezekiel 14:21, we learn that "pale green" is a symbol of death and decay. This above description in the sixth chapter of Revelation, and the reference in Ezekiel, may well have been among the sources for the development of the angel Azrael, or the *Malak Al-Mawt*, in the Islamic faith. This brings us to the places in the Muslim Holy Book, where the Angel of Death appears, the topic of the next section of this fourth chapter.

Angel of Death in Al-Qur'an and Hadith Literature

Death is represented by one of Allah's angels in the Holy Book of Islam, Al-Qur'an. The Holy Book's 70:4, 6:93, and 32:11–12, are three good examples where the Angel of Death is discussed. The first of these asks us this:

> Who is more vile than he who slanders Allah of falsehood, or says, "Revelation came to me," when no

such revelation came to him; or one who wishes, "I can reveal the like of what has been sent down by God?" If you could see the evil creatures in the agony of death with the angels thrusting forward their hands and saying, "Yield up your souls!" This day you will suffer ignominious punishment for uttering lies about Allah and by rejecting His signs and arrogance.[234]

At Surah 32:11–12, the Qur'an says, "The Angel of Death appointed over you will take away your soul [*nafs*], then you will be sent back to your Lord."[235] The Holy Book's 25:22–26 is a third passage that some Muslim scholars believe refers to the Angel of Death. This text tells us:

The day they see the angels there will be no happy tidings for the sinner, and they will say, "There is an unsurmountable barrier!" We shall turn to their deeds and scatter them like particles of dust. The inmates of Paradise will have a better abode that day and better resting place. The day the Heavens split asunder with a dazzling white cloud gathering and the angels descending in a continuous stream. The real sovereignty will belong to Ar-Rahman. How grievous will the day be for the infidels! The sinner will then bite his hand and say, "Would that I have taken the road with the Prophet."[236]

This passage clearly refers to the Day of Judgment, where unbelievers in Allah will be sorry that they did not live their lives with more moral goodness and virtue than they actually did. The name *Ar-Rahman* is one of the ninety-nine names for Allah. It means, "The Merciful," or the "Most Merciful." *Ar-Rahman* is the second most frequently employed name for God in Al-Qur'an. It often appears as a synonym for the word Allah. The 55th Surah of the Muslim Holy Book is named "Ar-Rahman. The Surah begins:

Ar-Rahman Who bestowed the Qur'an, created man, and taught him to express clearly. The Sun and the

Moon revolve according to His calculations; and grasses and trees bow to Him in adoration.[237]

Contemporary Yemini scholar Anwar Awlaki in his work *The Hereafter* describes the soul exiting from the body. He observes:

At this point the soul sits in the throat and smiles. The Angel of Death then gently calls for the soul to come out. If it is the soul of a believer, it comes out of the body like a drop of water sliding off the tip of a sprout of a jug. But if the soul was disobedient, the person fights back and refuses to leave the body. His soul is removed forcibly and comes out torn and fragmented like a piece of cloth being pulled off a thorny bush.[238]

Imam Al-Awlaki further sketches out his metaphor of the soul leaving the body:

When the soul of the innocent leaves the body voluntarily when called by the Angel of Death, the eyes of the dying watch it leave. If a person is a *Kafir* [non-believer], then the Angel of Death will look frightening to him and the dying person will be terrified to Death.[239]

Some scholars of Islam suggest it is the *Malak Al-Mawt*, or his minions, who are referred to at the Qur'an's Surah 16:32 that informs us:

Those people who the angels take in a good and wholesome state, they say to them, "Peace be upon you, and enter the Garden on account of the actions and things you used to do.[240]

Some traditions in Islam give the names *Nazi'at* and *Nashitat* to those angels who take the souls of the deceased at death. This *malakayn*, or pair of angels, is said to be described at the Muslim Holy Book'a Surah 79:1–2, a Meccan Surah that tells us: "I call to witness those who dive and drag, and those who undo the bonds gently." This is taken to mean the bond that keeps the *momin*, or soul, tethered to the body in life.

Several traditional Ahadith say the helpers of the Angel of Death cannot bear the sight of the most beautiful and handsome of all the *Mala'ika*, or they observe that these angels are among the most frightening, depending on the person's deeds in life. If a person led a good life, the angel looks beautiful. If the person had an evil life, the Angel of Death, or one of his assistants, looks frightening and foreboding. The Holy Book of Islam, at Surah 18:50, also speaks of the fear of the disbeliever before the soul is separated from the body. The text reveals:

> If only you could see when the angels take the souls of those who disbelieve, when the angels beat their faces and their backs.[241]

A Hadith from Ibn Abbas appears to make the same point. He tells us:

> So horrible is the appearance of Azrael when he comes to take the souls of sinners, that the strongest of men cannot bear the sight. It is said that prophet Ibrahim once asked Azrael to show him the aspect that he is in when taking the souls of the wicked. The angel told him that he would not be able to bear the sight, but Ibrahim said that he could bear it. The angel then asked him to turn aside and he did so. After a short while, the angel said, "Now look here," and Ibrahim looked toward him. When he met his gaze there was the most horrible giant, like a figure all dressed in black, with a dark complexion, and long hair, with each hair standing stiffly on end, and giving off a most disgusting smell, with flames leaping up from his mouth and nostrils. Ibrahim could not bear to look at the scene and he swooned.[242]

Ibn Abbas continues the Hadith about Azrael:

> When he regained consciousness, Azrael resumed his normal form, and Ibrahim then said, "Even if there were no other affliction for the wicked, the terrible ordeal of facing Azrael, in such a horrible form, should suffice for

their punishment. This is the form in which the Angel of Death appears when he visits wicked people; but when he comes to take the souls of the pious and the devout servants of Allah, he appears in the most handsome of forms, wearing a most pleasant look. When Ibrahim asked Azrael to appear before him in the form he adapts while visiting pious people , he saw, standing before him, a handsome young man, elegantly dressed, with perfumes all around his body. Ibrahim said, "Even if there was no other joy for the believer than the bliss of seeing the handsome face of Azrael at the hour of death, it should suffice for his pleasures."[243]

A number of other classical Hadith refer to the angel Azrael visiting some of the other prophets of Islam. In one of these Nabi Sulayman noticed that the Angel of Death was grieved. When questioned about the cause of the angel's sorrow, he answered, "I have been requested to take your soul to Hell [*Jahannam*]." On the following day, Sulayman asked the Angel of Death why he was full of mirth. He answered, "Because I was ordered to take your soul back to your Lord."[244]

In another Hadith, the Angel of Death appears to Musa (Moses) and said, "Give me your soul!!" Whereupon Musa replied, "Where I sit, you have no right to stand." And the angel retired ashamed. Then he is said to have reported back to Allah all that had occurred. The Hadith continues:

> Again, Allah commanded the Angel of Death to bring him the soul of Musa. The angel went and not finding him, inquired of the sea, of the mountains, and of the valleys, but they knew nothing of him. Musa did not die through the Angel of Death but through Allah's kiss— for it was Allah who drew his soul from his body.[245]

Another Hadith refers to the Angel of Death, Azrael visiting the Prophet Ibrahim:

> The Prophet Ibrahim once asked Azrael who had two eyes in the front of his head and two eyes in the back,

"Oh Angel of Death, what do you do if one man dies in the East and another in the West, or if a land is stricken by the plague, or if two armies meet in a field?" The angel said, "Oh Messenger of Allah, the names of these people are mentioned on the *Lawh al-Mafuz*. It is the Preserved Tablet on which all human destinies are engraved. I gaze at it incessantly. It informs me when the moment when the lifetime of a human being on Earth comes to an end, be it one of mankind or of the beasts. There is also a tree next to me called the Tree of Life. It is covered with myriad tiny leaves, smaller than the leaves of an olive tree and much more numerous. Whenever a person is born on Earth, the tree sprouts a new leaf, and on this leaf is mentioned the name of the person who was born. It is by this tree that I know who is born and who is to die. When a person is going to die, his leaf begins to wilt and die, and it falls from the tree and onto the Tablet. Then the person's name is erased from from the Tablet. This event happens forty days before the actual event, so we are informed forty days in advance of his impending death. The person himself may not know and may continue his life on Earth full of hope and plans. But we here in Heaven have that information, that is why Allah has said, "Your sustenance has been written in the Heavens and decreed for you, and it includes your lifespan. The moment in Heaven we see that leaf wilting and dying, we mix it into that person's provision, and from the fortieth day before his death, he begins to consume his leaf from the Tree of Life without knowing it. Only forty days then remain in his life in this world, and after that there are no more provisions for him. Then I summon the Spirits by Allah's leave, until they are present right before me, and the Earth is flattened out and left like a dish before me, from which I partake as a wish, by the order of Allah.[246]

The mentions of the "Preserved Tablet" and the "Tree of Life" deserve some explication in this Hadith. The *Lahwi-Al-Mahfuz* is a Divine Preserving Tablet on which the things that happen on Earth are recorded. It is a kind of mirror of the Knowledge of Allah, in that the Tablet acts as a Book of Fate. In fact, one of the ninety-nine names for God in Islam is *Al-Hafiz*, or "The Preserver."[247]

In regard to the Tree of Life, unlike the Biblical account where there are two trees in the midst of the Garden, in Islam there is only one tree. The Tree of Life is also called the "Tree of Immortality" in the Muslim faith. It is a tree that Allah specifically forbade to Adam and Hawa, or Adam and Eve. In Al-Qur'an, Allah does not refer to it directly as the Tree of Life or the Tree of Immortality. He merely refers to it as "the Tree." In Islam, it is Shaytan who calls it the Tree of Immortality, in order to trick Adam and Eve to eat from it.

A number of other Hadith speak specifically about the Prophet Muhammad and the Angel of Death. Another tradition tells us this:

> Once a man came to the Prophet and said, "I've come to take your life." This man was actually the Angel of Death in the form of a man; and the Prophet said to him, "Let me do my prayer first." Then both the Angel of Death and the Prophet said their prayers together. And then the Prophet's life was taken away, a beautiful end to a beautiful life.[248]

A second Hadith about the Prophet Muhammad and the *Malak Al-Mawr*, or the Angel of Death, relates:

> On the occasion of his impending death, Allah's Prophet has a small vessel of water placed before him. He began to dip his hands into the water and wiped his face with them. Then he said, "There is none worthy of worship except Allah. Indeed, death brings with it agony." Then he raised his hand up and kept repeating, "In the most exalted company" until his soul was taken and his hands went limp.[249]

This brings us to several other Hadith that speak of the *Malak Al-Mawt*, or the Angel of Death, in the Islamic faith. Many of these express a desire by humans to trick the angel in question, by asking to get one's affairs in order, or by offering to supply a substitute for the person designate to die soon.

Other Ahadith on the Angel of Death

Ukrainian-born Jewish scholar Dov Noy (1920–2013), in his book *Folktales of Israel,* suggests that Rabbinic literature produced three separate kinds of narratives about defying the Angel of Death.[250] In the first variety, the angel is defeated by deception on the part of humans. In the second kind, the Angel of Death appears as evil or cruel, or as a stubborn hero. Usually, in this second variety, Noy tells us, the humans submit passively to the Angel of Death. In the third kind, the Angel of Death is moved to feel compassion for the humans and changes his mind about claiming the person's soul.[251]

Professor Noy also speaks of the Angel of Death in ancient Judaism as having several attributes not mentioned in the above analysis. Among these are: nothing escapes him; he is depicted with many eyes and often as a diligent Reaper; he is sometimes shown as an old man holding a sword, from which poison drips into the mouths of mortals; and finally, he is sometimes shown as a fugitive, a wanderer, or as an ordinary man.[252]

Allama Sulayman Al-Jamal says in his *Tafsir al-Jalaylan*, "Azrael is not mentioned by name in Al-Qur'an, but he is referred to as the Angel of Death (*Malak Al-Mawt*).[253] The seventeenth-century Sufi scholar Al-Jamal continues his analysis:

> In reality, it is Allah the Most High who reclaims the souls of men from their bodies, but He does so by the means of the Angel of Death, whom He orders to take a person's soul when the proper time arrives.[254]

Qadi Iyad, in his *Kitab al-Shifa*, suggests that the Angel of Death is Azrael, and this fact is found in many of the earliest collectors of Hadith in Islam. Among these are Al-Tabarani, Ibn Abu al-Dunya, Abu

Nu'aym, and Ibn Abi Hatim's *Tafsir*, among others.[255] A tradition from Al-Tabarani tells us about the Angel of Death:

> When the Angel of Death takes someone, that person will not be able to take with him the worldly goods he or she has struggled to acquire throughout his or her life, nor the relatives nor friends they had held dear. On that day, when the people will come before Allah entirely alone, they will be confronted with everything they have done. Everybody, without exception, will realize at that moment that life on Earth was little more than a transient experience. Yet, it will be too late. This is also mentioned in a Hadith where the Prophet says, "He is a bad servant who is led by greed. He is a bad servant who is misled by passion. He is a bad servant who is debased by his worldly desires."[256]

Wahb Ibn Munabbah Rahmatullah, an eighth-century Yemini scholar, narrates the following story about the Angel of Death in Islam. He tells us:

> A King once decided to survey his Kingdom and his domain. He ordered out his stately robes and was presented a suit, but it did not please his fancy. So he called for another, then another, and after rejecting them all, he finally found one to his liking. He wore his most elegant suit, and then ordered his horse. A fine horse was brought, but he did not like it and he sent it back. Then two more horses were presented to him, one after the other, but he did not like them either. At last, the whole stable of horses was brought before him and he selected the best steed. The King then mounted the horse, and the accursed Shaytan infused pride and vanity into his mind as he rode off proudly, followed by his courtiers, attendants, and armored men, in a mighty cavalcade. But the King was too filled with disdain to take notice of them.

As he rode on, he came upon a decrepit old man, dressed in rags who greeted him, but the King paid no attention. At this, the old man took hold of the horse's bridle. The King fell into a rage and said to him in a threatening way, "Off with you. How dare you take hold of my horse's reins." And the man answered, "I have some business with you." Then the King said, "Be patient and wait until I dismount, for only then will I have time to listen to what you have to say." But the old man said, "I must tell you now," and saying this he gave the horse a violent tug and snatched it away. Then the King inquired, "What do you have to say to me?" The man said, "It is a secret I must whisper it in your ear. I am Azrael, the Angel of Death, come to take your soul.

Then, the King turned pale and his voice quivered, and he said in his flattering voice, "Could you give me a brief respite to go home and arrange my affairs?" And the angel said, "No, you will have no respite. Never again shall you meet your kinsmen, nor see your possessions." In saying this, the angel pulled out the King's soul from his body, and the King fell from his horse like a log of dry wood.[257]

A similar tale is told in the Islamic faith of a pious man:

After this, the Angel of Death went to a pious man who was going on a journey greeted the man and then said, "I want to whisper something in your ear. I am the angel Azrael." Then the man said, "Oh most welcome, blessed is your visit, for you have come after I have waited for so long. Of all those who are far away from me, you were the one I was most anxious to see." Then the angel said, "Go and hasten the task for what you have embarked on this journey." Then the man said, "I would dearly like to meet my Allah more than anything in the world."

Then the angel said, "Choose for yourself any state in which you would like to meet Death, and I will draw out your soul when you are in that state." Then the man said, "I will leave it to your choice." But the angel replied, "I have been commanded to follow your leave." Then the man responded, "If this is so, let me take *Wudu* and stand in *Salat*; when I lie prostrate before my Lord, you can pull out my spirit from my body." So, when the pious man was engaged in *Salat*, lying in *Sajdah*, his soul was taken from his body.[258]

The Arabic term *Al-Wudu* refers to a Muslim tradition of washing body parts in a kind of ritual purification. It involves washing the hands, mouth, nostrils, arms, head, and feet with water. *Wudu* is typically performed in preparation for formal prayer, or *Salat*, and also before handling or reading Al-Qur'an. *Wudu* is often translated into English as "partial ablution," as opposed to *Ghusl*, or "full ablution," the washing of the entire body. There is also the possibility of what is called *Al-Tayammum*, or "dry ablution," in which water may be replaced with sand or soil. In Islam, the purification of the body and one's clothes is called *Taharah*.

Thus, the pious man in the above narrative wishes to die after being in a state of *Al-Wudu wa Al-Salat*, or after being in a state of "ablution" and then prayer. The Arabic term *Sajdah* is a word employed in the Muslim faith to refer to the act of being in prostration in regard to the worship of Allah. It principally observed in the act of *Salat*, or Ritual Prayer.

Another Hadith about the Angel of Death comes from the collection of Hasan Al-Basri. He tells us that the Angel of Death visits during mourning. He observes:

When a person dies and a member of his household begins to weep and cry, The Angel of Death stands in the doorway and speaks to them. "I did not deprive him of his livelihood, he already had exhausted his decreed portion. I did not cut short his lifetime; I have been commanded to come and visit this house over and over again, until none of its inhabitants are left alive." Then Hasan Al-Basri said, "If the mourners could see the Angel of Death at that time and listen to his talk, they would forget about the deceased and begin to worry about themselves.[259]

Sometimes in these Hadith narratives on the Angel of Death, rather than the person being a pious believer, the human being is a miser. The following example is told among a number of Sufi thinkers:

A miser had accumulated by effort, trade, lending, three hundred thousand dinars. He had land, buildings, and all kinds of wealth. He decided he could spend a year in leisure, living comfortably, and then deciding what the future will bring for him. But almost as soon as he stopped amassing money, the Angel of Death appeared to take his life away.

The miser tried by every method he could to dissuade the angel who seemed quite adamant. Then the man said, "Grant me but three more days, and I will give you one third of all my possessions." The angel again refused and pulled at the miser's life by tugging to pull away his soul. Then the man said, "If you allow me two more days, I will give you two hundred thousand dinars from my personal store." But the angel would not listen to him. He refused to give the man even one more day.

Then the miser said, "Please give me time to write down one little thing." This time the angel allowed him this single concession, and the man wrote with his own blood, "Man make use of your life. I could not buy one hour more for three hundred thousand dinars. Make sure you realize the value of your time."[260]

Sachkito Murata and William Chittick speak of other attributes of the angel Azrael that they also find in Hadith literature. They observe:

The Angel of Death speaks to the soul. He announces that it is being accepted into God's forgiveness and good pleasure. Two of the attributes are mercy and gentleness. The angel wraps the soul in a Paradisal shroud, thereby concealing the soul's bodily dimensions which are dark and dismal in relation to angelic and Paradisal luminosity. The angel then goes on to soak the soul in a Paradisal perfume.[261]

Another Hadith on the Angel of Death comes from Ibn Abbas, one of the Prophet Muhammad's *Sabaha*, or companions. He tells us:

I saw the Angel of Death in my sleep and I asked him, "How much time do I have left?" The angel held up five fingers. Then I asked, "Does that mean five years, five months, or five days?" Before he had a chance to answer that question, Ibn Abbas awoke.[262]

Others end this Hadith by Ibn Abbas dropping dead. One final narrative about the *Malak Al-Mawt*, can be found in the Hadith collection of Sufi thinker Muhammad Hisham Kabbani's *Angels Unveiled*.[263] The narrative is about a great warrior named Dede Korkut and his meeting of the Angel of Death. Imam Al-Kabbani tells us:

Dede Korkut was the greatest warrior of his time. His exploits had reached the point where he considered himself invincible in the land, and challenged all of creation to defeat him, and his brave, young men in combat. Allah heard his words and was displeased with his pride. So He sent him the Angel of Death to take his soul. Azrael came to him as he was feasting in his place; and he stood before him without saying a word. Dede Korkut said, "I did not see you come in, who are you?" Then the angel replied, "I am not one who asks permission from the likes of you, and I came to teach you a lesson." Korkut immediately came to his feet and ordered that the visitor be caught. But the visitor changed himself into a bird and flew away through the chimney.

Dede Korkut ordered his horse to be saddled and everyone rushed into hot pursuit of the elusive bird. Soon he found himself lost in the middle of a deep forest, and the angel suddenly appeared again in front of him. "I got you now," exclaimed Korkut. "No," said the angel. "I got you," and he brought him down from the horse and he stood on his chest, pinning him to the ground. Dede Korkut began to weep and said, "I feel weaker than I have ever felt before. What did you do to me?"

Then Azrael said, "I am the Angel of Death, so prepare yourself to leave this life." Then Korkut said, "I beseech you to give me more time. Accept my apology if my boasting has offended you." Then Azrael said, "Do not apologize to me and do not beseech me; I am a creature as you are, and I only follow orders from the Almighty."

Then Dede Korkut said, "Then get out of my way and stop wasting my time." And he began to pray to Allah, "Forgive my boasting, Oh my God, and give me another chance, and accept my apology for offending you. You are the Almighty over Your creation."

Allah responded well to Korkut's comments, and he instructed Azrael to give him a respite. Azrael said, "God has decided to permit you to live on the condition that you will find someone else to die in your place." Dede Korkut said, "I will ask my father, he is old and will not refuse me." He went to his father and told him the story but his father replied, "Oh my son, I have slaved my whole life long in order to relish my old age. I am sorry, but I am not ready to die in your place."

Then Dede Korkut thought, "Surely, my mother will not refuse me." He went on to her but she said, "Oh my son, I gave my life for you many times already, when I bore you, fed you, raised you, and took care of you.

Now the rest of my life should be at your father's side, as company for his old age."

The young man was crestfallen and he went home, resigned to die. When his wife saw his sadness, she inquired what troubled him. "Oh my beloved wife, the Angel of Death is about to come and take my life unless I find someone else willing to die in my place. And my old father and mother refused me, so who can I find now?" His wife answered, "Oh my beloved husband, why did you not not ask me? I am happy to give you what even your own mother and father cannot give you. Take my life that yours might be spared." When Dede Korkut, the fierce warrior heard these words, his heart melted and tears came to his eyes. He turned to Allah and said, "Oh my Lord, take my life and spare my wife, for she is worthier and braver than me."

Allah was again pleased to hear these words, and he decided to spare both Dede Korkut and his wife. Instead, He sent Azrael to take the lives of his parents, as they had been blessed with long and happy lives. With this, Imam Kabbani finishes his tale this way: Allah wrote on the palms of the Angel of Death in letters of Light, "In the name of Allah, the Most Merciful, and Most Beneficient." Then He ordered the angel to take the soul of a Knower of Allah to show him those letters of Light which cause the soul of the Knower to come out of its body like an element attracted by a magnet or a Light returning to its source.[264]

The narrative told by Imam Kabbani contains a number of elements that all Hadith on the Angel of Death seem to have in common. First, some human being thinks he can trick or forestall the Angel of Death. Second, when humans act in their own self-interest, they rarely are seen as moral paragons in the Muslim faith. Witness the treatment of Dede Korkut at the close of his tale. In contrast, both Korkut and his wife at the end of the narrative show more concern for each other than they do for their own.

A third element that many narratives in Islam about the *Malak Al-Mawt* have in common is the strategy to find some willing human to take the person's place, a substitute soul for the Angel of Death to take. In Korkut's case, the mother and father are possible substitutes; but since they both act in their own self-interest, neither substitute is acceptable by Allah. Thus, in the close of Dede Korkut's tale, the Angel of Death takes the lives of the mother and father of the great warrior Dede Korkut.

Ulrich Marzolph, in his *Arabian Nights Encyclopedia*, gives three other versions of the cheating of the Angel of Death. He calls these "The King on His Throne," the "Devout Man," and the "Rich King." In all three scenarios, the human attempts to cheat Death by paying more money in the first and third cases, while in the second the man remains devout and thus is given a special place in Al-*Firdaws*, or Paradise.[265] The Arabic expression, *Al-Firdaws*, literally means "Paradise." A number of Hadith suggest it is the highest level of *Jannah*, or "Heaven."

At-Tirmidhi, for example, at Hadith number 3174, says, "*Al-Firdaws* is the highest part of Paradise, and the center and the best of it."[266] Ibn Al-Qayyim agrees. He relates:

> *Al-Firdaws* is the highest, noblest, most luminous and best part of Paradise because it is close to the Throne, for the Throne is its roof, and the further anything is away from it, the darker and more constricted it is. Hence, the lowest of the low is the worst of places and the most constricted and the fartherest from what is Good.[267] (*Al-Fawaa'id*, p. 27).

These Hadiths about the Angel of Death all appear to have two things in common. First, the emphasis in these narratives is on those who lead a believing life, as in the story of the pious man. The other conclusion we can make about these *Malak Al-Mawt* tales is that it is quite easy to give up one's faith and then to substitute for it some other worldly good. Thus, the narratives of the King and the Miser, both seem to reject the faith in lieu of wealth or money.

In addition to the Angel of Death (Azrael or Izrael) in Islam, a number of other *Mala'ika*, or angels are associated with *Mawt*, or Death, in the Islamic faith. Among these are Malik and Ridwan, the angels who rule Hell and Heaven, and Munkar and Nakir, the pair of celestial beings who interrogate the dead in the grave. We will move to an analysis of the first pair in the next section, followed by a section devoted to Munkar and Nakir.

The Angels Ridwan and Malik

Richard Burton, in the thirty-seventh of his *One Thousand and One Nights*, discusses both Malik and Ridwan, or as he calls the angel, *Rizwan*. Burton gives us a couplet that mentions the pair:

> I went to the house of the Keeper-man. He was out but others began to smile; I entered His Heaven and then His Hell; and I said, "Bless Malik and bless Rizwan.[268]

Burton gives footnotes to both angels, or *malakayn*, the dual form of "angel." About the angel Malik, Burton writes, "The angel who is the Door-Keeper of Hell; others say he especially presides over the torments of the damned."[269] (Qur'an 43:78.) In his note on Rizwan, Burton tells us, "The Door-Keeper of Heaven before mentioned who, like Guebre Zamiyad has charges of lasses and lads, and who is often charged by poets with letting them slip."[270] The *Guebre Zamiyad* is a Persian name for the angels who are responsible for tending to the young in the Persian Paradise.

The angel Ridwan in Islamic tradition is the angel in charge of maintaining *Jannah*, or Heaven. Sometimes the name is pronounced *Rizwan* in Farsi and Urdu. In Malaysia and Indonesia, the name of the angel in question is spelled *Riduan*. Among French scholars, the name of the Keeper of Paradise is called *Redouane*. Ridwan or Rizwan is not mentioned by name in Al-Qur'an, though there are a number Ahadith that mention the angel. Abu Hurayra speaks of Ridwan as *Qarib*, an Arabic verb that means close or near. Presumably, this is in reference to the angel's closeness to Allah. In fact, another Arabic word that Abu Hurayra employs to describe the angel Ridwan is the adjective *dhayyiq*, another word that means "near" in English.

In another Hadith from Ibn Kathir, he relates this about the Keeper of Jannah:

> Some lovers will be so absorbed in their yearnings for Allah that they will rush to the Gates of Heaven and ask the Gate-Keeper, the angel Ridwan, "We are told in the world that in Heaven one is granted the beatific vision of Allah." Then the angel Ridwan will ask Allah, "Oh Lord, the scales of justice have not yet been weighed yet these people seek entrance to Paradise." Then Allah will address them, "Oh my servants, you still have to account for your deeds, yet you wish to enter Heaven." Then the lovers will respond, "Oh Lord, Most Generous, you know well that we turned our backs on the material world, and then devoted ourselves only to You. Our hearts do not desire the goods of the world, and we always remain content. We loved You and we worshipped You throughout the night, our foreheads in prostration. We prayed and supplicated unto you from the depths of our hearts. We restlessly passed the night away, longing to attain Your pleasure. At the time of our death, we had nothing in our hearts but a love of You." Allah then addressed the angel Ridwan:"Ridwan, these are My lovers, what reckoning can there be for them? Open the Gates of Paradise and let them enter without having to account for their deeds."[271]

Several Ahadith and tales can be found on the angel Ridwan in Muslim literature. John Renard, in his book *Friends of God*, tells the story of a woman named Zayda, who serves Umar, a companion of the Prophet Muhammad. Zayda visits Muhammad one day and tells him that while she was gathering firewood, and having put a bundle of kindling on a rock, a messenger came from Paradise on a great steed. The angel told Zayda to tell the prophet that his community has only three kinds of people: Those going straight to Paradise, without judgment; those who will be judged mercifully; and those who enjoy Muhammad's intercessions.[272]

Then Muhammad turned to the stone of Zayda and instructed it to bear its contents to Umar's home. And immediately, the firewood found its new home.[273] Another narrative involving Rizwan begins with two lovers absorbed in their yearnings for Allah that they rush to the Gates of Heaven and say, "We were told in the world that in Paradise one is granted the Beatific Vision." Then the angel Ridwan will turn to Allah and say, "The scales of justice have not been weighed." Then Allah will say, "My servants, you must account for your deeds." Then The lovers will respond, "Oh Allah, Most Glorious, you know we have turned our backs on the material world. We loved You and worshipped You. We have longed to attain your pleasure.[274]

Then Allah will turn to Ridwan and say, "These are My lovers, don't make a reckoning of them. Open the Gates and let them enter." Then the Gates were opened and they were able to see the Lord, the Most Merciful.[275] Another tradition about the angel Ridwan is said about a particular tree in Paradise known as the "Tree of the Ridwan Pledge." All those who enter Paradise, this Hadith suggests, must make a pledge of allegiance to Allah and His Prophet beneath this tree. Muhammad is said to have taken the pledge when he was on his Night Journey. A number of Ahadith speak of the Ridwan Pledge, like this one from Said Ibn Al-Masaiyab (642–715), Medina-born expert on Islamic *Fiqh*:

> My father said, "I saw the Tree of the Ar-Ridwan and
> its Pledge of Allegiance, and when I returned to it later,
> I was not able to recognize it. Then the sub-narrator,
> Mahmijd said, "Al-Musaaiyab, then forget the Tree."[276]

Similar Ahadith are told by Tariq Ibn Ziyad (670–720), and by Abu Bukhari in regard to Ibn Abi Auf and Abbas Ibn Tamin. These Ahadith are usually tied to a verse in Surah four, "He who has obeyed the messenger has obeyed Allah."[277] These traditions may also be connected to the Holy Book's 48:18 that informs us, "Allah was pleased with the believers when they gave their *Bai'a*, or Pledge, under a Tree," an obvious reference to the Ridwan Pledge.[278]

In all of the Ahadith about the angel Ridwan, he usually is spoken of as being among the *Mala'ika* who are closest to Allah, and he is responsible for making sure that human beings account for their deeds when they enter Paradise. Although Ridwan is not mentioned by name in the Muslim Holy Book, his minions are mentioned in Al-Qur'an, where it tells us, "angels shall enter unto them from every gate saying, "Salaam alekum, excellent indeed is your final home."[279]

At the Qur'an's 14:22, the Holy Book speaks of the angel Malik and the reckoning in Hell, where humans will account for their deeds. It tells us:

> When the reckoning is over Shaytan will say, "The promise that was made to you by Allah was indeed a true promise; but I have gone back on that promise that I have made; for I have no power over you except to call you; and you responded to my call. So don't blame me, but blame yourselves. Neither can I help you nor give me help.[280]

The people in Hell will turn to the angels guarding there in an attempt to get their torments reduced, even if for just one day. The Qur'an's 40:49 tells us that, "And those in the Fire will say to the Keepers of Hell, 'Ask your Lord to lighten our punishment, even it is just for a single day.'"[281] Eventually, those in Hell lose all hope in reducing their torment, even if just for one day. Then, they will seek death, so they turn to the Chief Keeper of Hell, the angel Malik.

They plead with the angel for forty years, but to no avail. They will exclaim, "Oh Malik, let your Lord put an end to us." But Malik will give a curt response, "Indeed…you will remain here."[282]

The Qur'an also speaks of the angel Malik's compatriots. At Surah 74:26–30, the text tells us:

> I will cast him into the Fire of Hell. What do you think Hell Fire is? It leaves nothing, nor does it spare anything; it glows and burns the skin. Over it are nineteen guards.[283]

Several traditions in the Muslim faith confirm that the number of "Guards," or *Yuhafidh*, in Arabic, is nineteen. The Holy Book's 96:14–18 also speaks of these guards. It tells us:

Does he not know that Allah sees? And yet indeed, if he does not desist, We shall drag him by his forelocks, so let him call his associates. And we shall call the Guardians [*Yuhafidh*] of Hell [*Jahannam*].[284]

In some Hadith, these nineteen assistants to angel Malik are given the names *Zabaniyyah*. They are instructed by Malak Malik to bring torment to sinful humans and Jinn in *Jahannam*, for all of eternity. Two other mentions to the minions of Malik occur at Al-Qur'an's 40:49–50 and 71:25. The first of these informs us:

Those in the Fire will say to the warders of Hell, "Ask your Lord to reduce the punishment for us for a single day." They will say, "Did not your Apostles come to you with clear proofs?" They will answer, "Indeed, they did." "Then pray," the warders say. But the prayers of unbelievers will be in vain. Here the Arabic noun to represent Malik's helpers is *Muhafidh*, and the word for "punishment" is *Qisas*. The expression "in vain" in Arabic is *'abath*.

The Qur'an's 71:25 mentions the Keepers of Hell by describing certain humans who are condemned there, "They were drowned because of their habitual sinfulness, and sent to Hell and did not find any helper, other than Allah Himself."[285] The Arabic word "helper" here is *musa'ada*. One other reference in the Qur'an to the Keepers of Hell comes at Surah 66:6.

This ayat informs us:

Oh you who believe, save yourselves and your families from the Fire whose fuel is men and stones, over which are appointed angels stern and severe as wardens who never disobey what Allah commands them, and do whatever they are commanded.[286]

The Arabic word *Malik* is also employed in a number of other contexts in the Muslim Holy Book. *Al-Malik*, for example, is one of the ninety-nine names for God. He is *Al-Malik*, or "The King," in the most absolute senses. The word also is sometimes used in the expression *Malik ul-Shu'ara*, which means "King of the Poets," and *Malik ul-Tujjar*, or "King of the Merchants," an honorific title given to the Chief merchant of a village.

Finally, three important points may be made regarding the angel Malik and his followers. First, their primary roles are to deal with those who have been assigned to Hell by Allah and the angels, Munqar and Naqir, the pair of celestial beings who confront the dead in their graves. A second point about Malik and his minions is that the angels, like all other angels, were made to serve Allah. They do nothing except what Allah has willed them to do. In this sense, Malik and his followers, like the other angels in Islam, do not possess free will. And finally, in the Muslim faith, the angel Malik and his compatriots are not fallen angels, nor are they to be identified with Iblis or Shaytan. Malik and the other Keepers of Hell are not Devils.

The Roles of Munqar and Naqir and Barzakh in Islam

The Muslim faith teaches that there will be two different judgments after death. In the first of these, all human beings will face a personal judgment after death at which a pair of *Malakayn*, the dual form Munqar and Naqir, will scrutinize the individual's earthly existence. The second judgment will be the Final Judgment at the End of Time. These ideas are not dissimilar to what Thomas Aquinas in the thirteenth century called "Particular" and "General" Judgments.[287]

The final pair of angels, then, associated with Death in Islam are Munqar and Naqir. In Islamic eschatology, they are responsible for testing the faith of the dead in their tombs. After death, they prop up the deceased in an upright position and ask, "Who is your Lord? Who is your Prophet? And, what is your book?" A righteous Muslim will respond correctly by saying that Allah is his Lord, Muhammad his Prophet, and Al-Qur'an his Book. Then the person will be shown the place that has been reserved for him in Paradise, and where he would have gone if he went to *Jahannam*, or Hell.

An infidel, of course, will not respond in this way, and the angels will rebuke him; then, they will be told, "Neither did you know nor did you seek guidance from those who have knowledge."[288] Some

Muslim traditions suggest that these non-believers will be hit with an iron hammer between his two ears. Then, he will be shown the place he could have had in Paradise, before being thrown into the Hell Fire.

A number of other Ahadith are extant on Munqar and Naqir and their questioning in the grave. Al-Manuzi, for example, reports that Imam Ahmad said, "The punishment in the grave is a reality, and only he who is misguided or wants to misguide others is denied.[289] Another Hadith from fourteenth-century scholar Ibn Taymiyyah tells us this about the questioning in the grave:

> Each person will be questioned after his death, whether he is burned or not. Even if a person were eaten by carnivorous animals or burnt to ashes and thrown into the air or drowned in the Sea, he or she shall be questioned about his or her deeds, and rewarded with good or evil depending on his or her deeds in life. Both the body and soul together experience punishment or reward.[290]

Another Hadith from Ibn Al-Qayyim, a fourteenth-century Syrian scholar, agrees with the above judgment, when he writes:

> The early Muslim Community and its prominent scholars held that after death, a person is either in bliss or torment, both physically and spiritually. After its separation from the body, the soul endures a state of happiness or punishment.
>
> At times, when the soul rejoins the body, both of them receive torture or joy. On the Day of the Resurrection, the souls will be returned to their bodies and they will rise from the graves and stand before the Lord of the Worlds.[291]

A tradition from twelfth-century Egyptian scholar Al-Hafiz refers to the opinions of Ahmad Ibn Hazim and Abu Hurayra on Minqar and Naqir. Al-Hafiz explains:

> Ahmad Ibn Hazim and Abu Hurayra are of the opinion that the questioning of the soul after death is addressed

to the soul only, without its returning to the body. The majority of Muslim scholars, however, disagree with them. They say the soul is returned to the body, or some of it, as is confirmed by Hadith.[292]

Ib Book X, Hadith number 107, Jami' At-Tirmidhi, also makes reference to the *malakayn* of Munqar and Naqir, as the angels who question the newly dead in their graves, or *qubur*, in classical Arabic.

Finally, prominent North African scholar and prominent jurist Ahmad Ibn Al-Qasim (1570–1640) was asked, "Do you believe in Munqar and Naqir and what is related concerning the punishment in the grave?" He answered, "Glory to Allah, yes, we do confirm that, and we do declare it so." Then Al-Qasim was asked, "There is no mention of Munqar and Naqir in Hadith?" "Of course there is," he responded.[293] As we have seen, there is some confusion in Islam whether the soul, or the soul united with the body, is/are to be questioned by Munqar and Naqir in the grave. Whatever the answer is, the individual judgment will be followed by a collective judgment at the End of Time for everyone— much like Christianity in the Middle ages.

In some Muslim traditions, Munqar and Naqir are described as demons. They are sent throughout the world to visit the souls of the recently deceased while they still reside in their freshly buried corpses. Munqar and Naqir are traditionally described as being black in color with piercing blue eyes. One tradition says this about the pair:

> They are terrible to behold. They have twelve eyes that glitter like lightning, voices as loud as thunder, teeth like canines, horns like those of a cow, hair that drags to their feet, and shoulders as broad as the distance of a journey of several days.[294]

Another Hadith gives us a description of Munqar, Naqir and Azrael. It relates:

> If he is leaving this life and journeying to the hereafter, then the angels will descend upon him. Their faces will be black, and they will have with them a coarse woolen fabric made of fire. Then they will sit within eye-shot

of them. Then the Angel of Death will come and sit at his head and will say, "Oh you wicked soul, come out a anger of your Lord and a fury from Him." It will disturb throughout his body. Then it will be ripped out as a skewer ripped from a damp cloth. And along the way, it will tear and cut the nerves and the blood; and they will be cursed by all the angels between the heavens and the Earth; and the Gates of Heaven will be closed to them.[295]

In some Muslim accounts of Munqar and Naqir after death, a person's soul passes through a state that is known as *Barzakh*, where it lies in the grave, even if the person's body has been destroyed. Nerina Rustomji describes *Barzakh*, in a footnote to her work, *The Garden and the Fire*. She tells us:

In the state of *Barzakh*, the time and place between death and resurrection, there the realm on Earth, but must instead stay in that place until the next life, whether it is in *Jannah* or *Al-Nar*. *Barzakh* then acts as an intermediary space, but it does not have the same type of function as a Christian Purgatory that is an intermediate place between heaven and hell. Instead, *Barzakh* is temporary in nature, and once the believer has been located to *Al-Jannah* or *Al-Nar*, then *Barzakh* as a place, space, time, and experience is no longer available.[296]

Ms. Rustomji tells us, "The temporal link between the world and the afterworld begins at the onset of death. When a person dies, his or her soul is in the intermediate state of *Barzakh*. She goes on to describe the actions of Azrael, where she relates," Death is sometimes seen as an independent entity, but more often is personified in the terrifying angel Azrael, to which she adds, "Death is an anguished process."[297]

The soul rests near the place where the body lies. The questioning from Munqar and Naqir begins when the funeral is complete and the last person of the funeral procession has walked seventy steps away from the grave. A Hadith from At-Tirmidhi also describes the activity of Munqar and Naqir. He tells us:

> When the deceased or one of yours is buried, there comes to him two black and blue angels, one of whom is called Al-Munqar and the other Al-Naqir. And they say, "What did you say about this man?" And the man says what he is used to saying. If he is good, he will say, "I am the slave of Allah and His Messenger, Muhammad." Then the angels say, "We knew you would say that." Then his grave is made spacious for him, seventy cubits by seventy cubits, and it is illuminated for him. Then they say to him, "Sleep." Then he says back to them, "May I go back to my family and tell them?" And they will say, "No. Sleep like a bridegroom who will be awakened by none of the dearest of family members, until Allah raises him from that resting place."
>
> But if he is a hypocrite, he says, "I heard the people saying something like I do not know." Then the angels will say, "We knew you would say that." Then they will say to the Earth, "Squeeze him!" So it squeezes him until his ribs interlock, and he will continue to be tormented there until Allah raises him from his resting place.[298]

Albanian-born Imam Hasan Al-Albani (1914–1999), though he made his scholarly reputation in Syria, offers another Hadith on Al-Munqar and Al-Naqir:

> How will you deal, Oh Umar, with the two testers in the grave when they come to you digging at the earth with their eye teeth, stepping on their hair because it is so long? Their eyes will be like dazzling lightning, and their voices like deafening thunder, with a whip so heavy that if the whole world were to gather to lift it, they would not be able to do it.[299]

Although these two angels, Munqar and Naqir, do not appear in Al-Qur'an, they are mentioned in a number of traditional Hadith. One of these comes from the collection of Abu Hurayra. He relates:

> The angels of death arrive with a coffin for the soul, perfume with fragrance from Heaven. The soul is wrapped in the perfumed silk coffin and the angels ascend with it to Allah, traversing the Seven Heavens. At each level of Heaven, a door is opened with a greeting and the angel guard asks, "Who is this pure soul [momin] that lived in a pure body?" The spirit [Ruh] then returns to the Earth to remain with the body and it asks to be buried quickly.[300]

The Yemini-born member of the Sahaba, or Companions to the Prophet Muhammad, Abu Hurayra (603–681) continues his analysis, "In the grave the soul [momin] is returned to the body and Al-Munqar and Al-Naqir begin their intense interrogation."[301]

In the Sufi Tradition, a total of five questions, not three as above, will be asked to the soul of the dead. They also are asked, "Who is your Sheikh?" and "What is your Madhab?" The righteous believer should respond, "My Lord is Allah, Muhammad is my Prophet; and my religion is that of Islam." If the deceased answers correctly, the time spent awaiting the resurrection is pleasant. Those who do not answer faithfully will be chastised on the Day of Judgment at the End of Time.

A "Sheikh" in the analysis above was an Arabic word that originally was an honorific title to designate the leader of a tribe. In more modern Islam, it is closer to "Wise Man," or "Wise Teacher." A "Madhab," is a school of thought within Islamic Fiqh, or "Islamic Law." In Sufi theology, there were many different Madhab in the Medieval period and beyond.

In many Islamic traditions, the angels Al-Munqar and Al-Naqir have appalling aspects. If the inquisition of the soul is a good one, then it is gently drawn out through the lips, and the body is left to repose in peace. If the soul answers the questions incorrectly, then the body is beaten about the back and head with iron clubs, and the soul is wrenched forth by racking torments.

There is also sometimes a remarkable post-funerary custom observed in some branches of Islam involving Munqar and Naqir. The ceremony is called the "Chastisement of the Tomb." It is believed by some Muslims that on the night following the burial, the two angels, or *Mala'kayn*, enter the tomb and ask their questions. If the answers are faithfully given, they open a door in the side of the tomb for the soul to pass to his repose in Al-*Firdaws*, or Paradise. The name of the state in which the soul resides after death is called *Al-Barzakh,* as mentioned earlier.

The Arabic word *Barzakh* means a "space" or a "partition" between two things. In this case, it is a barrier that keeps the soul from its former life, as well as its eventual salvation or damnation. The soul is said to be in the state of *Barzakh* when it is interrogated by the two angels. The word *Barzakh* appears a number of times in Al-Qur'an. At the Holy Book's 55:20, it speaks "of a *Barzakh* which they [the souls] cannot traverse."[302] The Muslim Holy Book's 23:100 tells us of an "intervening *Barzakh* stretching all the way to the Day of the Resurrection."[303] The Qur'an's 25:53 also employs the word *Barzakh*. It reveals:

> It is He who made two bodies of water flow side by side, one fresh and sweet while the other is brine and bitter; and He has placed a *barzakh*, a barrier between the two.[304]

The Holy Book also employs the word *Barzakh* in making a similar point at Surah 55:19–20 that reveals: "He has set two Seas in motion, that flow side by side together, with a *barzakh* between them which they cannot cross."[305] In this metaphor for the grave, the state of *Barzakh* is like a barrier between a body of saltwater and another of freshwater. The afterlife is the same way. The *momin*, or soul, cannot return to the life on Earth, nor can it yet enter the life beyond the grave that will begin on the *Yom al-Qiyamah*, or the "Day of Judgment."

In the meantime, the soul resides in a state of *Al-Barzakh*, where it will be interrogated by the *Mala'kayn* of Al-Munqar and Al-Naqir when its fate will be decided. It will remain in this temporary state until the End of Time. Abdullah Yusuf Ali, in his English translation of Al-Qur'an, renders the word *Barzakh* as "quiescent state."[306] In this state, the soul is unaware of anything that occurs in this life. This is confirmed by Surah 35:22 that tells us:

> Equal are not the living and the dead. Verily, Allah makes those He wishes to listen. But one cannot make those hear who are in their graves.[307]

Some contemporary Muslim scholars such as African Sayyid Rizvi, for example, point out that not all souls will be interrogated in the grave by the two angels. Children, the mentally impaired, and others lacking the capacity to choose right from wrong are not subject to questioning or punishment. Instead, Imam Rizvi argues, "These souls will continue in a deep sleep until the Final Judgment Day."[308] Rizvi also maintains that the interrogation process may be avoided if the *Talqin al-Mayyit*, or "instructions to the dead," are recited over the grave after burial. The *Talqin* is to remind the deceased of his beliefs in Allah, the Prophet Muhammad, Isla, and Al-Qur'an. If properly recited, Imam Rizvi says, the *Talqin* is acceptable by the angels as proof of the *Momin's* faith.[309] This brings us to a discussion of one final *Malak*, or angel, associated with *Mawt*, or Death in Islam, *Malak Ruman*.

The Angel Ruman and Death in Islam

One final celestial being associated with death in the Islamic faith is an angel named Ruman. Muslim lore tells us that he works along with Munqar and Naqir, and he resides in the infernal regions. He is said to be the angel that greets each condemned person. He forces them to sit down and to write out each and every deed they performed during their time on Earth. In some cases, the writing of these evil deeds takes a long time, even though Ruman is fully aware of all the wicked deeds done by them, from the smallest to the largest evil deed. He is to patiently and cruelly to wait while the sinners scribble down their sins.

Once the sinners are finished with the recording of their bad deeds, the poor souls of these people are handed over to Al-Munqar and Al-Naqir, whereupon they are inflicted with eternal punishment. Like Munqar and Naqir, the angel Ruman does not appear in the Holy

Qur'an, but he does appear in several Ahadith in traditional Islam, particularly in Shiite collectors.

In his *Sahifat al-Sajjaiyyah*, a work of the fourth Shiite Imam, Zayn al-Abidin Ali Ibn Husayn, eighth-century Shiite scholar and leader, for example, left a remarkable prayer often recited by the pious, asking Allah to bestow blessings upon the various angels. Among the *Mala'ika* he mentions are Jibril, Mika'il, Israfil, Azrael, Al-Munqar, Al-Naqir, and the *Malak Ruman*.[310] In the account that Al-Abadin gives of the angel Ruman, he described the angel as being wicked and demanding on those who are brought before him.[311]

The fourteenth-century Sufi thinker 'Izz al-Din Kashani, author of a well-known Persian paraphrase of Abu Hafs Suuhrawardi's *Awarif al-Ma'arif*, also discusses the angel Ruman.

He says that Ruman "works in tandem with Munqar and Naqir." He adds that:

> Ruman's treatment of the dead is even more wicked than the angel Azrael, when he separates the soul from the body.[312]

The famous thirteenth-century cosmographer Al-Qazwini, in his *'Aja'ib al-Makhiuqat*, or *The Wonders of Creation*, gives a detailed description of fourteen kinds of angels. Imam Al-Qazwini mentions angel Ruman along with Munqar and Naqir, as angels related to death.[313]

Contemporary scholars Smith and Haddad tell us that, "Ruman is shiny like the Sun."[314] They add:

> When the Prophet was asked, "What is the first thing a person encounters when they are put in the tomb?" He replied, "That is Ruman, roaming around the graves."[315]

Smith and Haddad also agree that the angel Ruman appears before the arrival of Munqar and Naqir, and his primary task is to get the evil souls to write down his bad deeds while on Earth before the arrival of Al-Munqar and Al-Naqir. Some scholars of Islam suggest that this tradition of the angel Ruman is not an essential element of the Faith. Again, Smith and Haddad tell us in their book *Islamic Understanding of Death and Resurrection*:

He [the angel Ruman] arrives before Munqar and Naqir, but then gives information to suggest that it is not a tradition integral to the most commonly accepted sequence of events.[316]

Jane Smith and Y. Y. Haddad, then, find the narrative of the angel Ruman not to be an essential part of the drama that goes into the Islamic faith when someone dies. This brings us to the major conclusions we have made in this fourth chapter. Chapter Five of this study is taken up with another class of beings in the Islamic faith known as the *Houris*.

Conclusions

In this fourth chapter, we have described and discussed the major angels in the Islamic faith associated with Death, or *Mawt* in Arabic. The first of these angels was Azrael (or Izrail), who is often called *Al-Malak-Al-Mawt*, or the Angel of Death. We began the chapter by exploring the places in Al-Qur'an where the angel Azrael appears, including Surah 6:93, 18:50, 32:11, and 25:26, among other portions of the Holy Book.

In the second section of this fourth chapter, we have explored a number of places where the Angel of Death appears in traditional Hadith literature. There we saw traditions from Sulayman Al-Jamal, Al-Tabarani, Hasan al-Basri, and Ibn Abbas, among other traditional collectors. These Ahadith about the *Malak Al-Mawt* have two major elements in common.

First, those who fair the best with the Angel of Death are those who are committed believers in the Muslim faith. And secondly, those who have given up their faith are consigned to the tortures of Hell because they have substituted over things, like prestige or money, in the place of the worshipping of Allah.

As we have shown, a number of Islamic traditions of Azrael and his followers show the souls of the devout being gently removed from the body, while the souls of non-believers are ripped from their bodies. We also have shown in this fourth chapter that the angel Azrael is said to have visited many of the Muslim prophets, including Ibrahim, Sulayman and Musa, among others. We also described in this chapter the roles of various angels in the Muslim faith who play roles in the process of death and dying, as well as on Judgment Day, including greeters at both the Gates of Heaven and of Hell.

Additionally, we have spoken in this fourth chapter of several ways in the Islamic tradition, where people have attempted to cheat or forestall the Angel of Death, including a Hadith from Ibn Abbas where he asks the angel how long he has left, only to have the angel hold up five fingers. When Ibn Abbas asks if that is five years, five months, or five days, by the time he asked, he died!

In subsequent sections of this chapter, we have described and discussed the roles of several other angels associated with death in Islam, including Ridwan, the Keeper of the Gates of Heaven; Malik, the Keeper of the Gates of Hell; Munqar and Naqir, the pair of celestial beings who interrogate the dead in their graves; and the angel Ruman who interviews the dead before the arrival of the two interrogating *malakayn.* Although Ruman does not appear in Al-Qur'an, he is mentioned in a number of Ahadith.

Above all, what we have tried to show in this chapter is to give some indication of the complexity and the depth of what Muslim scholars have to say about the roles of angels in the process of dying and death. Islam is concerned with these processes down to the number of assistants that Malik has in performing his duties (nineteen) and the number of questions that are asked of the dead while being interrogated in the grave (three for Sunnis, and five for Shiites.)

In Chapter Five, we shall explore and discuss a group of beings in the Islamic faith known as the *Houris.* Traditionally, these beings have been seen as comely maidens who greet believers when thet enter Paradise. But in Chapter Five, we reject that traditional view in favor of a thesis recently offered by philologist Christoph Luxenberg.

Chapter Five:
Houris in the Faith of Islam

These maidens of Paradise are described in various passages in the Qur'an. In Surah 2:25, 3:15, and 4:57, they are called "Purified Wives."

—Christoph Luxenberg, *The Syro-Aramaic Reading of the Koran*

Although there is a wide range of interpretations about the houris, there is no definitive account of what constitutes the meaning of the term.

—Nerina Rustomji, *The Garden and the Fire: Heaven and Hell in Islamic Culture*

Announce to those who believe and have done good deeds, glad tidings of gardens under which rivers flow and where they eat the fruits that grow they will say, "Indeed, they are the same that we were given before," so like in semblance the food would be. And they shall have fair spouses [*Houris*] there, and will live there abidingly.

—The Holy Qur'an 2:25 (Author's translation)

Introduction

In this fifth chapter, we shall explore the uses in Muslim tradition of the employing of the noun *Hur*, or *Huriyah*, as used in the Holy Qur'an and traditional Hadith literature. Christoph Luxenberg begins his discussion of the Houris by quoting the article in the *Encyclopedia of Islam* on the Hur. He tells us:

> *Hur*, plural of *hawra*, fem. of *Ahwar*. Literally, "the white ones," i.e., the maidens of Paradise, the black irises of whose eyes is in strong contrast to the clear white around it. The *nomen unitatis* in Persian is *hur* (also, *huri-bihishti*), Arabic, *Huriyah*. The explanation of the words found in Arabic "those at whom the spectator is astounded (*hara*)" is, of course, false and therefore rejected even by other Arab philologists.[317]

This entry from the *Encyclopedia of Islam* continues:

> The maidens of Paradise are described in various passages in the Qur'an's 2:25, 3:15, and 4:57; they are called "purified wives"; according to the commentators, this means that they are free alike from bodily impurity, and defect of character. In Surah 55:56, it is said that their glances are retiring, i.e., they look only upon their husbands. Neither man nor Jinn have ever touched them; this is interpreted to mean that there are two classes of them, one like man and the other like Jinn. They are enclosed in pavilions (55:72). They are compared to jacinths and pearls (Surah 55:58).[318]

Noted scholar of Islam, Bernard Lewis and B. E. Churchill give us this from the glossary of their book, *Islam: The Religion and the People*:

> *Houri*. From the Arabic *hur*, the plural of *hawra*, an adjective form from an Arabic Root with the general meaning of "whiteness." The term is used to describe the beautiful virgins of Paradise whose companionship is promised to the believers as part of their eternal reward. They are described in some detail in those passages of the Koran, where the joys of Heaven are contrasted with the torments of Hell.[319]

Lewis and Churchill continue their description of the *Houris*, or Virgins of Paradise:

> In the Koran (52:20, 55:56, 55:72–74, and 56:22–23), the function of the immaculately chaste *houris*, as of the perpetually fresh youths, is to attend and serve the blessed in Heaven. Some later commentators and traditions specify the number of Houris and assign them a more explicitly sexual role, their virginity being miraculously reconstituted after each encounter.[320]

A number of Muslim scholars describe the Houris' relationship to one's good deeds on Earth. If a believer led an exemplary life while alive on Earth, then these deeds are changed to lovely companions, reflecting the goodness of the deeds, particularly expressed in physical attributes. In some traditions, this metaphor is said to obtain for both humans and Jinn in Paradise, after being recreated anew in the Hereafter.[321] Islam also has a strong mystical tradition that places these heavenly delights in the realm of ecstatic experiences, like the Beatific Vision.

The primary goal of this fifth chapter is to analyze and discuss how the terms *Hur, Houri* and *Houris* have been employed in the history of Islam, as well as discussing a new theory about the Houris promulgated by German philologist Christoph Luxenberg in relationship to these Arabic terms. As we shall see, Luxenberg's view goes far beyond the traditional Islamic interpretations of the Houris and may shed some new light on the original meanings of these terms.[322]

In classical Arabic, the noun *Hur'in* is made up of two words, *hur* and *in*. The first of these is the plural of both *ahwar* (masculine) and *Hawra* (feminine), which literally means, "white-eyed," that is persons distinguished by *Hawar*—that is, "an intense whiteness of the eyes with lustrous, black pupils." The word *Houri* has entered the English language through modern French, where the word means "a voluptuous, beautiful, alluring woman." In classical Hebrew, the corresponding adjective is *Hiwer*, which means "pale" or "white in color." This classical Hebrew term comes from the same HWT Semitic root. This brings us to the places in the Holy Qur'an, where the Houris are mentioned, the topic of the next section of this chapter.

Houri and Houris in the Qur'an

The Houris variously have been described in the Qur'an. They are called "chaste females," (55:56); who "restrain their glances (37:48 and 55:56); they have a "modest gaze" (38:52); with "wide, beautiful, and lovely eyes" (56:22–23, 37:48, 52:20 and 56:22); their eyes "shine like pearls" (56:23); they are called "virgins" (56:36); who are free from "pregnancy and breast-feeding" (56:38). The Houris are called "Companions of an equal age" (56:38), suggesting that both believing male Muslims, as well as their Houris in Paradise, will look young and virile.

Among the places in the Muslim Holy Book where Houri and Houris appear are the following passages: 2:25, 37:40–48, 44:51–55, 47:15, 52:17–20, 55:56–57, 55:70–77, 56:7–40, and 78:30–34. We shall discuss a number of these passages in our analysis below.

Most of the passages in the Qur'an where the Houris are discussed come from the Prophet Muhammad's Meccan period, where much stress was placed on the Last Judgment, the pleasures of Paradise, and the torments of *Jahannam*, or Hell. Among the Mecca passages on the Houris are the following: 37:47–48, 38:52, 44:54, 52:20, 55:58 and 72; 56:22–24, 56:30–34, and 78:30–34.

There are also a number of passages in the Holy Book that most likely came from Muhammad's Medinian period. These include 2:23–24, 3:13–15, 4:57–60, and 61:12. Unlike the ayats in the Meccan period, the passages in the Medinian period tend to address the new followers of Islam. These passages often begin with the salutation, "Oh you believers!" Often what follows are verses related to Islamic Law, like the "Five Pillars" and the "Six Articles of Faith" of Islam, for example.

The Arabic terms *Hur, Houri, and Houris* (singular and plural) are used several times in the Muslim Holy Book. In most of these references, the noun is employed in its plural form. The Qur'an's 37:40–48 is the most extensive description of the Houris. The text tells us:

> Except the chosen creatures of Allah whose provisions are predetermined, fruits of every kind, and they will be honored. In the Garden of Delight, sitting on couches face to face, with cups from a flowing stream being

passed around, clear and delicious to drink, neither dulling the senses nor intoxicating. And with them, maidens of a modest look and large, lustrous eyes.[323]

The Muslim Holy Book, at Surah 44:51–55, also gives an extensive passage on the Houris:

Surely those who fear and follow the straight path will surely be in the place of peace and security. In the midst of gardens and springs, dressed in brocade and shot silk, facing one another, just like that; we shall pair them with companions with large, black eyes. They will call with every kind of fruit with satisfaction.[324]

A third passage on the Houris comes at 52:17–20. These *ayats*, or verses, reveal:

Those who fear Allah and follow the straight path will surely be in Gardens and bliss. Rejoicing at what their Lord has given them; and the Lord will preserve them from the torments of Hell. "Eat and drink with relish," they will be told as recompense for what they have done. They will recline on couches set in rows, paired with fair companions, clean of thought and bright of eye.[325]

Another reference to the Houris, at the Qur'an's 55:55–57, gives us more information about the nature of the Houris. It asks:

How many favors of your Lord will then both of you deny? In them maidens with averted glances and undeflowered by man or by Jinn before them. Which of your favors, then, will both of you deny?[326]

This notion that the Houris are virgins (*adhara*, in Arabic) is confirmed by Surah 55:57–58 and 55:70–77. The latter passage reveals:

In each there shall be virgins chaste and fair. Dark-eyed virgins sheltered in their tents who neither man nor Jinn have touched.[327]

The Qur'an's 56:35–38 confirms the virginal status of the Houris, where it says, "We have made them in a distinctive fashion, and made them virginal, loving companions matched in equal age, for those of the right hand."[328] In the Qur'an and early Islam, the right/right-hand is preferred to the left/left-hand. It is related to the Good in Islam, as opposed to Evil. The Arabic expression, *Ma malakat aymanukum*, or "What one's right hand possesses," an expression employed many times in Al-Qur'an, is another example of the preference for the Right/Right hand.

In several other passages in the Qur'an, we get a sense that young boys will be available to people in Paradise. The Holy Book's 52:24, 56:17 and 75:19, for example, tell us that not all of the companions in Paradise will be females. The first of these passages reveals, "And round them will serve handsome boys like well-guarded pearls."[329] Al-Qur'an's 56:17 speaks of "serving boys of perpetual freshness,"[330] And 76:19–20 says that:

> And boys of everlasting youth will go about attending them. Looking at them you would think they are pearls dispersed. When you look around, you will see delights, and great dominion.[331]

Scholar Malise Ruthven, in his *Islam in the World*, points out that some Muslim thinkers believe that the passages in Al-Qur'an about the Houris are entirely allegorical. He writes:

> Some Muslim commentators were at great pains to point out that these descriptions were purely allegorical. Bukhari, Muslim, and others record Hadiths in which the Prophet is said to have stated of Paradise, "I have readied for my righteous servants what no eye has ever seen and what ear has never heard, and no heart of man has ever been conceived."[332]

Yusul Ali, prominent contemporary Qur'anic translator and commentator, insists that the Houris, who have feminine gender in Arabic, are purely spiritual beings. Mr. Ali comments: "…less grosser ideas of sex would intrude. It is made clear that these companions for heavenly society will be of a special creation—of virginal purity, grace, and beauty, inspiring and inspired by love, with no question of time or age."[333]

Other Medieval Muslim interpreters, however, like Al-Ghazali and Al-Suyuti, believe that the ayats about the Houris in Al-Qur'an are to be taken literally. Imam Suyuti advises us:

> The food of Paradise is everlasting. When the elect have eaten or drunk something, they will perspire a little with sweat, and they will be as fresh and perfumed as musk. The dwellers in Paradise have no anuses. They were made for defecating, but in Paradise, there is no defecation.[334]

Malise Ruthven continues his description of the Houris. He writes:

> The Houris, or female companions, come in a variety of colors, including white, green, yellow, and red. Their bodies are made of saffron, musk, amber, and camphor, and their hair is as raw as silk. Each of the elect may have seventy Houris in addition to his earthly lives and other women he found attractive. All become more beautiful each day. A man's virility becomes greatly increased. Couples make love as on Earth, but each moment of pleasure lasts for twenty-four years.[335]

The Irish scholar Ruthven completes his description of the Houris in Paradise:

> Paradise, however, is not just a place of sensual delights in Suyuti's vision. Its God, when the faces of the elect will be "bright with happiness looking up to its Sustainer," while the faces of the damned will be "overcast with despair, knowing that a crushing calamity is about to befall them."[336]

The Muslim Holy Book's account of companions in Paradise seems to make three principal points. First, those who go the straight path and follow the prescription of Allah are promised a collection of young companions in the afterlife. Second, they will be virgins. And finally, they may not all be female. There may be young boys for women, as well as men who prefer them. This brings us to the places in the major collectors of Hadith literature, when the Houris are the topic of conversation.

The Houris in Hadith Literature

Christoph Luxenberg speaks of the Houris in later Islam when he tells us:

> Later literature is able to give many more details of their physical beauty; They are created of saffron, musk, amber, and camphor, and have four colors, white, green, yellow, and red; they are so transparent that the marrow of their bones is visible through seventy silken garments. If they expectorate in the world, their spittle becomes musk. Two names are written on their breasts. One is the name of Allah, and the other of her husband. They wear many jewels and ornaments, etc., on their hands and feet. They dwell in splendid palaces surrounded by all possible luxury.[337]

A Hadith from ninth-century collector Al-Tirmidhi speaks of the Houris, as well as other females in Paradise, as well. He observes:

> Al Basri says that an old woman came to the Messenger of Allah and made a request. "Oh Messenger of Allah, make dua [ritual prayer] that Allah grants me entrance into *Jannah* [Paradise]. The Messenger of Allah replied, "Oh mother, an old woman cannot enter Paradise." Then the woman began to cry and she turned to leave. Then Muhammad said, "Tell the woman that no one will enter Paradise in a state of old age; but Allah will make all women in Jannah as young virgins.[338]

Another Hadith from Mishkat Ul-Massabih, in his *Al-Hadis,* tells us, "There is a market in Paradise where there will be no buying or selling, but will consist of men and women. When a man desires a beauty, he will be provided with her and have intercourse with her.[339] (Vol. IV, p. 172, no. 34). A Hadith from the collection of Al-Tabari also speaks of meeting the Houris in the afterlife. He informs us:

> Yet, by Allah, I feel happy that we shall soon meet, for, by Allah, if all that here is between us and the maidens of Paradise (*ah hur al'ayn*) is that these people should come out against us with swords, then I want them to come out against us with swords.[340]

Muhammad Al-Tabari confirms this judgment in another Hadith that says, "All righteous women, however old and decayed they may have been on Earth, will be resurrected as virginal maidens, and like their male counterparts will remain eternally young in Paradise.[341] A Hadith from ninth-century Persian scholar Sunan Ibn Maja speaks of the attitudes of the Houris to earthly wives in Paradise. He informs us:

> Houris do not want wives to annoy their husbands, since the Houris also will be their wives in the afterlife. Ibn Jobal reported that Allah's Messenger said, "A woman does not annoy her husband but his spouse from among the maidens with wide eyes intensely white and deeply black will say, 'Do not annoy him, may Allah annoy you if you do. He is with you as a passing guest. Very soon, he will part with you and come to us.'"[342]

A Hadith from Ibn Kathir suggests that, "The Houris are delightful virgins of a comparable age. They will not have sexual intercourse with anyone before their husbands, with either humans or Jinn."[343] Another Hadith from Ibn Kathir, fourteenth-century Syrian collector of Hadith suggests:

> In the other life, after they have become old in this life, they will be brought back to a youthful, virginal state. They will be delightfully passionate and compassionate with their husbands. They will be beautiful, kind, and cheerful.[344]

Abu Bukhari, one of the six traditional collectors of Sunni Hadith, writes of the Houris in several of his traditions. In one of these, he observes,

> "The first group of people who will enter Paradise will have wives of the Houris. All of them will be Muslim men, and they will look alike. They will resemble their father, Adam [in stature], sixty cubits high."[345]

In another tradition from Abu Bukhari, he speaks of certain believers, "Who will have twin wives. The marrow of their bones in their legs will be seen through the flesh of excessive beauty.[346]

In another place, Abu Bukhari tells us that, "Their wives [the Houris] will be so beautiful that they will be pure and transparent, and the bones in their legs will be seen through their flesh."[347]

Ninth-century Persian Sunni scholar Sahih Muslim tells us the following about the Houris:

> Muhamad reported that some persons stated with a sense of pride and discussed whether there will be more men or women in Paradise. It was upon this that Abu Hurayra said, "The members of the first group to get to Paradise would have their faces as bright as a full moon during the night; and next to this group will have the faces as bright as shining stars in the sky. And everyone will have two wives or husbands."[348]

Another tradition from Abu Bukhari tells us that, "The Houris have intensely black eyes and intense whiteness in their eyeballs; and they are extremely beautiful."[349] Not all traditions about the Houris are in the Sunni tradition. According to some Shiite Hadith, Fatima became a Houri in Paradise after her death. All believing Muslims in Heaven will have as many wives as they wish, but among the Shiite believers, Ali will only have Fatima. A Shiite text called *Omn al-Kitab* tells us that Fatima, "appeared at the creation of the material world, crowned and seated on a throne, and holding a sword."[350] The same text tells us:

> She was ornamented with a million varicolored shimmering lights, which illuminate all of Paradise.

She was the first to occupy the Seal of Dominion, the resting place of Allah, the Most High. Her symbol is the crescent moon, and she is called, "*Al-Zahra,*" or "Bright Blooming," a former title of the Great Mother God.[351]

The *Encyclopedia of Islam* also mentions this tradition of Fatima becoming a Houri in Paradise. It tells us:

Fatima [Hazrat Ali's wife] gave birth through her left thigh, while Maryam [Mary] is said to have given birth to Isa [Jesus] through her right thigh. Fatima became a Houri in Heaven. All the Muslims in Heaven will have as many Houris or wives as they wish, except that Ali would have no other wife but Fatima. Some see a similarity between the veneration of Fatima and the Roman Catholic veneration of the Virgin Mary. Fatima has been called the "Mother of her father" by 12er Shiites.[352]

Among the followers of the Druze Faith of Western Asia, who see their beginnings in the patriarch Jethro of Midian, as well as the Ba'hai faith, are beliefs that Fatima, the wife of Ali in Shiite Islam, became a Houri in *Jannah*, or Heaven, upon her death. Other Ahadith on the Houris appear in the collection of Ibn Habib, a fifteenth-century commentator. Nerina Rustomji speaks of Al-Habib's treatment of the Houris, when she writes:

It includes more common traditions, one that the Houris are so fair that the marrow of their bones can be seen through their clothing, just as a red liquid can be seen in a glass of water. Yet there are other traditions that present strikingly new material. For example, one tradition introduces a Houri named La'bh around whom the other Houris gathered. Houris also interact with believers. In these exchanges, houris are active beings who receive believers in new abodes and greet them as their rewards.[353]

Thus, Al-Habib suggests that the Houris may have other roles and jobs besides the traditional view of satisfying the sexual desires of believers in Paradise. In a later section of this fifth chapter, we suggest that one of those jobs is to aid Muslims on the battlefield. Other Ahadith on the Houris in the history of Islam include entries from the collections of Hadith from Al-Tirmzi and Mishkat. Al-Tirmzi tells us, "Every man who enters Paradise shall be given 72 Houris." He adds:

> No matter at what age he had died, when a man is admitted to Paradise, he will become a thirty year old man, and he shall not age any further. A man in Paradise shall be given virility equal to that of one hundred men.[354]

In addition to the emphasis on sexual virility in these passages from Al-Tirmzi, he is also one of the first of Hadith writers to suggest that the number of Houris given to the believing Muslim upon entering Paradise is seventy-two. More will be said about this number in a subsequent section of this chapter. It is enough now to say, however, that many suicide bombers in contemporary life appear to have been motivated by, among other reasons, this claim about the seventy-two comely maidens, for those who practice Jihad. In another tradition from Al-Tirmzi, which is a nickname for Al-Tirmidhi, ninth-century Sunni Jurist, he again gives a description of a Houri in Paradise.

He relates:

> A Houri is a most beautiful young woman with a transparent body. The marrow of her bones is visible like the interior lines of pearls and rubies. She looks like red wine in a white glass. She is of white color and free from routine physical disabilities of an ordinary woman such as menstruation, menopause, urinal and offal discharge, childbearing and related pollution. A Houri is a girl of a tender age, having large breasts, which are round and pointed and not inclined to dangle. Houris dwell in places of splendid surroundings.[355]

Noted Islamic philosopher, Al-Ghazali, also speaks of the bodies of the Houris. The great philosopher relates:

> The Houris of Paradise will be pure women—free from menstruation, urine, stool, cough, and children. They will sing in Paradise on Divine purity and praise, "We are most beautiful Houris, and we exists for the pleasures of honored husbands."[356]

The Persian Sunni philosopher Al-Ghazali (1056–1111) also tells us that the maidens of Paradise will be "sixty meters tall and seven meters wide."[357] In another Hadith, Al-Tirmidhi informs us that the Houris will be "hairless, except for the eyebrows and the head, and they will be pure."[358] He also suggests that the Houris "will be transparent to the marrow of their bones."[359] Sahih Bukhari calls the Houris, "splendid and beautiful."[360]

In another tradition, Muhammad Al-Bukhari (810–870) again speaks of the maidens of Paradise when he observed, "Everyone will have two wives from the Houris, who are so beautiful and pure and transparent, that the marrow of the bones in their legs will be seen through their flesh."[361] Abu Bukhari again speaks of the Houris in a section called "The Prophets" of his Hadith collection. Abu Bukhari observes:

> People who enter Paradise will not urinate, relieve nature, spit, or have any nasal secretions. Their combs will be of gold, and their sweat will smell like musk. The aloeswood will be used in their censers. Their wives will be Houris; all of them will look alike and will resemble their father Adam, sixty cubits tall.[362]

Sahih Muslim Ibn Al-Hajjaj Nishapuri (821–875), one of the traditional collectors of Hadith in Sunni Islam, also repeats many of the facts listed above about the nature of the Houris. He tells us:

> Muhammad reported that some persons stated with a sense of pride and some discussed whether there will be more men in Paradise than women...Then the Prophet said, "The first group to enter Paradise will have their

faces as bright as the full moon during the night. And next to this group, are people who will have their faces as bright as the shining stars in the sky, and every person would have two wives [*Houris*] and the marrow of their shanks would glimmer beneath the flesh and there will be none without a wife [*Houri*] in Paradise.[363]

Another Hadith from Abu Bukhari also speaks of the great height and the transparency of the Houris. He relates:

A tent in Paradise is like a hollow pearl which is thirty miles in height; and on every corner of the tent the believer will have a family that cannot be seen by others.[364]

Al-Bukhari again speaks of the pavilions in Paradise occupied by the Houris. Abu Bukhari reveals:

In Paradise there is a pavilion made of a single, hollow pearl sixty miles wide; In each corner there are wives who will not see those in the other corners; and the believers will visit and will enjoy them.[365]

Finally, a Hadith from *Hadith Mishkat* also speaks of the radiance on the faces of the Houris in Paradise. The tradition tells us:

If a Houri looks down from her abode in Heaven onto the Earth, the whole space shall be filled with light and fragrance. A Houri's face is more radiant than a mirror, and one can see his image in her cheek; the marrow of her shins is visible to the eyes.[366]

This brings us to a discussion of the seventy-two Houris promised to believing male Muslims in the afterlife, the topic of the next section of this fifth chapter. We call it "The Houris and the seventy-two Virgins."

The Houris and the Seventy-two Virgins

Perhaps the most famous Hadith on the Islamic Houris comes from fourteenth-century collector Ibn Kathir. In his *Tafsir* on Surah al-Rahman, 55:72, he comments:

> The Prophet Muhammad was heard saying, "The smallest reward for the people of Paradise is an abode where there are 80,000 servants and 72 wives, over which stands a dome decorated with pearls, aquamarine, and ruby, as wide as the distance between Al-Jabiyyah and Sana'a."[367]

Al-Jabiyyah is a suburb of Damascus, Syria, and Sana'a is a city in the Southwest portion of Yemen. This Hadith from Ibn Kathir has been widely understood to mean that if someone dies in the name of Allah during a Jihad, or in other circumstances, he will receive seventy-two virgins, or Houris, in the afterlife. Later in this chapter, we will explore the interpretation of this Hadith recently made by philologist Christoph Luxenberg in his book *The Syro-Aramaic Reading of the Koran*.[368] As we shall see, Luxenberg thinks this is a misreading of the Hadith in question, and the corresponding verses from Al-Qur'an, and so do we.

In August of 2001, just a month before 9/11, CBS News aired an interview with Hamas activist Muhammad Abu Wardeh, who recruited terrorists for suicide bombings in Israel. Mr. Wardeh was quoted as saying, "I described to them how God will compensate the martyr for sacrificing his life for his land. If you become a martyr, God will give you seventy virgins and everlasting happiness."[369] Mr. Wardeh was, in fact, short-changing his recruits, since Ibn Kathir and Al-Tirmidhi both say the number of virgins is seventy-two.

Since September 11, 2001, news stories have repeated the story of suicide bombers and their heavenly sexual rewards. Muslim scholars and Western apologists of Islam alike have repeatedly said that suicide is forbidden in Islam. Although suicide, or *qatlu nafsi-hi* in Arabic, is not explicitly mentioned in Al-Qur'an, it is clearly forbidden in a number of traditions in classical Hadith literature. Mr. Wardeh, however, correctly uses the word *Shahid*, which means "Martyr" in Arabic. Thus, these suicide bombers see themselves as dying for the holiest of purposes, for *Jihad*, an incumbent religious duty established in Al-Qur'an and in subsequent Hadith. While suicide is explicitly forbidden, martyrdom is everywhere praised, welcomed and sometimes even urged. Nevertheless, there are two points about the virgins available to martyrs in Paradise. First, there is no mention anywhere in Al-Qur'an that the number of available virgins for believing Muslim men is seventy-two. And secondly, the dark-eyed damsels are available to all Muslim men, not only to martyrs. It is only in Ahadith from Ibn Kathir and from Al-Tirmidhi, that we find seventy-two "wives," or "houris," not virgins, are specified.

Modern apologists of Islam try to play down the emphasis on materialism and sexuality in these passages. Even theologians like Al-Ghazali (twelfth century) and Al-Ash'ari (tenth century) have admitted the abundant sexual delights in Paradise. Sensual pleasures also are graphically described by scholar Al-Suyuti, Qur'anic commentator and polymath, in the early sixteenth-century. Al-Suyuti wrote, "Each time we sleep with a Houri we find her a virgin." He adds:

> Besides, the penis of the elect never softens, the erection is an eternal one. The sensation you feel each time you make love is utterly delicious and out of this world. Were you to experience it in this life, you would faint. Each chosen one will marry seventy Houris, besides the women he married on Earth, and all of them will have appetizing vaginas.[370]

Contemporary scholar Margaret Kleffer Nydell, in her book *Understanding Arabs: A Guide for Modern Times*, says that the belief in the seventy-two virgins should be understood by Christians in the same way that some believe that after death they will be issued wings, a halo, harp, and then begin to walk on clouds."[371]

Other scholars of Islam, however, like Hafiz Salahuddin Yusuf, for example, suggest that the traditions about the seventy-two virgins in Paradise is based on a weak chain of narrators. Yusuf uses the word *Da'if* to describe the train of transmission. This Arabic word might be translated as "extremely weak."[372] This brings us to a discussion of another problematic pair of verses in the Holy Book of Islam. These verses are in reference to Surah 78:33–34, as we shall see next.

The Breasts of Surah 78:33-34

In addition to the Ahadith mentioned above, there also has been considerable scholarly disagreement concerning Surah 78:33–34. A simple English translation of these ayats give us something like this:

> And graceful maidens, of the same age, and cups of wine full and flowing. They will hear no blasphemies there or disavowals, a recompense from your Lord, a sufficient gift.[373]

Some commentators have taken this passage to refer to the Houris and a description of their breasts, particularly verse 34. Translations from Palmer, Rodwell and George Sale, for example, say that the Qur'an's 78:34 speak of "swelling breasts."[374] A Hadith from Ibn Kathir tells us this about the line:

> This means "round breasts." They meant by this that the breasts of these girls will be fully rounded and not sagging because they will be "virgins of an equal age."[375]

Abdullah Yusuf Ali, however, renders the Qur'an's 78:34 as "maidens of an equal age,"[376] without making any references to their physical attributes. Muhammad Asad, on the other hand, says this about the passage in question:

> As regards my rendering of *kawa'ib* as "splendid companions," it is to be remembered that the term *ka'b* from which the participle *ka'ib* is derived, has many meanings and that one of those meanings is "prominence," "eminence," or "glory." Thus, the verb *ka'ba*, when applied to a person, signifies "he made another person prominent, glorious, or splendid." Based on this topical meaning of both the verb *ka'ba* and the noun *ka'b*, the participle *ka'ib* has often been used in popular parlance to denote, "a girl whose breasts are becoming prominent or are budding;" hence, many commentators see it as an allusion to some

sort of "female companions" who would entertain the
presumably male residents of Paradise.[377]

Then, Mr. Ali goes on to argue against this view. He says in his
notes to Surah 78:

> ...This interpretation of *kawa'ib* overlooks the purely
> derivative origin of the above popular usage—which
> is based on the topical connotation of "prominence"
> inherent in the noun *ka'b*—the subject for this
> obvious tropism the literal meaning of something that
> is physically prominent; and this, in my opinion, is
> utterly unjustified. If we bear in mind that the Qur'an's
> description of the blessings of Paradise are always
> allegorical, we realize that in the above context that
> the term *kawa'ib* can have no other meaning than
> "glorious" or "splendid beings."[378]

The most important conclusion that Mr. Ali makes about Surah
78:34 is that he believes the passages on the Houris are "always
allegorical." For him, the verse in question is a small allegory that
goes into the making of a larger allegory—that the Houris are not to be
understood literally. Nevertheless, what to make of the Arabic sentence,
"*wakawa'iba atraban*" is not entirely clear. It is a conjunction followed
by an accusative, feminine, plural noun, followed by an accusative
feminine plural, indefinite adjective.

Other interpreters translate the noun in question and its adjective as
"mature breasts," (Al-Tabari) or "voluptuously, fully-matured breasts,"
(Muhammad Habib Shakir, 1866–1939), or Muhammad Sarwar (1910–
1948), Pakistani scholar, and his rendering of "pear-shaped breasts."
Arberry prefers "maidens with swelling breasts."[379]

Again, at the close of this chapter, we shall explore the recent
scholarship of philologist Christoph Lexenberg and his book *The Syro-
Aramaic Reading of the Koran*, where he argues, quite convincingly,
that these traditional views of "swollen breasts" in the Qur'an's 78:31–
34 are misplaced, as we shall see in a subsequent section of this chapter.
Before we get to that section, however, we first will explore another
context for the Houris in Islam, the role on the battlefield.

The Houris on the Battlefield

In some Islamic traditions, both angels and Jinn have been suggested to have aided the Muslim Army in the earliest of its battles. In some traditions, those aides have been given the name *Jundullah*, or "Those who helped Muhammad on the Battlefield." What is not clear is whether this term refers to angels, to Jinn, or to both.

In addition to the Houris playing a role in Heaven as voluptuous maidens, they also have been thought of in the Muslim tradition to have played a role on the Battlefield in some Islamic contexts. In these situations, the role of the Houris is like that of the angels involved in skirmishes like the Battle of Uhud, the Battle of Badr, and the Battle of the Ditch. The Battle of the Ditch was an extension of the Battle of Uhud, as the Battle of Uhud was fought by the Quraysh to get revenge for the defeat at Badr. The conflict at Uhud proved to be indecisive for the early Muslim Army.

When the Prophet Muhammad came to know of the war preparations made by the Quraysh, he held a Council of War. They concluded that in light of the large force of the Quraysh, who had allied themselves with a number of Arab tribes, it was not advisable to face the enemy out in the open. The city of Medina had natural defenses on three sides, so the Muslims built a ditch on the fourth side. Thus, the origin of the battle's name.

An old account of the Battle of the Ditch is an epic ode called the *Sirat'antar*, or the "Thirsty Sword." It speaks of the role of the Houris in the battle. It also speaks of the bravery of the Muslim soldiers. One of these was a man named Utba who lost a leg at the Battle of the Ditch. Nerina Rustomji speaks of the warrior Utba and the battle:

> In the poem, Utba's amputated leg is exchanged for his future life. The next life is located in the highest garden, characterized by its proximity to God and the Houris, who are like beautiful artworks. Within this description is an implicit hierarchy where Utba's actions gain the very best of rewards, as opposed to a possibly lower level of reward in the garden. This much-awaited fate is framed as a type of commercial transaction. He bought

the Highest Heaven with the sacrifice of his leg... He
loses his leg and gains the Houris.[380]

In another account, the Houris are mentioned as having occupied
the battle space as "ethereal nurses" who tend the sick and the slain. A
Hadith from Jordanian collector Abdullah Ibn Abu Najih reveals that:

When a martyr is slain, his two wives from the dark-
eyed houris pet him, wiping off the dust from his face,
saying all the while, "May Allah put dust on the face of
the man and slay him who has slain you. The Houris
then have a special place on the battlefield, acting not
only as an indication of the promised life that will soon
arrive but also as a precursor to that life within the
earthly moment of dying.[381]

Ms. Rustonji also speaks of another tradition about the Houris on
the battlefield. She observes:

In another instance, Muhammad sees some Houris.
He turned away from a fighter who recently had died.
When questioned about why he turned away from the
man, Muhammad replied, "With his two wives from
the dark-eyed Houris," and he averts his gaze out of
respect.[382]

Ms. Rustomji continues her analysis:

The Houris function may have been akin to wives in the
actual battle; however, given their other-worldly origin,
their visibility is curious. The appearance of the Houris
suggests that death is a type of intermediate state
where attributes of the garden can be experienced
within earthly time. Here the garden is not just an
extension of eschatological time, but it also acts as a
frame of meaning within Earthly time. After all, the
Houris does not appear in any mundane moment or
natural death. Instead, Houris are visible on Earth only
with the soiled blood on the battlefield.[383]

Whatever the role of the Houris on the battlefield may be is not clear, but some Hadith suggest they act as nurses for the wounded and the dead and may help the latter on their way to Paradise, particularly if the soldiers were numbered among the righteous.

In the final two sections of this chapter, we shall explore the work of philologist Christoph Luxenberg on the nature and function of the Houris. As we shall see, it is a perspective radically different from Islam's traditional view of the virgins in Paradise with "swelling breasts." Before moving to Luxenberg, however, we will first discuss the idea of Jesus' mother Maryam as one of the Houri in Paradise.

Maryam as a Houri in Paradise

One other issue concerning the Islamic views of the Houris is a tradition that suggests that Maryam, the mother of Isa (Jesus), is to be one of the wives of the Prophet Muhammad in the Great Beyond. This tradition can be found in a Hadith from Ibn Kathir's *Qasas al-Anbiya*, or "Tales of the Prophets," in which Imam Kathir says, "The Messenger of Allah said, 'God married me in Paradise to wed the daughter of Imran and to the wife of Pharaoh, and to the sister of Musa.'"[384]

This comment of Ibn Kathir's comes in a chapter entitled, "Allah Choosing Maryam, peace be upon her." After mentioning a number of traditional Hadith concerning Maryam's status in Islam among the women of Paradise, then Imam Al-Kathir indicates that Maryam, the mother of Isa, will be a wife of the Prophet Muhammad in Paradise. This has led Ibn Kathir and others to conclude that after her death, Maryam became a Houri in the Great Beyond. Some Muslim critics also maintain that the Prophet Muhammad met Prophet Maryam during his Night Journey. At any rate, this brings us to a discussion of the philological work of German scholar Christoph Luxenberg on the Houris.

Christoph Luxenberg on the Houris

Christoph Luxenberg is the pseudonym of a philologist writing in German. He is the author of *Die Syro-Aramaische Lesart of the Koran*, first published in Germany in 2004. In this work, Luxenberg tries to show that many of the obscurities of the Qur'an disappear if we view certain words as Syriac, rather than Arabic. In Luxenberg's analysis, which leans heavily on the hymns of Ephrem, the Syrian, a prolific Christian hymnographer in the fourth century.

Ephrem the Syrian, or *Mar Aprem Suryaya* in Syriac, was born around 306 CE in the city of Nisibis, now Nusaybin, in Turkey. Ephrem wrote a wide variety of hymns, poems and sermons in verse in addition to Biblical commentaries. He also constructed works of practical theology for the edification of the church in difficult times. Ephrem is called the most significant of all Syriac writers working in the early church.

In Luxenberg's analysis, the Muslim males who dream of sensual bliss in Islamic *Jannah*, or Heaven, are actually "white raisins of crystal clarity," rather than the doe-eyed and ever-willing virgins of Islamic interpretation. Luxenberg claims that the contexts of Qur'anic passages related to the Houris make it clear that it is fruit that is being offered, and not "buxom, virginal Houris." Writing in *Hugoye: The Journal of Syriac Studies*, Robert Phenix and Cornelia Horn give an in-depth review of Luxenberg's book, including the following paragraph:

> In the forward, Luxenberg summarizes the cultural and linguistic importance of written Syriac for the Arabs of the Qur'an. At the time of Muhammad, Arabic was not a written language. Syro-Aramaic or Syriac was the language of written communication in the Near East from the second to the seventh centuries AD. Syriac, a dialect of Aramaic, was the language of Edessa, a city-state in upper Mesopotamia. While Edessa ceased to be a political entity, its language became the vehicle of Christianity and culture, spreading throughout Asia as far as Malabar and Eastern China. Until the rise of the Qur'an, Syriac was the medium of wider communication and cultural dissemination for Arameans, Arabs, and to a lesser extent, Persians. It produced the richest literary expression in the Near East from the fourth century (Aphrahat and Ephrem) until it was replaced by Arabic in the seventh and eighth centuries. Of importance is

that Syriac-Aramaic literature and the cultural matrix in which that literature existed was almost exclusively Christian. Part of Luxenberg's study shows that Syriac influences on those who created written Arabic was transmitted through a Christian medium, the influence of which is fundamental.[385]

In Luxenberg's book, the most important of these early Syriac-Aramaic works for our purposes was Ephrem the Syrian's "Hymns of Paradise."[386] In strophe eighteen of this long poem, Ephrem gives us this in an English translation of his Syriac:

Whoever has abstained from wine on Earth
For him do the vines of Paradise yearn.
Each one of them holds out to them bunches of grapes.
And if a man had lived in chastity, they [feminine] receive him
In a full bosom.[387]
Because he is a monk he did not fall into the bosom
And bed of Earthly love.

A little earlier, in the same text, at strophe fifteen, we find a solitary virgin, abstinent in her earthly life, being surrounded by male beings (prophets, angels, apostles) in the Heavens:

The virgin who rejected
The marriage crown that fades
Now has the radiant marriage chamber
That cherishes the children of light,
Shining out because she rejected
The works of darkness.
To her who was alone
In the lonely house
The wedding feast now grants tranquility:
Here angels rejoice
Prophets delight
And apostles add splendor.[388]

Using the original Syriac text of Ephrem's hymns, Luxenberg suggests that these hymns may have been the origins of the Houris in

Paradise in Islam. He compares the language of the oldest fragments of Al-Qur'an that contains language about the Houris to the Syriac poems and concludes that the latter is the source of the former. Given these early Syriac sources, in addition to the Houris being "raisins" or "grapes," he also suggests that the "full bosoms" of the Holy Book's 78:31–34 should be rendered this way:

31. The pious will in days to come have a place of felicity.

32. Gardens and grapes.

33. And indeed, lush, succulent fruits,

34. And a brimming full (wine cup).[389]

Luxenberg begins his analysis of the Houris by commenting on the Holy Book of Islam's 44:54. The Arabic text gives us this: *wa zawwajnahum bi hur'n*, which is usually rendered, "We shall wed them to maidens with large, dark eyes." Luxenberg treats the Arabic expression *zawwajnahum*, "we shall wed them," as "*rawwahnahum*," or "We shall let them rest." Luxenberg's suggestion is only a difference of two diacritical marks. The confusion arose, the German scholar argues, because early Muslim interpreters, because of the preposition, *bi*, or "to," so early Arabic interpreters gave us, "We shall marry them to." But Luxenberg points out that the Syriac *bi* means "to," as well as "under" and "among."

Thus, Luxenberg suggests the phrase in question should have said, "We shall let them rest among," or "We shall let them rest under…" If Luxenberg's analysis is correct, then *hur'in*, which is usually rendered as the feminine plural of "eye" or *'ain*, whose plural form is *'uyun*.

Thus, for Luxenberg, the *hur'in*, or Houris, can no longer refer to "virgins" or to "comely maidens." As mentioned above, the word *'ain* is traditionally rendered as the feminine plural for "eye." Thus, the expression *hur'in* is sometimes rendered as "wide-eyed." Thus, the end of the Qur'an's 44:54 might be translated as Marmaduke Picktshl does as "fair women with wide, lovely eyes." Or, as Muhammad Yusuf Ali translates, "fair women with beautiful, luscious, wide eyes" or even "lovely eyes," or as Shakir renders the verse, "Houris, pure, beautiful ones."[390]

Luxenberg does not deny that *hur* also can mean "white," nor that *'in* usually means "eye." But he proposes through Syriac a different translation of *bi hur 'in*. He suggests that *'in* may also mean "grape." Consequently, what has been for thirteen centuries "married to comely maidens," now becomes "white grapes that are under, or among something."[391]

Luxenberg goes on to interpret the seven other major passages in Al-Qur'an that speak of the Houris in a consistent manner what he has said about 44:54. He also deals with the three passages that refer to male youths in Paradise (52:24, 56:17–19 and 76:19). He argues that they are not male versions of the comely maidens, either.

In conclusion, then, Christoph Luxenberg suggests that what has been understood since the beginning of Islam as comely maidens of Paradise are actually "luscious grapes" that may well have been popular and desirable in seventh – and eighth-centuries Arabia and the Near East.

The response to Christoph Luxenberg's book has been mixed. By and large, traditional Islamic philologists and exegetes have been critical of the book. Some Semitic language scholars, like ourselves on the other hand, find the thesis to be intriguing. One way or the other, Luxenberg's research, whether good or bad, forces other contemporary scholars to reconsider how to make sense of the Houris of Paradise in the future.

Several contemporary Islamic scholars have attempted to refute the claims of Luxenberg. Maher Hathout, for example, the senior advisor of the Muslim Public Affairs Council, argues that Luxenberg has misinterpreted the Hadith in question. Dr. Hathout describes the Houris as "Allegorical, symbolic beings of bliss in Paradise."[392] He goes on to explain, "It seems that what he [Luxenberg] was referring to as 'raisins' is *kawaib*. He challenges what he claims as the Arabic meaning of 'swollen breasts,' while if he had known Arabic, he would have understood the term as 'beings with distinction.'"[393]

This conclusion is quite consistent with the rendering of Surah 78:31–34, which was suggested earlier in this chapter. Our conclusion about the Houris, then, is that it is quite likely that these ayats do not describe "buxom maidens in Paradise," but rather they are pieces of succulent, or prominent fruit, that will be offered to the faithful in the Great Beyond.

Christoph Luxenberg's conclusions about the relationship between the early Syriac language and the Arabic of Al-Qur'an, is part of a larger tradition that stretches back to the work of Alphonse Mingana (1878–1937), an Iraqi-born scholar and priest who wrote voluminously on the issue at hand. Mingana advocated an approach to Al-Qur'an that parallels the historical-critical method in the study of the Old Testament. In an essay called, "Syriac Influence on the Style of the Qur'an," Mingana wrote:

> The time has surely come to subject the text of the Qur'an to the same criticisms as that to which we subject the Hebrew and Aramaic of the Jewish Bible and the Greek of the Christian scriptures. Apart from some stray comparative remarks by a few eminent scholars, the only comprehensively critical work on the subject is still that of Noldeke, printed in 1860.[394]

The Noldeke to whom Mingana refers is Theodor Noldeke (1836–1930), German philologist and linguist who wrote extensively on the origins of Al-Qur'an, and other related issues. Both Noldeke and Mingana wrote a great deal on the relationships of the Syriac language to the Arabic of Al-Qur'an, as well as Biblical names in the Bible. They argue that names like Solomon, Pharaoh, Isaac, Ishmael, Jacob, Noah, Zachariah, and Mary, all appear in Al-Qur'an as figures reflecting the Syriac spellings of these names, rather than the Hebrew or Greek of the Bible.

Other religious languages of Al-Qur'an also appear, in their view, to have been borrowed from the Syriac renderings of these same words. Among these religious categories are words for priest, scribe, parable, salvation, sacrifice, resurrection, the Garden, soul, spirit, and the Kingdom of Heaven. The dependence of Al-Qur'an upon the Syriac language is also visible in certain theological expressions, such as "light upon light," at the Qur'an's 24:35. The same applies to Biblical events and facts such as the flood, manna, tribes, the verb to crucify, and the word Apostle. The forms of these words in Syriac are much closer to the Arabic of the Qur'an than they are to the Hebrew and Aramaic of the Old Testament and the Greek of the New Testament.

Many other common expressions and names in the Muslim Holy Book are much more reflective of ancient Syriac than the Biblical languages. Mingana, for example, tells us this about the Arabic word *Iblis*, one of the names for the Demonic in Islam. Mingana relates about Iblis:

We believe it is quite possible that the word *Iblis*, the "Evil One," is derived from *Diabolus*, through a confusion of the initial *dal* with an *alip*, by the early Kari, or the first editor of Al-Qur'an.[395]

Thus, Alphonse Mingana believed that the Arabic term *Iblis* had its origins in the Greek-Syriac *Diabolus*, a word from which we get the English "Diabolical." Mingana and Noldeke before him, also suggest that the orthography, as well as the construction of sentences in the earliest forms of written Arabic, are more indebted to Syriac than to Hebrew or Aramaic. This is also true, they argue, when it comes to foreign words, as well. The Syriac name for the mountain on which Noah's ark came to rest, for example, is much closer to the Syriac than to the Hebrew.

The Muslim Holy Book's 30:10 employs the Arabic word *Rum*, which is used to express the Byzantine or Greeks of Constantinople. Mingana says of the word *Rum*:

Whatever our views may be as to the linguistic peculiarities of the word, we are not at liberty to deny that it is derived from the Syriac *Rumaya*.[396]

Mingana goes on to argue that the Arabic word for "soldier," *Rumaye*, is most likely a form derived from the Syriac *Rumaya*. Similarly, the Arabic word *Shirk*, meaning "idolator," is originally derived from a Syriac source. The word *Shirk* comes from the same Semitic root SHRQ that is the source for many words in Arabic and Syriac related to unbelief. Mingana also believes the Arabic words *Jinn, Isa, Maryam, Malik,* and *Yahya*, or Spirit, Jesus, Mary, King, and John the Baptist, are also Arabic terms derived from Syriac.

Thus, the word of Christoph Luxenberg is part of a long tradition that goes back to the mid-nineteenth century that holds that the Arabic of Al-Qur'an was greatly influenced by the earliest forms of Christianity that employed the Syriac language. Luxenberg's thesis is not a new one. It goes back to the 1840s to the 1860s, beginning with Theodor Noldeke and continuing in Alphonse Mingana.

Because of the appearance of an article on Luxenberg's book in the *New York Times*, and another in the international edition of *Newsweek*, in 2003, the Pakistani government banned both the book and that edition of *Newsweek* on the grounds that it was offensive to Islam. This fact was reported by a number of international news organizations, including a CBS News story called "What Does the Qur'an Really Say" that aired on July 25, 2003.[397] This brings us to one final question in regard to the Houris—Should they be interpreted literally or Allegorically?—the topic of the final section of this chapter.

Houris Interpretation: Literal or Allegorical

In the vast array of the history of Islam, there are a number of Islamic thinkers that suggest that the Houris are not to be understood literally; rather, they are to be understood in an allegorical way. Chief among these traditional interpreters who held this view are thirteenth-century Persian scholar Al-Baydawi, as well as Muhammad Ibn Al-Shaffi, who died in 820, Az-Zamakhshari (1075–1143), Ar-Razi (1149–1209), and Al-Suyuti (1445–1505).

Each of these thinkers, in their own way, suggest that the description in the Qur'an about the Horis is not to be taken in a literal sense. Rather, they argue that these celestial beings, the Houris, are better understood in a metaphorical or allegorical fashion. Each of them, to that end, employs the Arabic word *Qiyas*, which means "metaphor" or "analogy," in describing the Houris. Both mystic Al-Rabi'a (714–801) and Persian philosopher Al-Ghazali (early twelfth century) also maintained that much of the language, concerning a range of eschatological issues, is to be understood in the language of metaphor. Al-Rabi'a called Hell a "veil," and Al-Ghazali implied that many eschatological issues should not be understood as literal truth. He says the language in Al-Qur'an about the Houris is more about spiritual realities than about material ones.[398]

This same view has been held by a number of contemporary thinkers, writers and scholars, including Joan DelPlato, John Updike and Islamic expert Oliver Leaman. DelPlato, in her book *Multiple Wives and Multiple Pleasures*, raises the issue of whether the Houris are to be understood literally or metaphorically.[399] Ultimately, she opts for the latter in her book.

John Updike, in his 2007 novel *The Terrorist*, also has a central character that makes the point that the Houris are simply a metaphor.[400]

Oliver Leaman, Islamic scholar and editor of *The Qur'an: An Encyclopedia*, also implies that the best way to understand the idea of the Houris is in an allegorical fashion.[401] Leaman also points out that this was the understanding of the Houris held by both Montgomery Watt and Richard Bell, two of the greatest scholars of Islam in the twentieth century. Watt's *Free Will and Predestination in Early Islam* and Richard Bell's *The Origins of Islam in a Christian Context*, both held the view that it is better to see the Houris as a metaphor for passionate love.[402]

Contemporary French scholar Jacques Jomier seems to take a similar view in his *Bible and the Qur'an* published in 1959. In discussing the Houris, Father Jomier writes:

> We will not quote the texts about the Houris, those maidens of Paradise mentioned in a few places. The word means that the white of their eyes is intensely white, and the black of their eyes is intensely black. For a brief description of these beings of perfect beauty allotted to the Elect, the Companions of the Right, see Q. 56:33–36.[403]

Jomier adds to his analysis, "The text has been used and misused by controversialists and apologists beyond reason. It suffices to know that they give the Muslim Paradise a very different aspect from that of the Christian concept. For analysis, we should rather look to the millennium of Earthly happiness."[404] Again, like the other thinkers mentioned earlier, Jomier implies that the best way to understand the phenomenon of the Houris in Paradise in Islam is to search for proper analogies or metaphors, particularly those related to human happiness on Earth. Thus, not all historical and contemporary comments on the Islamic Houris suggest that they should be understood literally.

Conclusions

We began this fifth chapter by exploring the nature and uses of the Arabic terms *Hur*, *Houri* and *Houris*. We then described at some length the chief places in the Muslim Holy Book where the Houris are mentioned or discussed. Subsequently, we also examined many of the places in the traditional collectors of Hadith where the "comely virgins" are discussed. In this literature, we discovered that traditional Hadith literature has tended to understand the Houris in terms of literal truth. We also have shown that three passages imply that there will be young males in the Afterlife for women or men who prefer them.

In the next section of Chapter Five, we spoke specifically about the guarantee in Hadiths from Ibn Kathir and At-Tirmidhi that Muslims who die in the cause of Jihad will be given seventy-two Houris in the Afterlife. In another section of this chapter, we have explored and discussed the Holy Book's 78:31–34 and the traditional understanding in Islam that the Houris have "swollen breasts." In that section, we rejected this view and pointed ahead to an understanding of the Houris recently offered by Christoph Luxenberg.

In the next section, we introduced and then discussed a view that the Houris had a role on the Muslim battlefield. We maintained that this role is to act as nurses for the wounded and the deceased in battle and that they may also accompany believing Muslims to Paradise. In the final section of this chapter, we described and discussed the philological work of scholar Christoph Luxenberg in relationship to the origins of certain Arabic passages in Al-Qur'an. These passages are many of those connected to the appearances of the Houris in their soldiers' trips to *Jannah*, or heaven. Among these passages Luxenberg examines are 2:25, 3:15, 4:57, 44:54, 52:20, 55:56, 56:36 and 78:31–34.

In this section of Chapter Five, we described and discussed the view of Christoph Luxenberg's that passages in Al-Qur'an where the Houris are mentioned may well have been derived from Christian scholar Ephrem the Syrian and his poem "Hymns of Paradise." We pointed out that what Islamic tradition sees as buxom maidens with large breasts may, in fact, be "pieces of succulent fruit." What traditionally has been understood as "swelling breasts" may be "cups of wine flowing over."

We will now turn our attention to Chapter Six, introducing and discussing the roles of two other classes of *Mala'ika*, or angels, in Islam. These are called "Guardian" and "Recording" angels. As we shall see, both of these classes of angels have played significant roles in the history of Islam.

Chapter Six:
Guardian and Recording Angels in Islam

This allusion here is to the guardian angels attached to every soul guarding him or her from harm, unless Allah wishes otherwise.

—Ishaq Al-Ma'ani, Commentary on Al-Qur'an, 13:11

These angels are with us all the time, except when we have intercourse or we have gone to the bathroom.

—Ibn Kathir, *Hadith*

He has power over his creatures and appoints guardians to watch over them. When death comes to one of you, Our messengers come and take away his soul and they do not falter.

—The Holy Qur'an 6:61 (Author's translation)

Introduction

Our chief goal in this sixth chapter is to describe and discuss the roles of two types of angels in Al-Qur'an known as the *Kiraman Kitibin*, or literally, "the honorable angels that write down our deeds," and the *Hafaza*, a type of *mala'ika*, or angels, comparable to the idea of guardian angels in Christianity.

Annemarie Schimmel, in her book *Islam: An Introduction*, writes of the tradition of protective angels in Islam. She observes:

Humans are surrounded and protected by angels during
one's whole lifetime. The pious believe in the presence
of two, sometimes four, or sometimes even a whole
host of protective angels.[405]

Ms. Schimmel goes on to describe the recording angels, as well:

Two recording angels are placed on one's shoulders;
the angel on the right notes down one's good actions,
while the one on the left takes notes of his evil actions.
However, the angel on the left hesitates a while before
completing his work, and if the sinner repents during
a certain space of time, his mistakes and sins are not
entered in the record.[406]

Thus, Ms. Schimmel tells us that the recording angel on the left
hesitates to write down the person's sins because the Muslim faith
allows the idea of forgiveness right up to the eleventh hour before those
evil deeds are recorded in the record. This idea, as we shall see later in
this chapter, is connected to the notion that in Islam, good deeds and
bad deeds are not of the same intrinsic value. In fact, good deeds are far
more valuable than are evil actions in the Muslim faith.

The guardian angels, as we have indicated earlier, are also known
as the *Hafaza*. An article on the "Hafaza" in *Hastings Encyclopedia of
Religion and Ethics* tells us this about these *Mala'ika*:

A *Hafaza* in Muslim lore is a term designating angels.
The *Hafaza* constitutes a special class of four angels in
number who protect humans from Jinn, other humans,
and from the *Shayatin*, or Satans.[407]

The Arabic word, *Hafaza*, comes from the Semitic root HFZ,
which is generally related to words expressing, guarding, keeping
or memorizing. The Arabic word *Hafiz*, for example, is a term used
in Islam to designate one who has memorized the entire Al-Qur'an,
usually at an early age. Thus, the *Hafiz* is memorizing and guarding the
integrity of the sacred text.

The Arabic root *Ha-Fa-Za,* or HFZ, is employed forty-four times
as various parts of speech, including the verb *hafiza*, which means

to order someone to do something (Qur'an 4:34). The expression *wahif'zan*, at 2:238, means "they should guard." At 12:64, the noun *Hafizan* is employed to designate a "Guardian," and at the Holy Book's 86:4, we see the noun *Hafizun*, which means "Protector."

The Semitic root HFZ is employed thirteen times as an active participle *hafiz*, three times as the noun *haf'z*, seven times as the Arabic verb *hafiza*, four times as the verb *yuhafiza*, and twice as the passive participle *Mahfuz*. Among the other Qur'anic passages where the root is used are 5:89, 6:92, 12:65, 13:11, 15:17, 23:9, 24:30 and at 34:70.

In addition to the terms *Kiraman Katibin* and *Hafaza*, a third name in Arabic that is sometimes used for a set of angels who guard or protect people is an angel called *Moakibat*. In pre-Islamic folklore, the name *Moakibat* was employed to designate a set of angels who protect or accompany human beings, as well as recording both their good and bad deeds. This brings us to a more detailed discussion on the etymologies of the terms mentioned above, the topic of the next section.

Etymology and Origins of the Hafaza and Kiraman Katibin

The Arabic word *Kiraman* comes from the Semitic root KRM, or *kaf-ra-mim* in Arabic. In classical Arabic, it connotes words related to "nobility," "honor," "generosity," and "comfort." The phrase *Dhul-Jalai wa Ikram*, for example, means "A Lord of Majesty Who is Generous." The KRM root is used forty-seven times in Al-Qur'an in eight different derived forms. The word *Akrimi*, to cite another example, which appears at the Holy Book's 12:21, means "to make comfortable." The Arabic word *Karimun* is used several times at Surah 8:4. It means someone who is "Noble." At the Qur'an's 25:72, we find the word *Kiraman*, which signifies "dignified beings."

The Semitic and Arabic root KTB, or Qaf-ta-ba in Arabic, is employed 319 times in the Muslim Holy Book, 260 of those is the noun *Kitab*, or "Book." The root is related to words related to writing, books and decrees. *Kataba* means, "He wrote." *Kateb* is "the one who writes." And *Kitibat* is the classical Arabic word for "writing." When the KTB root is not used to express books and writing, it is also employed to speak of *Katabna*, "we have decreed," or *Kataba*, "He was decreed," or even *Kutiba*, the verb, "is recorded," referring to Decrees of Allah.

From all of this, we conclude that the Arabic expression *Kiraman Katibin* means something like "illustrious recorder or writer." It specifically refers to the angels who are assigned the task of writing down the deeds of human beings, both good and bad. It is likely that this idea originally came from the idea of guardian spirits in Babylonia, as well as the *daena* and *fravarti*, or *fravashi* of the ancient Persians. In both of these traditions, we see the idea of guarding or guiding spirits who assist human beings in their moral lives. A similar role is employed by the *Kiraman Katibin* in Islam, as we shall see in the course of this sixth chapter.

Our principal task in this chapter, then, is to describe and to discuss the roles of the two classes of *Mala'ika* known as the *Kiraman Katibin*, or recording angels, and the *Hafazin*, or "Protecting angels." We will attempt to show how these words are used in Al-Qur'an, in traditional Hadith literature, as well as in subsequent Islamic scholarship and history. This brings us to the question of the origins of these two varieties of angels, the topic of the next section of Chapter Six.

Sources for Recording and Protective Angels in Islam

The major sources for the ideas of protective and recording angels in Islam are the Old and New Testaments. The Old Testament's Ezekiel 9:3–4 and Malachai 3:16 are good places to begin. The former passage speaks of the angel Gabriel as the recording angel of Judaism, where he is "like a man clothed in linen who has his writing case by his side."[408] In the verse from Malachai, there is a description in Heaven of there being "angels in conference," and the Lord took note and listened, and a "book of remembrances was written before Him of those who revered the Lord and thought well of His name."[409]

This idea of a "Book of Remembrance" in the Old Testament, on which are written the deeds of human beings, appears in a variety of places in the Hebrew Bible. Psalm 56:8 speaks of "God recording every action in His book."[410] The Psalmist asks at 69:28, "Let them be blotted out in the book,"[411] And Exodus 32:32 refers to a "book which He has written."[412]

The Old Testament also speaks of guardian angels and protective angels, protecting individuals, as well as entire nations. At the Book of

Daniel 10:10–21, for example, God tells Daniel that his "words have been heard," an indication that the Almighty knows all that Daniel did.[413] Other passages in the Old Testament that may be sources for the idea of recording angels in Islam are the Book of Job 37:7 and the Prophet Ezekiel 9:4. The verse from Job tells us, "He seals up the hand of every man that all men will know his work."[414] The verse from Ezekiel refers to angels passing through the city of Jerusalem and putting an X on the foreheads of those who practice abomination.[415]

There is also a series of passages in the Babylonian Talmud that speak of a ledger of the deeds of human beings. These come at Abot. III, 20; Ta'an 11a; Ber. 6a; Meg. 16a; and Shabb. 55a. In the reference from Abot III, 20, Rabbi Akiba tells us:

> Many buy in open shop where the dealer gives credit;
> the ledger is open, and the hand writes.[416]

Rabbi Shila tells us at Ta'an 11a, "Two attending angels follow men as witnesses, and when a man dies, all his deeds are enumerated with places and dates of events, and the man himself even endorses the record."[417] In a separate place, writing in relationship to Malachai 3:16, Rabbi Shila also tells us, "Whenever two people on Earth discuss the Law [*Torah*], their words are recorded above."[418] Finally, in the *Secrets of Enoch*, an apocryphal work, also known as Second Enoch, a recording angel is known as Pravuil, "whose knowledge was quicker in wisdom than the other archangel, who wrote down all of the deeds of man for the Lord."[419]

An entry in the royal annals that record the acts of merit or Mordecai in saving the life of Ahasuerus tells us that something "has been erased by the Royal secretary, a man named Shimshai. Later, it was said to have been restored by the angel Gabriel, the champion of Israel. This incident is said to have brought the fall of Haman in Chapter Seven of the Book of Esther.[420]

Of these ancient Jewish sources, the comments from Rabbi Shila and the other materials from the Talmud, as well as Malachai 3:16's mention of a "Book of Remembrances." These Jewish sources are strikingly reminiscent when placed alongside the Muslim Holy Book's Surah 18:49, that tells us:

> The Ledger of their Deeds would be placed before them. Then you will see the sinners terrified at its contents, and say, "Alas, what a written revelation this is; nothing has been left unaccounted, not even the smallest or the greatest thing. They will find in it whatever they have done. Your Lord does not wrong anyone."[421]

Kaufmann Kohler, in an article entitled, "The recording angels," for the *Jewish Encyclopedia* (vol. 10, pp. 343–344) also examines these ancient Jewish sources for both the protective and the recording angels. In regard to the former, he quotes Psalm 91:11.

Regarding the latter, Kohler cites the Book of Isaiah 63:9, which speaks of an "Angel of Presence" that also may be a recording angel.

At any rate, in addition to these possible Old Testament sources, there are also some materials in the New Testament that may be sources for the Muslim *Kiraman Katibin*. Among these in the Gospel of Matthew's 18:10, that speaks of a guardian angel who will speak the words of God when Jesus' followers are captured and turned over to the authorities.[422] This text, as well as Saint Luke's account of the angel Gabriel appearing to Mary, as well as the angels at the empty tomb, are also possible New Testament sources for the Islamic recording angels.[423]

Although the idea of recording angels can be found in both the Old and New Testaments, one scholar, M. A. Palacios, in his book, *Islam and the Divine Comedy*, believes that the influence goes the other way. That is, that Islam influenced the Christian tradition. Dr. Palacios points out:

> It is noteworthy that the features of the two Books of Record do not appear in the legendary lore of the West until the time of Bede, or the eighth century of our era.[424]

Whether or not Palacios is correct about which way the influence goes, we now shall discuss the places in the Holy Book, Al-Qur'an, where the *Hafaza* and the *Kiraman Katibin* appear, the topic of the next section of this sixth chapter on the Islamic views on angels.

The Hafaza and Kiraman Katibin in Al-Qur'an

As we have mentioned above, the Arabic word for the protective of guardian angels in Islam is the *Hafazin*. They are a class of angels whereby they are appointed to human beings to protect and defend them. The Kiraman Katibin, on the other hand, is a category of *Mala'ika* whose job is to report the good and bad deeds of human beings. There is a pair of angels that perform this function during the day, and another pair that do it at night. Like the protective angels, the recording angels also are said to protect people from assaults and to keep them free from accident and injury.

The Kiraman Katibin appear in the Muslim Holy Book in six principal Surahs. These come at Surah 6:61, 13:11, 18:49, 43:80, 50:17–18 and 82:10–12. The first of these is used as an epigram for this sixth chapter. It suggests that Allah has appointed guardians to watch over human beings until, eventually, an angel messenger will come to drag away the souls of believers and nonbelievers alike. The second passage listed above, the one at Surah 13:11, looks something like this in English translation:

> His angels keep watch over him in succession night and day, in front and behind, by Allah's command. Verily, Allah does not change the state of people until they change it themselves. When Allah intends a misfortune for a people, no one can avert it, and no savior will they have apart from Him.[425]

This passage suggests that there are two sets of guardian or protective angels, one pair that works at night and the other during the day. It also tells us that there are angels in front, and behind, human beings, in their struggles to the Afterlife. Finally, and most importantly, this ayat in Surah 13 points out that ultimately it is human beings who are responsible for their final destination, not Allah.

The third passage in the list above, the one from the Holy Book's surah 18:49, already has been quoted in the above analysis. The fourth passage that mentions the guardian/protective angels, the one at the Qur'an's 43:80, asks the question of whether nonbelievers think that Allah does not know their every move. This ayat reveals:

Do they think that we do not hear their secrets and their sneaky consultations? In fact, Our Messengers who attend them record everything they do.[426]

The two most lengthy accounts of the guardian/recording angels in the Muslim Holy Book come at Surah 50:17–18 and at Surah 80:10–12. The former provides a little more information about the *Kiraman Katibin*. It relates:

When the two angels who keep the account, one sitting on the right and the other on the left, take it down, there is not a word that he utters that an observer is ready to make note of it.[427]

This passage in Surah fifty is similar to the one in Surah eighty, ayats ten to fourteen. In these ayats we are told:

Surely, there are Guardians over you, illustrious Scribes who know what you do. The pious will surely be in Heaven [*Jannah*], and the wicked surely will reside in Hell [*Jahannam*.][428]

This Surah goes on to say that on the Day of Judgment, each person will be given a book, a complete account of all of his or her deeds, while the person is alive until he experiences Death (*Mawt*). From all of this, we may make the following conclusions. First, every human being is assigned both *Hafazin* and *Karsmin Kitibin*, or protective and recording angels (*Mala'ika*). These angels protect humans and record their every deed. Secondly, some of these angels perform these tasks at night and others during the day. Thirdly, it ultimately is the human beings themselves that determine their fate, not Allah. And finally, one of the recording angels, the one who writes down good deeds, sits on the right shoulder of the person. While the other, who writes down the human's bad deeds, sits on the left shoulder, or, alternatively, one is in the front and the other behind the human.

Two other passages from the Holy Book's Surah 83, also speak of the recording angels. These come at verses 8–12 and 19–20. The former asks:

How will you comprehend what *Sijjin* is? It is a repository of a distinctly written record. Ah, the woe that day for those who deny and call the Day of Judgment a lie! None deny it but the sinful transgressors.[429]

A few ayats later, at 19 and 20, a similar question is asked:

But how will you comprehend what *Illiyum* is? It is a repository of a distinctly written record. Written by those who are honored, verily, only the pious will find themselves in Heaven [*Jannah*].[430]

The word *Sijjin* has two meanings in the Qur'an. The first is that it is a synonym for the registry of a person's good and bad deeds. The other Arabic meaning of the word is a "deep pit." The word *Sijjin* is sometimes employed to speak of the deepest parts of *Jahannam*, or Hell.

The Arabic word *Illiyun*, on the other hand, designates the "Seventh Heaven" in Islam. The word is a cognate of the ancient Hebrew, *El Elyon*, or "God the Most High," in the Hebrew Bible.

These Qur'anic verses, 83:8–9 and 19–20, are clearly a matched set. The first pair asks about those entering Hell after death, and the second pair, those entering Paradise. The following chapter, or Surah 84 of Al-Qur'an, verses 7–10, there is another reference to the recording angels. This text tells us:

The faithful will return to his people full of joy; but he who is given his ledger from behind his back will pray for death but will then be roasted in the fire [*Nar*].[431]

Two other ayats from Surah 36, also refer to the job of the *Kiraman Katibin*. The first of these comes at the Holy Book's 36:12, which tells us, "It is We indeed who bring back the dead to life, and write down what they send ahead of their deeds and traces that they leave behind. We keep an account of all things that happen in a lucid registry.[432] This points out what is, at times, a confusion concerning who records a person's deeds. Some passages suggest the recording angels, while others seem to imply it is Allah Himself.

This same ambiguity can also be seen in the Biblical materials. In some Muslim traditions, the *Kiraman Katibin* are given the names *Raqib* and *Atid*. In this view, the former sits on the person's right shoulder recording good deeds, while the latter rests on the human's left shoulder. *Atid* is said to record the evil deeds and blasphemies of the humans to whom he is assigned. Both *Raqib* and *Atid* are said to report words, actions, as well as moral deeds.

This brings us to the places in traditional Hadith literature, where the protective and the recording angels can be found—the topic of the Next Section of this Sixth chapter.

Protective and Recording Angels in Hadith Literature

In addition to the mention of the *Kiraman Katibin* in Al-Qur'an, there are also a number of discussions of guarding and recording angels in the principal collectors of Hadith in the Muslim faith. Among these are entries by Abu Dawood, Sahih Bukhari and Ibn Kathir. The latter is employed as an epigram for this chapter. It suggests that the only time that guardian angels leave the humans they protect is when they have intercourse or go to the bathroom.

A Hadith from Sahih Bukhari, ninth-century Sunni collector of Hadith literature, tells us this about the guardian angels:

> One of these angels is positioned at the front, while the other is at the rear. They change their duties morning and evening. There are two others, one at the right and the other at the left. These two write down the deeds. The one on the right records good deeds, while the other records evil deeds. Thus, every person has four angels with him at all times, four during the day and four at night.[433]

In Abu Bukhari's view, then, each human is accompanied by four angels, both night and day, one behind, one in front, one on the right to record good deeds, and the other on the left to write down sins and evil acts. A Hadith from Abu Dawood speaks of the roles of protection these angels also seem to have. The ninth-century Afghani collector of

Hadith says, "These angels guard people from falling into potholes, from slipping on the tops of walls, and to escape from falling objects. Life would be impossible if Allah removed these angels."[434]

Another Hadith from Abu Dawood also speaks of the recording angels. He relates:

> Recording angels stay with a person all the time and never leave him, whether the person is a Muslim or a nonbeliever, ritually pure or impure. However, the angels do leave the person in a state of ritual impurity. These are called the "Angels of Mercy."[435]

In another tradition from Abu Dawood, he relates this about ritual impurity:

> There are three types of people that angels do not approach among whom are those in a state of ritual impurity, unless he performs ablution.[436]

Shams Al-Haq Al-Abadi agrees that these angels are called Angels of Mercy. He says of them:

> These angels are those who descend with mercy and blessings on the children of Adam. They are the recording angels because they never leave a person.[437]

Another Hadith from Persian Ibn Kathir tells us much of what already we have seen about the recording angels. He observes:

> By the command of Allah. Allah states that there are angels who take turns guarding each servant, some by night and some by day. These angels protect each person from harm and accidents. There are also angels who take turns recording good and bad deeds. Some do this by day and others by night.
>
> There are two angels, one on the right and the other on the left of each person, recording the deeds. The angel to the right records good deeds, while the angel to the left records evil deeds. There are also two angels

that guard and protect each person, one in the back and one in the front.

Therefore, there are four angels that surround each person by day, and they are replaced by four others at night, two Scribes and two Guards.[438]

Al-Abadi agrees with the major conclusions we have seen so far about the Recording and Protective, or guardian angels. One pair of *mala'kayn* record the good and bad deeds of humans; one sits on the right shoulder, the other on the left shoulder of the person. Another *mala'kayn* protect, or guard, the person, one in front of the particular human, and the other is behind the person.

Another Hadith from Abu Hurayra also confirms much of what we have concluded about what Abu Bukhari and Ibn Kathir have said earlier in this sixth chapter. He tells us, "From him (each person) there are angels in succession, before and behind him."[439] The remainder of this Hadith repeats verbatim the entry from Ibn Kathir discussed above. Thus, the principal collectors of Hadith, Ibn Kathir, Abu Bukhari, Sahih Dawood, and Abu Hurayra, all seem to agree that each human being is accompanied by four angels.

Two other Ahadith that mention the recording angels come from Wahb Ibn Al-Ward, eighth-century exegete, and seventh-century traditionalist, Shahri Ibn Hanshab. Al-Ward tells us, "To everyone at his death there appear two angels who during his life were the guardians of his deeds."[440] Ibn Hanshab, on the other hand, believes the number is four:

Two white angels seat themselves on the right of the sickbed, and two black angels on the left. And they dispute over the soul. An examination of the dying man's tongue, which shows traces of having uttered certain prayers, finally settles the dispute in his favor.[441]

Two other Ahadith on the recording angels come from the prophet's wife Aisha and another tradition recorded by both Sahih Bukhari and At-Tirmidhi. The first of these observes:

> Malik related to me that he heard that Aisha, the wife
> of the Prophet, sent a message to one of her family
> after the evening prayer, saying, "Will you not allow the
> recording angels to rest?"[442]

The other Hadith is narrated by Abu Huraya, who said that Allah says:

> Whenever my slaves intend to do a bad deed, I say
> to the angel reporting these deeds, "Do not record
> it against him until he actually commits the act. If he
> has done so, write it down exactly as one in his record
> book. But if he refrains from it for My sake, write it
> down as a virtue on his part. And when he intends to
> do a good deed but does not actually do it, write it
> down as a virtue for him. And if he puts it into practice,
> write its rewards equal to, from ten to seven hundred
> times in his accident."[443]

We will speak more about this Hadith, and others like it, on the relative value of good versus bad deeds in a later section of this sixth chapter. It is enough now, however, to point out that Islam puts far more emphasis on the value of good deeds that come along with good intentions (*maqasid* in Arabic) than the relative value of evil acts or deeds with bad intentions.

The recording and protective (guardian) angels are also discussed among a number of more minor collectors of traditions. One example from Ishaq Al-Man'ani, while referring to the Holy Book's 13:11, relates, "The allusion here is to the guardian angels attached to every soul, guarding him or her from harm, unless Allah wishes otherwise.[444] Another Hadith from seventh-century collector Habib Ibn Zayd Al-Ansari, a member of the Sahaba (Companions) of Allah and a *Shahid*, or Martyr of the Faith, relates:

> Angels take turns around you, some at night and some
> during the day. All of them assemble during the time of
> the *Fajr* and *Asar*. Then those who have stayed with
> you throughout, ascend to Allah Who asks them, "How

have you left My servants?" They reply, "As we have
found them praying, we left them praying."[445]

Another Hadith from Abu Hurayra also speaks of the guardian
and the recording angels.

He relates:

We are assigned several angels in our life; they have
two shifts. Some watch over us in the day, and some in
the night. There are two times when all the angels of
the day and night assigned to each of us, meet. The first
time is between *Fajr* and *Ishraaq,* and the second time
is between *Asar* and *Maghrib.*[446]

The Arabic terms *Fajr, Ishaaq, Asar and Maghrib* refer to four
times of the ritual requirement of *Salat.* The *Fajr* is the first of the
prayers. The word means "Dawn" in Arabic. The time for *Ishaaq,* the
second prayer of *Salat,* begins when the sun appears on the horizon
until the sun is at its meridian.

Contemporary scholar Ruqaiyyah Waris Maqsood describes the
time for *Asar* and Maqhrib:

Like many in a hot climate of the Middle East, the
Prophet made up for a lack of sleep by taking a siesta
during the heat of the day, after the mid-day prayer, the
Zuhr. Late afternoon was the time when the heat drops
again and a major time for prayer—with the *Asar* as
the light begins to change, and then the *Maghrib* after
sunset. The last formal prayer was during the hours of
darkness, the *Isha.*[447]

Thus, the five daily prayers in Islam are known as *Fajr,* between
dawn and sunrise; *Zuhr,* at the height of the noonday sun; *Asar,*
during the afternoon when shadows have lengthened; *Maghrib,* just
after sunset; and *Isha,* during the hours of darkness. An entry from the
Hadith Qudsi tells us another tale about the guardian angels:

A certain person had committed 99 murders. He went
to a scholar and asked him, "Is there any chance that

I might be forgiven?" The scholar told him no, he had committed too many sins, so the man killed the scholar. But the man's heart was restless, so he went to another scholar and asked the same question. This time he was told yes, but he must leave this town of bad people and go to live in the next town that is filled with good people.

So the man set out for the next town and on the way, he died. A man passing by saw two angels who were arguing over the dead body. The angel from Hell said, "His body belongs to me since he had no good in his life." Then the angel from Heaven said, "His body belongs to me because he had repented and had set out to be with good people."

Now the man who was the passer-by said, "Let us measure the distance of his body from the town he left and from the town he was going to." After this was done, they found that he was nearer to the town he was going.[448]

In other Muslim versions of the same tale, the Earth is ordered by Allah to shrink, so that the distance was shorter so that the man could be admitted to Paradise. We introduce this narrative in this sixth chapter because these *Mala'kayn*, one from Heaven (*Jannah*), and one from *Jahannam*, or Hell, are thought to be the recording angels who write down every deed, both good and bad, performed by every human being. This brings us to a discussion of the relative intrinsic value of good deeds versus bad deeds in the Islamic faith.

Relative Value of Good Versus Evil Deeds in Islam

A number of Islamic traditions disagree about the relative value of good and evil deeds. Some scholars suggest that every good deed is worth at least four evil deeds. Others say the rate of good deeds is more like ten to one. All Muslim thinkers who comment on this question agree that the ratio is clearly in favor of the value of good deeds over bad deeds.

The value of good deeds is mentioned in several places in the Muslim Holy Book, including Surah 42:26 that tells us:

> He answers prayers for those who believe and who do the good, and He gives them more of His bounty; but for the nonbelievers, there is to be very, severe punishment.[449]

Al-Qur'an tells us that Allah's bounties are not closed to anyone. Surah seven, ayats twenty and twenty-one relates:

> We bestow the gifts of Our Lord on these and on these, for the gifts of the Lord have no restrictions. See how we favor one over the other, and, in the life to come there are higher ranks and favors even greater still.[450]

Surah 39:14 tells us that one must "worship Allah with the greatest devotion, all-exclusive of Him."[451] The Holy Book's 40:14–15 agrees. These verses tell us:

> So call on Allah with exclusive devotion and obedience, however the disbelievers may dislike it. Most exulted of positions, Lord of power, He directs inspiration by His command to any of His creatures as He wills, to warn men of the Day of the Meeting.[452]

Although Islam, for the most part, is quite clear about the intrinsic values of good versus bad deeds, a number of principal Hadith discuss how these deeds are to be recorded, as well as how good and bad deeds are related to good and bad intentions. Abu Hurayra, for example, relates:

> Allah ordered the appointed angels over you that the good and bad deeds are written down. He then showed the way how to write. If someone intends to do a good deed, and he does not do it, then Allah will write for him a full good deed.
>
> If someone intends to do a good deed and then actually does it, then Allah will write for him in his account

its reward equal from ten to seven hundred times. If someone intends to do a bad deed and he does not do it, then Allah will write a full deed in his account. And if he intended to do a bad deed and actually did it, then Allah will write one bad deed in his account.[453]

Thus, Abu Hurayra speaks of the relative value of a good deed over an evil deed. He says the former is worth ten to seven hundred times more valuable than the latter. Abu Hurayra also seems in this Hadith to speak of the value of having good intentions when it comes to doing morally good deeds. Like Immanuel Kant, as well as other traditional thinkers in Western ethical theory, Islam takes the value of moral intentions very seriously when it comes to moral discourse. In Islam, moral intentions, or *Maqasid* in Arabic, are as important for moral discourse as is Kant's idea of the "Holy Will." In his *Groundwork for the Metaphysics of Morals* he says:

> In addition to Islamic traditions speaking of the relative value of good and bad deeds, at times, some thinkers also speak about the possibility of good deeds wiping out, or canceling out, evil deeds."[454]

This phenomenon can be seen, for example, at Surah 11:114 of the Muslim Holy Book. The text tells us:

> Stand up for the service of prayer at the two ends of the day, and the first watch of the night. Remember that good deeds nullify the bad. This is a reminder for those who are observant.[455]

Both Imams Bukhari and Abu Muslim also report another Hadith about the issue at hand. They observe:

> Tell me, if there were a stream at your door in which you take a bath five times a day, will any filth remain on the body? They replied, "No dirt would remain." Similar is the case of the five compulsory prayers. Allah obliterates all sins as a result of the offering of these prayers.[456]

Several other Ahadith make the same point. In each of these, there is an emphasis that good deeds cancel out, or replace, evil deeds. Another Hadith from Abu Tharr, for example, instructs us to "Follow a bad deed with a good deed that will wipe out the bad one." In another narration, Abu Tharr asks the Prophet Muhammad, "Give me some advice." Then the prophet said, "If you do a bad deed, then follow it with a good deed that will wipe it out."[457]

Other Ahadith specify that certain good deeds that are of a character to cancel out the bad deeds. Among these "cancel out" actions are repentance, praying *Salat*, and the seeking of forgiveness; as well as perseverance through hardship and crisis; supplication at the end of every meeting; performing the *Wudu* (ablution) perfectly; performing the five daily prayers well with humility; attending Friday prayer services without speaking; fasting during the month of Ramadan; as well as fasting during other Muslim holidays, like the Feasts of Arafah and Ashura, for example.

The Arabic word *Wudu* is a term for ritual purity with water. Sometimes it is pronounced *Wuzu*. It refers to the cleansing of certain parts of the body in running water. This process is described at Surah 5:6 of Al-Qur'an. The Holy Text informs us:

> Oh you who believe. When you rise up for prayer, wash your face and your hands up to the elbows; and wipe your head and wash your feet to your ankles; and if you are under an obligation to perform a bath [that is ritually clean after sex, menstruation, or childbirth] then go through a complete wash; and if you are sick or on a journey. Or, if you have come from the bathroom or have been intimate with another, and you cannot find water, then take clean dirt from the Earth and wipe your face and hands with it. Allah does not wish to put you into difficulties, but he wishes to purify you that He might complete His favors upon you.[458]

Abu Dawood also speaks about canceling out bad deeds. He says, "If a person does a bad deed, and then he makes a good *Wudu*, and prays twice, and then seeks the forgiveness of Allah, then Allah will forgive him."[459] Imam At-Tirmidhi reports that "Whoever sits in a gathering which indulges in useless talk before getting up and supplicating and then saying, 'There is no God but Allah and Muhammad is His Prophet,' he will be forgiven immediately."[460]

Abu Muslim reported that the Prophet Muhammad said, "If anyone performs the ablution perfectly, then, according to Sunnah, his sins will come out of his body, even from under his nails."[461]

In another tradition from Sahih Muslim, he comments on performing the five daily prayers. He tells us:

> When the time for a prescribed *As-Salat* approaches and a Muslim observes its ablution and acts of bowing and prostrating are done properly, this *Salat* will be an expiation for his past sins, as long as he does not commit major sins, and this is for always.[462]

A Hadith from Abu Bukhari tells us that, "He who observes fasting during the month of Ramadan, out of sincerity of his faith and in the hope of earning a reward will have his past sins pardoned."[463] Sahih Bukhari adds, "Whoever adds optional prayers during the month of Ramadan will be given a great blessing."[464] Imam Muslim reports that "He who fasts during the Day of Ashura will receive an expiation for his sins of the preceding year."[465] And both Abu Bukhari and Imam Muslim tells us about performing the *Hajj*, or the Pilgrimage to Mecca:

> Whoever performs the *Hajj* and does not have sexual relations with his wife, nor commit sins, nor disputes unjustly (during Hajj), then, when he returns from the Hajj, he is as pure and as free as he was the day his mother gave birth to him.[466]

Other acts that some Ahadith suggest absolve or cancel out bad deeds are the giving of charity and the remembering of the many names of Allah. At-Tirmidhi observes that "Charity puts out bad deeds the way that water puts out a fire."[467] Both Abu Bukhari and Sahih Muslim report that:

> He who utters, "There is no God but Allah and Muhammad is His Prophet," one hundred times a day,

his sins will be obliterated even if they are equal to the extent of the ocean.[468]

Both Abu Bukhari and Sahih Muslim give a report that "The performance of *Umrah* is an expiation for the sins between this and their previous *Umrah*; and the reward for this, as well as the Hajj, is nothing but *Al-Firdaws*, or "Paradise."[469] The Arabic word *Umrah* means "to visit a populated place." It is a technical term to perform the *Tawaf*, or circumambulation around the Kaa'ba. The Hajj is considered the Larger Pilgrimage, while the Umrah is sometimes called the Smaller Pilgrimage. In some schools of Islamic thought, however, the performance of *Umrah* is not obligatory, but it is highly recommended. Other moral acts that cancel out bad deeds in Islam include, as Sahih Muslim says, "anyone who repents before the Sun rises from the West, will be forgiven by Allah."[470]

Both Bukhari and Sahih Muslim report that a believer "is never stricken with discomfort, illness, anxiety, a grief, or mental worry, or even the prickling from a thorn, then that believer's sins are to be expiated for him."[471] Sheikh Sayyed Ibn Al-Sabiq speaks of the prophet's view of fasting during the Day of Arafah. Al-Sabiq writes:

> It is confirmed that the Prophet did not fast on the Day of Arafah. The Prophet said, "Verily, the Day of Arafah, the Day of Sacrifice, and the days of *Tashriq* are our days of festivals. These are the days for eating and drinking.[472]

Abu Hurayra also reports that "Muhammad forbade fasting on the Day of Arafah for anyone who is actually at Arafah."[473]

This had led some Muslim scholars to conclude that if Muhammad forbade fasting during the Day of Arafah, this gave believers a more focused devotion for worshipping and supplication on that day.

Sahih Muslim and Abu Bukhari, in separate Hadiths, make the same claim about praying during the Night of Al-Qadr:

> Whoever offers *Qiyam* during the Night of Al-Qadr with faith, while being hopeful of Allah's rewards, will have his former sins forgiven.[474]

The Night of Qadar, or Night of Power, is a night in the month of Ramadan when the angel Jibril first brought down Al-Qur'an to Muhammad. It is believed this same night occurred during Ramadan, so as to become a month of fasting. A Hadith from Ibn Hibban speaks of the connections among these particular revelations:

> The Torah was revealed on the sixth night of Ramadan; the Gospels on the thirteenth night, the Zabur on the eighteenth night, and Al-Qur'an on the twenty-fourth night of Ramadan.[475]

The *Zabur* is a collection of ancient hymns and spiritual songs. Islam believes this is a book that was worshipped by King Sulayman, or Solomon, in his temple in Jerusalem. It is sometimes referred to as Dawud's *Zabur*, or "David's Psalms." The *Zabur* is mentioned three times in Al-Qur'an. There are also a number of Ahadith from Abu Bukhari and Abu Hurayra that tells us this:

> The reciting of Al-Zabur was made easy for Dawud. He used to order his riding animals to be saddled and would finish reciting the Zabur before they were saddled, and he would never eat except from the earnings of his manual labor.[476]

The Day of Ashura comes on the tenth day of Muharram. It marks the celebration of the Remembrance of Muharram, a day of mourning that symbolizes for Shiites the martyrdom of Husayn Ibn Ali, the grandson of Muhammad. Ali died at the Battle of Karbala on the tenth of Muharram in 680 CE. Sunni Muslims believe that Musa, or Moses, fasted on this day to express his gratitude to God for bringing the Jews out of Egypt. Some Sunni scholars argue that from this day on, Musa asked his followers to fast that day. In some Muslim lands, Ashura is celebrated as a national holiday. This is true in Pakistan, Lebanon, Iran and Iraq, among other places.

Finally, Sahih Muslim wrote a series of aphorisms about good deeds canceling out or negating bad deeds. Among these are numbers 813, 614, 615, 620, 621 and 622. The first of these tells us, "One who is happy by doing a good deed and sad by a bad deed, is a true believer."[477] In Aphorism number 614, Abu Muslim again relates:

He does not belong to us who does not call himself to account, that is, if he has done a good deed and he should be praised for it, and then he wishes further good deeds. And if he has done something wrong, he then should ask for the greatest forgiveness.[478]

The Islamic faith in Al-Qur'an in Hadith literature, as well as in later developments in Islam, has taken great pains to show that the value of certain good, moral deeds is infinitely more important than the value of morally bad actions. In fact, as we have seen, there are some Muslim scholars who say that a morally good deed is worth ten to seven hundred times more than an evil action. We also have shown in this section of Chapter Six, that certain kinds of moral actions like fasting, ablution and prayer, may cancel out, or negate the damage of evil moral actions.

Guardian Angels and Bringing Good Deeds to Heaven

One final tradition concerning the guardian and recording angels in Islam pertains to go through a process by which these *mala'ika* are said to bring the good deeds of humanity to the awareness of Allah and to His Heavenly Court. One tradition from Sahih Muslim begins this way:

> The guardian angels record man's deeds, day and night, and send them up while it is as bright as the Sun. When they reach the sky of the world, they purify the deeds and add to it, but then all of a sudden the angel will say, "Wait! Throw the deed in the face of the doer, for with this deed, he was following mean objectives in the world. I am the angel of Worldly Affairs and will not let the deeds of this person pass on to the others from here."[479]

Sahih Muslim continues his analysis:

> Then the next day, while carrying good deeds, the angels return and pass by the former angel, purify the deed and add to it until it reaches the Second Heaven, where an angel will say, "Stop here. Throw the deed in the face of the doer, for with this deed, he was following

mean objectives in the world. I am the angel of Worldly Affairs and will not let the deed of this person pass on to others from here."[480]

Then the angel said, "The next stage angels, take up the deed of Allah's servants from whose charity and prayer they are happy. But when they reach the Third Heaven, the angel will say, "Throw this deed in the face of the doer. I am an angel recording arrogance. This person has good deeds, but he was very arrogant to people. My Lord has ordered to let this man's deed pass from here.[481]

Then he said, "The guardian angels took up the deed of God's servant while it was still shining like a star," and his voice was up like the glorification of Allah, fast and Hajj pilgrimage. They were taken it up to the Fourth Heaven when an angel said, "Stop here. Throw it before the face and the belly of the doer. I am the angel that records self-admiration. He was self-conceited. He had good deeds, but he was self-complacent. My Lord has ordered to let his deeds pass on to the others from here."[482]

Then is followed by Imam Muslim taking the man's deeds to the Fifth Heaven, followed by the Sixth Heaven, but again, the man's deeds were rejected at both the Fifth and the Sixth Heavens. Then, Abu Muslim completes the tale:

At this point, the man began weeping, and then he said, "What can I do to show devotion in my deed?" Then Muhammad, who was telling the story, said, "Follow your prophets in being certain about the unity of Allah."[483]

In this narrative, we get some sense of the relative, moral weight of certain deeds in the Islamic faith. It is clear that the emphasis in Islam is to be placed on alms, fasting, prayer and the making of the

Hajj. In some Islamic traditions, as we have shown, these moral acts are valued somewhere between ten and seven hundred times higher than evil acts. Ultimately, these acts, alms, fasting, etc., are those in Sahih Muslim's tale that reach all the way to the Seventh Heaven, while evil acts are canceled out or left to dissipate into oblivion.

This central belief that good deeds may cancel out or annul any evil or blasphemous actions or words a person may have done or said is an indication of how valuable believing Muslims think that morally good versus morally evil actions are intrinsically worth, the former being infinitely more valuable than the latter, as we have shown throughout this section of this sixth chapter.

The idea of the Oneness of Allah, or *Tawhid* in Arabic, is a category that has been in the Islamic faith since the seventh century. *Tawhid* is the indivisible Oneness of the concept of the Monotheism. The Arabic word *Tahwid*, also spelled tawheed, touched, or even *Tawvid*, is an infinitive noun that means "God asserts or declares that He is One." At the Holy Book's Surah seven, ayat 180, we learn that Allah has many "glorious names." Islamic tradition says the number is ninety-nine. Among those names are *Al*-Ahad, or "God is One," and *Al-Wahid*, that "God is Simple."

The Unity and the Oneness of Allah, or *Tawhid*, then, is the central and most important concept of the Islamic faith. It was devised, apparently, to counteract the polytheism of other traditions in the Arabian Peninsula, as well as the concept of the Trinity in the Christian Church. This brings us to the major conclusions we made in this sixth chapter. In the seventh chapter, we shall explore the roles that the *mala'ika* have played in Islamic art from its beginning to the twentieth century. As we shall see, this material is rich and diverse.

Conclusions to Chapter Six

Our chief aim of this sixth chapter has been to describe and discuss the roles of the guardian and recording angels in the Islamic faith. We began this chapter by suggesting that two passages from the Hebrew Bible, Ezekiel 9:3–4 and the Book of Malachai 3:16, were most likely the original sources of these two types of angels in Islam. In the second section of this chapter, we enumerated and then discussed at some length the places in Al-Qur'an where the guardian and the recording angels appear in the Muslim Holy Book. These passages come, for the most part, from Surahs six, thirteen, forty-three, fifty, and eighty-two.

In the third section of this chapter, we described and discussed those places in Hadith literature, where discussions of guardian and recording angels may be found. As we have seen, many of the traditional collectors of Hadith, Al-Bukhari, Abu Hurayra, Sahih Muslim, Abu Dawood Al-Ansari, Al-Abadi, and Ibn Kathir, among others, all have made some general and specific comments about the roles of guardian and recording angels in the Muslim faith.

For the most part, as we have seen, these aHadith point to the central roles of these angels, particularly in relation to salvation and the end times, that we saw in the Muslim Holy Book, Al-Qur'an. In the next to final section of this chapter, we explored and discussed Muslim thinkers who suggest that good deeds such as fasting, alms, praying *Salat* and making the Hajj to Mecca, are far more valuable than the evil deeds that humans perform. Some scholars say that these good moral deeds are worth between ten and seven hundred times more than evil deeds. In fact, as indicated, we have shown that certain good moral deeds cancel out or annul bad acts.

In the final section of this sixth chapter, we have shown and discussed a process described by Sahih Muslim in which the deeds of believing Muslims are brought to Heaven for a perusal by Allah Himself. In this section, we saw that the same deeds that Muslims value the most are precisely the same deeds that eventually reach Allah in the Seventh, or Highest Heaven. These deeds include those related to the "Five Pillars of the Faith," as well as the "Six Articles of Faith," discussed in earlier chapters.

As we have shown, one of the roles of the guardian and recording angels in Islam is to safeguard the good acts of human beings, particularly believing Muslims, while at the same time to dissuade those believers from moral sins and evil acts. Above all, the jobs of the guardian and recording angels are to assist human beings to attain a place in Paradise, and to safeguard the moral deeds they do, so that they may be evaluated at the end of time and the coming of the Final Judgment. In the following chapter, Chapter Seven of this study, we shall explore and discuss the uses of angels in Islamic iconography. As we shall see, depictions of *mala'ika* in Muslim art have tended to be tied to several particular historical events in the history of the Muslim faith. Among these are Jibril and Muhammad on their Night Journey; Jibril bringing Al-Qur'an to the Prophet Muhammad; the Houris in Paradise; whether angels drink alcohol in Heaven; and many other Muslim scenes.

Chapter Seven:
Angels in Islamic Art

History is a mirror of the past and a lesson for the present.

—Persian Proverb

Art is the mirror of its culture and its world view.

—Elizabeth Siddiqui, "Islamic Art"

Any attempt to make sense of Islamic art and architecture as a whole while retaining a chronological framework runs the risk of distortion.

—Robert Hillenbrand, *Islamic Art and Architecture*

Introduction

In this seventh chapter, our major goal is to explore and discuss the ways that the *Mala'ika*, or the angels, have been depicted and rendered in Islamic art. In the opening section of this chapter, we shall make some very general remarks on the history of Islamic art and architecture. This section will be followed by many of the major ways in which angels have been employed in Muslim art and architecture. The analysis in the opening section of this chapter mostly comes from an appendix entitled, "Biblical Figures in Islamic Art," from *Biblical Figures in the Islamic Faith*, published by Wipf and Stock in 2008.[484]

As we shall see, the earliest years of Islam produced very little original art of its own. Instead, the Muslim Arabs who conquered parts of Asia, Europe and North Africa, in the late seventh and early eighth centuries. In fact, Islam incorporated elements from Byzantium, Coptic and Persian art, fusing them into a distinctive decorative style centered mostly on the art of calligraphy—particularly in relation to the Muslim Holy Book, Al-Qur'an.

These early traditions laid down by Muslims created devout crafts whose sole purpose was to glorify Allah. Islamic doctrine was at the heart of early Islamic art, whether it was the decorative arts, representational art or calligraphy. In the early years of Islam, sculpture was prohibited, and carvers turned their attention to exquisite in-lay and fretwork, notably on screens and doors, as well as large Islamic monuments, such as the Alhambra Palace in Granada, Spain, and the Taj Mahal in India. Today, Islamic art is found predominantly in Egypt, Iran, Iraq, Turkey and the Indian sub-continent, as well as the central republics of Asia.

In the opening section of this chapter, we give a short overview of the history of Islamic art. In the second section, we describe and discuss the earliest and most predominant form of art in Islam—calligraphy. The remainder of this chapter is taken up with the places in Muslim art, where the *Mala'ika*, or angels, have been a central subject matter. At the close of this chapter, we shall describe and discuss many of the illustrations of the Turkish *Siyer-i-Nabi*, a biography of the Prophet Muhammad that was completed in the fourteenth century. Along the way, we also explore the many places, primarily in Persia and Turkey, where the *Mala'ika* have been represented in Islamic art.

The History of Islamic Art

The Islam faith began in the early seventh century and rapidly spread throughout the Middle East and North Africa. Before the close of the eighth century, it had moved to Byzantium, Persia, Eastern Europe, and some parts of Africa and Asia. In the first thousand years of Islam, from Muhammad's first revelation in 610 to the period of the Empires, the Religion of Islam flourished. While Western Europe suffered through the Dark Ages, from 500 CE to 1000 CE, scholars in cities like Jerusalem, Damascus, Alexandria, Fez, Tunis, Cairo and Baghdad made remarkable advances in philosophy, science, medicine, literature, poetry and the visual arts.

Indeed, Islam, in its early history, was very adept at incorporating elements from other cultures into its art. Thus, paper came from China; Arabic numerals from India; and classical, philosophical, and scientific texts from the ancient Greeks, and all of these were shared in the Islamic world from very early on.

Under the Abbasid Caliphate, which followed the Umayyads (661–750), the center of political and cultural development in Islam shifted from Syria to Iraq, where, in 762, the capital was established in the city of Baghdad. The first two centuries of Abbasid rule saw the emergence and dissemination of a new style of art, including textiles, pottery, architecture and painting.

Robert Hillenbrand writes of this period as a "Gilded Age." He tells us:

> This gilded age was underpinned by a complex financial machine to which capital investments, liquidity, and long-term investments, were familiar concepts.[485]

Professor Hillenbrand goes on to argue that this guaranteed the first necessary condition for the development of fine arts—financial support. Hillenbrand observes: "Perhaps the major extinguishing feature of the early Abbasid Empire was its immense wealth."[486] Hillenbrand adds,

> "But this idyll was short-lived. Squabbles over succession pinpointed much deeper rifts."[487]

Among these squabbles were conflicts between Arabs and Persians, and between and among Shiites and Sunnis.

The art of pottery was greatly advanced in the Muslim world in the ninth and the tenth centuries, chiefly because of the influence of Chinese ceramics. The Abbasid Empire also practiced the art of "lustre painting," a process by which pottery is made to look like precious metals. The process of lustre painting was expensive, complicated and time-consuming, but these objects were regarded as luxury wares and status symbols.

For a short time, a city north of Baghdad called Samarra served as the capital of the Empire. Hillenbrand comments on the developments in Samarra:

> It was at Samarra that Islamic Art came of age; and
> from that center, it spread virtually throughout the
> entire Muslim world, also influencing local Jewish and
> Christian art.[488]

The town/city of Samarra had existed since ancient times on the Tigris River. In fact, prior to Mesopotamia, the city of Samarra, between 5500 and 4800 BCE, may have been the largest city in the world. The Samarran culture had fine pottery that was disseminated throughout the Middle East.

In 836 CE, when the Abbasid Caliph Al-Mu'tasim was pressured to leave Baghdad, he made Samarra the new capital. He built a palace and gardens there and a city that stretched for over twenty miles. In 892, the capital was transferred back to Baghdad, which caused subsequent decline in the city of Samarra. By the year 1300, most of the city was in ruins. It has since been revived.

The move of the Caliphate from Baghdad to Samarra was brought about, as indicated earlier, by Caliph Mu'tasim, who died in 866. The distance from Baghdad to Samarra was about sixty miles. At Samarra, eight Caliphs lived in a short period of fifty-six years. Mu'tasim was responsible for a number of building projects, including a great palace that he built on the site of an abandoned Christian monastery. A main avenue, with many other royal residents, ran along the banks of the Tigris. The name "Samarra" comes from the Syriac, *Surra man raa*, which means, "He who sees it rejoices."

Scholar Al-Tabari, in volume XXIII of his *History*, which he called *Storm and Stress Along the Northern Frontier of the Abbasid Caliphate*, describes in great detail the rise of the aesthetic in Samarra. Al-Tabari observes:

> The new aesthetic at Samarra is best expressed by wall
> decorations fashionable in grand palaces and houses
> alike. Polychrome painted stucco was both carved and
> molded. The Samarran palaces were grand. They were
> mostly made of mud and brick, which was cheaply
> disguised by mass-produced decorations. The urban
> palaces quickly uprooted palace cities conceived in

the Perso-Sasanian model, where massive scale is dominant. Indeed, for many centuries, the Mosque at Samarra was the largest Mosque in the world.[489]

By the beginning of the tenth century, the Abbasid Empire had begun to crumble, and Abbasid power was now limited to Iraq. Meanwhile, new styles in art began to appear in Egypt, Spain and Iran. This new empire was called the Fatimid, which lasted from the tenth to the twelfth centuries. The Fatimids carved vessels of rock crystal, a type of transparent, colorless quartz whose surface could be brilliantly polished. Hillenbrand describes the importance of the developments in Fatimid art:

> From the art historical point of view the importance of the Fatimids is due both to geography and to chronology—for the art of this period forms a bridge in time and space between east and west in the Muslim World, between the pervasive influence of the Umayyad and the Abbasid Art which was rather different entirely.[490]

In the Fatimid Period, Old Cairo, then known as *Al-Fustat*, became the center of production of pottery, glass, metalwork, rock crystal, ivory and textiles. The lusterware techniques were now used on jewelry, as well as ceramics. Wood carving also was very popular in this period.

The Fatimids created new decorative techniques, and they made greater use of figural forms, both of humans and animals. In the Fatimid Period, these figures were stylized to look as though they were alive, with traditional vegetal and geometric patterns employed in the Fatimid art.

By the eleventh century, the Seljuk Turks briefly ruled over a vast empire that stretched from Iran throughout the Middle East, and west to Turkey. By the end of the century, this vast empire had given way to different branches of the empire. The Ghaznavid—one of those branches—defeated the Byzantine army in eastern Anatolia in 1071. Another branch of the Turkish Empire established itself in Central Asia, where Islam flourished until the coming of the Mongols in the thirteenth century. The Seljuks built structures of immense proportions, as well In

Central Asia, Islamic artists made great innovations in Muslim pottery. In fact, they reinvented a technique that combined clay, quartz and potash, which was first employed by the ancient Egyptians. Meanwhile, back in Iran, the earliest and most distinctive forms of painting were being produced. There was also a new style of painting employed in Baghdad, which later was referred to as the "Baghdad School." These early styles of painting in Iraq and Iran mainly were decorations for manuscripts of the Muslim Holy Book, Al-Qur'an.

The Baghdad School was a relatively short-lived school of Islamic art from the late twelfth century until the early fourteenth century, during the Abbasid Caliphate. The style employed strong, bright colors, better sense of design and decorative quality, and linguists who cooperated with artists to produce an art form derived from mostly non-Muslim sources.[491]

The earliest of these Iranian Qur'an paintings were produced in the first half of the thirteenth century. Iranian miniatures, fine and small drawings, began to be produced after the fall of Baghdad in 1285. Since the beginning of the fourteenth century, handwritten books were adorned with battle scenes, feasts and hunting scenes. Among the illustrated books in the Baghdad School, the *Kelileh and Demneh* was one of the finest.[492] Images are painted much larger than their actual size and are not proportional. Only a bare number of colors are used in these paintings. Most of these handwritten books of the thirteenth century were enriched with images of animals, vegetation, and illustrations of fables and stories.

The Ottoman Empire inherited the art of miniature painting from the Seljuks. During the Ottomans from 1389 until 1402, he went a step further by setting up workshops in his palace.

The art of miniature painting in Turkey reached its peak in the sixteenth century. Then, by the seventeenth century, influences from European painting can be seen in the Turkish miniatures.

At the beginning of the eighteenth century, what is sometimes called the "Tulip Period," wall paintings now were used as architectural decorations instead of tiles. Fruit and vegetation often adorned the walls, as in the "Fruit Room" of Ahmet the Second's Topkapi Palace in the city of Istanbul.[493]

The "Tulip Period," 1718–1730, was a transitory era of the Ottoman Empire. It is marked by cultural innovations and new forms of elite consumption and sociability. The Tulip Period coincided with the latter half of the Ottoman rule of Sultan Ahmed III, who ruled from 1703 until 1730. This brings us to a discussion of calligraphy as a Muslim art form, the subject matter of the next section.

Calligraphy as a Muslim Art Form

In addition to the art forms mentioned above, the most venerated form of Islamic art always has been Arabic, Farsi and Turkish calligraphy. Early Muslim calligraphers concentrated on finding styles that were worthy of the words they were putting down. Most of these came from Al-Qur'an. R. W. Maqsood tells us something of these early Arabic scripts:

> The earliest scripts were the *Ma'il* or slanting, and the *Mashq*, or the extended script. The most famous of early scripts are the *Kufic*, from the Islamic Center in Kufa, and the *Naskhi*, or the inspirational script.[494]

Dr. Maqsood goes on to tell us that the first written Qur'ans had no artwork because the scribes believed it was wrong to make representations of Heavenly, or even Earthly, beings—particularly the Prophet Muhammad. They did not wish to call attention to the decorations, rather than the Sacred Text. Later, wealthy patrons, kings and sultans mostly, commissioned lavish and colorful Qur'ans, resplendent in gold, green, red and blue. A superb ninth-century Qur'an in gold script on blue vellum, for example, survives almost intact in the city of Kairouan in Tunisia.[495] The bulk of the manuscript is preserved in the National Library of Tunisia. A number of missing leaves can be found in other libraries, as well as private collections around the Middle East.[496] By the eleventh century, the twenty-eight letters of the Arabic script began to be modified and employed as ornaments and new geometric designs, adding plaiting, knotting and braiding.

During the thirteenth and fourteenth centuries, Square Kufic script was developed, and it began to be used in buildings, as well. Islamic calligraphy reached its height in the sixteenth century Turkish

Empire. By this time, texts now were accompanied with pictures, many of which were of Qur'anic origins.

From very early on, a style of calligraphy was developed in Mosques. It was there that the characteristic Arabesque Mosque calligraphy style was developed. Arabic calligraphy frequently was written on the walls and ceilings, both inside and outside these structures. The subject matter of the calligraphy was derived from the Muslim Holy Book, from Hadith literature, as well as Arabic folktales.

The most common phrase found in Mosque calligraphy was/is the *Bismillah*—"There is no God but Allah and Muhammad is His Prophet." The Arabic phrase is beautifully poetic, and it offers both deep insight and brilliant inspiration for those who see and read it. It is sometimes said that this phrase is the essence of the entire Al-Qur'an, and thus the essence of the one true religion.

The United States' Library of Congress possesses a number of fragments of single folio items of calligraphic compositions, illuminations and paintings in Arabic, Persian and Turkish.

Many of these exist in pages extracted from the Safavid Period (1501–1722), and just following it. Some of these compositions survive in albums. Item number 1-2000-154, for example, contains an intricately designed composition of human figures accompanied by angels, with registers bearing inscriptions.[497]

During the eighteenth and nineteenth centuries, new types of calligraphic compositions emerged in Iran and in Muslim India. Many of these compositions contain explicit Shiite invocations and poetic verses in Farsi. Calligraphers composed panels as a tribute, or *pishkas* in Farsi, or as New Year's presents to honor benefactors or sponsors to support their causes. Item number 1-84-154-96, for example, composed by Farid al-Din, is a text to honor the Prophet Muhammad's son-in-law, Ali.[498]

Another of these Shiite texts, item number 1-85-154-96, composed by Hafiz Nur Allah, compares his patron's military career to Ali's military prowess, using the analogy of Ali's nickname, *Haydar*, or "The Lion," and his sword that was called *Dhu-Al-Fiqar*, or "The Sword of the Holy Man."[499]

In the twelfth century, and beyond, calligrapher scribes continued to make Arabic masterpieces by hand. Modern advancements in computer technology and graphics have led to a new flourishing of styles and techniques in the arts, creating new dimensions for this ancient form of art brought up to date. One of these new forms is called the *Kashkoi*, or "Diary." It is the on-going record of important family events, including the births of children, marriages and deaths. A *Kashkoi* often uses one of the new Arabic, calligraphic scripts. It may be the record of one man, or an entire family over generations.

Many of these diaries also include remedies for various ailments like stomach ache or headache, passed down from generation to generation. These *Kashkois* now often include calligraphic styles of Arabic that did not exist until the late twentieth century. A recipe to help with memory loss, for example, suggests a treatment of a medicine that combines rose hips, turmeric and the poppies of opium.[500]

Other items popular among contemporary Islamic calligraphers are pages from Al-Qur'an, as well as collections or histories of the Islamic prophets. The latter usually begins with the name of the prophet, then works its way down the page, telling facts about the prophet's life, where he was born, who his parents were, where and when he lived, and what he may have written or otherwise produced.

These items are also completed in many new Arabic, Farsi and Turkish scripts, completed as computer graphics. Also popular in some Muslim lands is a revival of very old, Arabic scripts, popular in the beginning of Islam up through the Middle Ages. This is particularly true among calligraphers in contemporary Egypt, Syria and Iran.

Angel Images in Early Islamic Art: Ninth to Twelfth Centuries

One of the earliest pieces of Muslim art and architecture related to angels can be seen in the late seventh-century Dome of the Rock Mosque completed between 684 and 691 in Jerusalem by architects Yazid Ibn Salam and Raja Ibn Haywah. Wijdan Ali, in his book, *The Arab Contribution to Islamic Art*, writes of the symbolism of the Dome of the Rock Mosque. He writes:

> In this Muslim monument, the celestial sphere of the Dome joins the temporal sphere of the octagon, which stand for the right angels described in the Qur'an as bearing the Divine Throne.[501]

In this quotation, Wijdan Ali mentions the *Arsh*, or "Throne" of Allah. The word *Arsh* appears twice in the Muslim Holy Book, at Surah 85:15 and 107:2. The Throne of Allah is discussed, however, in a variety of other passages of Al-Qur'an. Many of these include the mention of the *Hamalat Al-Arsh*, or the eight angels "who bear the throne." Among these Qur'anic passages are Surah 7:54; 11:7; and forty, ayat seven.

A number of other themes involving the *Mala'ika* have been employed in Muslim architecture, particularly in Mosque art, from the seventh to the tenth centuries. Often depictions of Muhammad's "Night Journey," accompanied by the angel Jibril, or Jibril bringing Al-Qur'an to the Prophet Muhammad, can be seen on the walls of many early Mosques in the Muslim faith.

Among the earliest of Islamic images of angels is a ninth-century depiction of "Muhammad Riding Buraq Accompanied by Jibril." The angel hovers over the prophet with his enormous wings spread.[502] Another version of the same theme can be found in Rashid Al-Din's *Jami'al-Tawasrikh*, which is likely a redrawn lithograph of the original.[503] S. Rappaport has produced a version of this same scene in his *History of Egypt*.[504] Muhammad sits astride Buraq, sword in his right hand, the angel Jibril hovering above them.

Another early image of angels can be found in an eleventh-century Persian manuscript of the Night Journey. In the painting, Muhammad atop Buraq, along with Jibril, encounters a multi-headed creature in Paradise. Both Muhammad and the angel Jibril are dressed in Oriental garb, and they both are adorned with crowns.[505]

A third early Islamic depiction of angels is another eleventh-century Persian text, a miniature from a volume entitled *The History of Muhammad*. This text was produced around 1030. The manuscript is owned by the Bibliotheque Nationale in Paris.[506] One of the illustrations of this text is called *Muhammad's Paradise* and includes a rendering of the seven levels of *Jannah*, or Heaven, with *mala'ika*, with extended wings at the center of each of the bottom three levels. Below Heaven, in a lower register, is a scene of the Earth. Various people congregate around the Mosque at Mecca.

Finally, in a fourth image of angels in early Islam, from a twelfth-century Sufi manuscript, shows the Prophet Muhammad, along with the angel Jibril who appears to be bringing the revelation of Al-Qur'an to the prophet. Jibril is on the right of the image. He is kneeling and wears a crown. His wings are folded behind him. Muhammad sits on the left; a blazing halo is around his head.[507] This brings us to angel images from the thirteenth to fifteenth centuries.

Angel Images in Islamic Art: Thirteenth to Fifteenth Centuries

In the thirteenth to fourteenth centuries, Islamic renderings of angels come mostly from Iran and Turkey. Many of the themes of these images are extensions of the earlier period. One fourteenth century image of the "Birth of Muhammad," for example, is a miniature illustration on vellum from the book, *Jami' al-Tawarikh*, or "The Compendium of Chronicles," but it is often referred to as *The Universal History* or *The History of the World*, by Rashid Al-Din.[508] The manuscript in question comes from Persia and is dated to the year 1307. The text is owned by the Edinburgh University Library.

In this rendering, two angels, or *mala'kayn*, with spread wings, peer down at Muhammad's mother and the baby prophet. The infant and mother are surrounded by family and friends. This image is related to a Muslim tradition that the baby Muhammad was visited by a *mala'kayn* shortly after his birth. The depiction in question looks very much like versions of the Christian Madonna and Child from the same period.[509] A second group of Persian images are depictions of the angel Jibril bringing the revelation of Al-Qur'an to the Prophet Muhammad. One of these is another image from Rashid Al-Din's *Universal History,* which was produced in Tabriz around 1310. In this Persian miniature, a seated Muhammad is on the right, while on the left, an enormous Jibril stands, his left hand pointing to the prophet. The angel wears a crown that looks like the horns of a bull. His left wing is bent and pointed down, while his right wing is spread behind him.[510]

In another folio from the same manuscript, the prophet sits atop his steed Buraq, during the Night Journey, on the left of the depiction. On the right, the *Malak Jibril*, holding a copy of Al-Qur'an, stretches the book forward for the perusal by Muhammad. Behind the angel, to the right, another angel can be seen. Buraq wears a crown in the image. The Prophet Muhammad is dressed in the Oriental garb of the day.

Another fourteenth-century Persian depiction of the Night Journey again shows Muhammad seated on a crowned Buraq. They are located atop a modern building in Iran. Buraq has the face of a woman and the tail of a peacock. The Farsi inscription that accompanies the image says, "The Messenger mounted at a mainland shiny door village [*yzdlaan kyvry*] blinds to ascension wine river."[511]

Needless to say, what to make of this caption is incomplete and not clear; it can be found, however, on the website of the Iranian newspaper *Hamshahri* that was sponsoring a contest of cartoons in response to what they saw as irreverent cartoon depictions of the Prophet Muhammad in the west.[512]

Another fourteenth-century Persian image that shows angels is entitled *Muhammad Exhorting His followers Before the Battle of Badr*. The depiction is dated 1314–1315 and is owned by the Nour Foundation's Nasser D. Khalili Collection of Art in London. In the image, Muhammad is on the left, a sword in his right hand. A group of mounted soldiers, carrying lances and swords, are on the far left of the depiction. Between Muhammad and the warriors float three angels who appear to be aiding the Muslim Army against the Quraysh Tribe, Islam's enemy.

There are also a number of extant Turkish renderings of angels. For the most part, they show scenes we have discussed earlier. One fourteenth-century Turkish manuscript, owned by the Topkapi Museum in Istanbul, shows the Prophet Muhammad and the angel Jibril standing before a giant angel. The image comes from Tabriz and is dated between 1360 and 1370.[513]

Another fourteenth-century Turkish depiction of angels shows Muhammad borne on the shoulders of Jibril arriving at the Gates of Paradise. The angel Ridwan, the Gate-Keeper, holds out his left hand, inviting the prophet to enter. Jibril's wings are outstretched, and he wears a golden crown. This depiction comes from another manuscript owned by the Topkapi Palace in Istanbul.[514]

A large variety of Islamic images of *mala'ika* can be found in Turkish art from the fifteenth century, including depictions from Afghanistan, Iran and Turkey. Two separate Afghan images of the Night Journey, both owned by the National Library in Paris, show the Prophet

Muhammad arriving on the shores of the White Sea. In the center of the first depiction, the prophet sits atop a crowned Buraq who has the face of a woman. Muhammad is in Eastern dress and has a flaming halo around his head. The angel Jibril is on the left of the depiction.

His wings are outstretched, and rays of light emanate from them. The angel seems to be leading the prophet and Buraq on their Night Journey.[515]

In the other Afghani image, Jibril brings Muhammad's first revelation to the prophet. This depiction is a leaf from a copy of the *Majmac-al-Tawarikh*, or "The Compendium of Histories," produced by Timurid around 1425.[516] The manuscript in question is owned by the Metropolitan Museum of Art in New York City. In the image, the Prophet Muhammad kneels on the right, while the angel Jibril delivers the revelation on the left. The angel Jibril is standing, his left hand pointing with the message. His large wings are spread behind him.[517]

A number of fifteenth-century Persian images of angels are extant, including a pair of depictions of the Night Journey, an image of angels at war, and a fifteenth-century Persian representation of the *Houris*. The first Persian depiction of the Night Journey shows Muhammad flying over the city of Mecca at the beginning of the Mi'raj. A large, square building, probably the Kaa'ba, stands in the center of the city. Muhammad rides a Buraq with a golden crown. The pair is surrounded by angels with light (*Nur*), emanating from their wings.

The manuscript is entitled, the *Khamseh*, and was painted by an artist named Nezami, at the very end of the fifteenth century. This manuscript is owned by the British Library in London.[518]

In the other fifteenth-century image of the Night Journey, Muhammad is on the right, astride Buraq, and the angel Jibril is in the center of the depiction talking with Prophet Ibrahim, on the left. All three figures—Muhammad, Jibril, and Ibrahim—have blazing haloes. In the lower right is a group of human believers, or angels, huddled together and looking toward the others.[519] The fifteenth-century Persian image depicts Muhammad, and the angel Jibril shows Muhammad on a horse with a sword in his right hand. He receives the permission of the Banu Nadir, a Jewish tribe defeated at Medina. Above Muhammad, suspended in the air, is a menacing-looking angel who appears to have aided the Muslim Army in battle. This depiction is from a manuscript of the *Jami'al-Tawarikh*, dating from the early fourteenth century. It is part of the Nasser D. Khalili Collection of Islamic Art in London.[520]

Another fifteenth-century Persian image produced around 1436 shows the Prophet Muhammad being greeted into Paradise by four angels, the first of which greets the prophet with a handshake. Behind the scene of the five figures is a host of other *mala'ika*, waiting to greet Muhammad into Paradise.[521]

Two other final fifteenth-century Persian depictions of angels— one of the Night Journey and the other of the *Houris*— are also extant. The first, *Muhammad Flying Over Paradise During the Night Journey*, shows the prophet flying over Paradise on his steed, Buraq. The angel Jibril is leading them. Below these figures, several *Houris* are harvesting flowers.[522] The other fifteenth-century Persian depiction also shows the Night Journey and the Houris. Muhammad, on the upper-right, visits Paradise with Buraq. They are accompanied, of course, by the *Malak Jibril*, on the upper left. Below them are several Houris riding camels. They have beautiful, female faces and wear Eastern headdress. Each Houri carries flowers to give to the prophet, as he enters *Jannah*, or Paradise. This painting comes from a manuscript called the *Miraj Nama,* which is owned by the National Library in Paris.[523]

A number of other representations of the Houris are extant in Islamic art. One of the best is a depiction from a manuscript owned by the British Library, catalogued as Or. 12964. This eighteenth-century text shows the Prophet Muhammad bowing in worshipping Allah, and then he ventures on to the Seventh Heaven, where a number of Houris are frolicking in a garden. The Houris seem to be enjoying the bounty of the garden, with flowering trees and flowing streams. Some pick flowers, while others are conversing with ease. Nerina Rustomji says of this image:

> There is such a peace in this composition that even the birds come to them and sit on some of their heads [the Houris], unperturbed.[524]

Among the mosaics of the Great Mosque in Damascus, there is a painting of the Houris in Paradise. Seven Houris bow in the direction of Allah, gifts in hand for the Almighty. The Mosque was built during the reign of Caliph Walid, the First, between 705 and 715, though some scholars attribute it to the time of his uncle, Walid, the Second, who ruled from 743 to 744.

The 253-foot tall Mosque is on a site that originally was a first-century Hellenic Temple dedicated to the god Jupiter. Later, it was a Syriac, Christian church to honor Saint John the Baptist.[525]

The most celebrated Umayyad desert complex of Jordan is the bathhouse of Qasar' Amra, a small structure nestled in a broad depression about fifty-five miles east of Amman. The walls and ceilings of this rectangular building are covered in preserved frescoes depicting a variety of scenes that were typical of Umayyad decorations, like battle and hunting scenes, for example. The Audience Hall of Qasar' Amra also has a number of frescoes, including one depicting a military victory, attended by servants and flanked by peacocks, heavy-set wrestlers, pacing lions, and most important for our purposes, flying angels.[526]

Other of the fresco images at Qasar Amra include an impressive depiction of the Zodiac, a large naked woman, and an image of six kings. The west first became aware of the Jordan structure at Qasar Amra when Czech explorer Alois Musil reported having traveled there. The site at Qasar Amra is now a UNESCO World Heritage Site.

There are also a number of extant fifteenth-century Turkish images of angels. Two of the most impressive are a Turkish version of the Night Journey and another depiction of angels presenting the Prophet Muhammad with a miniature city. In the former image, the angel Jibril carries Muhammad on his shoulders, while flying over mountains, where angels are shown among golden flames. This depiction is from a manuscript owned by the Topkapi Palace Library in Istanbul.[527]

In the other fifteenth-century Turkish image, an angel presents the Prophet Muhammad and his *Sahaba*, or companions, with another miniature city. The enormous angel, with wings stretched wide, holds the small city in his two hands. Below are Muhammad and his two companions. The pair at the far right are standing, while others are kneeling or sitting. This brings us to an analysis of sixteenth-century angel images in Islamic art.

Angel Images in Islamic Art: Sixteenth Century

A variety of Muslim images of angels can be seen from the sixteenth century, some from Persia, some from Turkey, and one from Uzbekistan. Muhammad sits atop a crowned Buraq. He is surrounded by a bevy of angels, about two dozen in all, with light reflected in their wings. Below this scene, in a lower register, three Muslim scholars on Earth are discussing some matter of importance.[528] Among sixteenth-century Persian depictions of the *Mala'ika* are a number of renderings of the Night Journey. One comes from a manuscript dated around 1570. It is an opaque watercolor and gold on paper. The manuscript is owned by the Fine Art Museum of San Francisco. Muhammad sits atop Buraq, and they are surrounded by Jibril and six other angels.[529]

Another sixteenth-century Persian depiction of the Mi'raj shows the prophet surrounded by Jibril and other angels, as well. Jibril is holding something in his right hand, possibly the Al-Qur'an. This manuscript was completed around 1517. The image in question is part of a text known as the *Khamza* by an artist named Nizami.[530]

A third sixteenth-century Persian image of angels comes from a mid-century miniature. In the depiction, the Prophet Muhammad is ascending to Paradise riding on Buraq and surrounded by *Mala'ika*. This manuscript was completed in Tabriz between 1539 and 1543. There are eleven angels in all, above, below and on the sides of the prophet.[531]

One final sixteenth-century Persian image of the same scene also features Muhammad and Buraq surrounded, this time, by nine *Mala'ika*. The manuscript from which the image comes is owned by the Seattle Art Museum.[532]

Beginning in the mid-sixteenth century, the most important of the Ottoman miniaturist painters was a man named Nakkas Osman. Details of Osman's life are scant, but the earliest known of his illustrations were made between 1560 and 1570, for a Turkish translation of a Persian manuscript known as the *Firdawsis Shahnama*.[533] It is an illuminated text owned by the Albright-Knox Art Gallery in Buffalo, New York.

Nikkas Osman is important for our purposes because he was one of the first illustrators of the *Sebi-i-Nebi* written around 1388, but not illustrated until the mid-1590s. Noble prize winner Orhan Pamuk gives a fictional account of the life of Osman in his novel *My Name is Red*. In the novel, Osman blinds himself with a needle, apparently emulating the life of miniaturist Bihzad.[534] Critic Zeren Tanindi, writing about the miniaturist style of Nakkas Osman, observes:

> Osman's illustrative style has been described as "plain, yet perceptive." His illustrations show careful attention to the most minute detail, always depicting events in a realistic style.[535]

There is a variety of sixteenth-century Turkish images of angels. One is a 1595 illustration in a manuscript that shows the angel Jibril making his Annunciation to the Prophet Muhammad. The depiction in question comes from an illustrated edition of the *Siyer-i-Nebi* that is owned by the Topkapi Palace Library in Istanbul.[536] The same manuscript has an image of Muhammad and His companions traveling to Mecca. The prophet and his entourage are accompanied by four large, standing angels.[537]

Another Turkish manuscript from the same period around 1594 or 1595 shows a flying Jibril delivering Al-Qur'an to the prophet. Jibril is suspended in air above the prophet. The angel wears a gold crown. Around the scene is a gathering of earthly believers, two dozen or so, in all.[538]

Another sixteenth-century Turkish work that includes Islamic illustrations of angels is called the *Epitome of Historical Works* that was completed in 1583. Among the illustrations in the *Epitome* are the following:

1. *Flying angels*, from the *Zubdeit ut-Tevarih* (late sixteenth century).
2. *Ibrahim and His Son Ishaq and an Angel Bringing a Ram for Sacrifice. Zubdeit ut-Tevarih* (1583).
3. *The Descent of Christ with Two Angels*, Miniature in Damascus (1583).
4. *Angels and Adam and Eve. Zubdeit ut-Tevarih* (1583).[539]

The latter of these images is owned by the Museum of Turkish and Islamic Arts in Istanbul. It shows four angels, all with female faces, descending on the Garden of Eden on Earth. All four angels wear gold crowns. They sit on the branches of what most likely is the "Tree of Life." Item number two above suggests that the son of Ibrahim for sacrifice is Ishaq (Isaac). Usually, however, the Islamic tradition prefers that the sacrificed son is Ismail, of Ishmael in Hebrew, the progenitor of the Arab people.

There is also a variety of other sixteenth-century Turkish depictions of angels. One is another Turkish miniature of the Prophet Muhammad and the angel Jibril. The angel kneels before the prophet, his enormous wings spread behind him. Jibril wears a gold crown, and Muhammad has a flaming halo around his head.[540] Another sixteenth-century Turkish image shows Muhammad on a blue donkey, most likely Buraq while touching hands with the angel Jibril. This depiction is from an illustrated edition of the *Siyer-i-Nebi*, also owned by the Topkapi Palace Library in Istanbul.[541]

Another sixteenth-century Turkish rendering of Islamic angels shows the angel Jibril cleansing the heart of Muhammad from impurities in preparation for the Night Journey while other angels watch. This image comes from a book entitled *The Progress of the Prophet*. The illustrations for this manuscript were completed in Istanbul in 1595.[542] Finally, a miniature painted by Herat around 1520 for Sultan Muhammad that illustrates a *Mala'kayn* drinking wine in Paradise, is the most controversial of angel images in Islam. The Muslim Holy Book, Al-Qur'an, at several places, including Surah two: 219, 4:43, 5:90–91 and 16:67, outline a prohibition against intoxicants. Yet, in the rendering created for Sultan Muhammad shows several *Mala'ika* tipping a cup of wine and drinking.[543]

It is not entirely clear what to make of the painting in question. What is clear is that in the images from this manuscript, on four separate plates, angels are drinking wine. Perhaps that fact is nothing more than to indicate that in Paradise, all beings of Allah will enjoy themselves to the fullest. Another explanation is to point out that many of the Sufi thinkers have pointed out that the state of intoxication is closer to mystical states of consciousness in which one understands, or experiences a Beatific Vision. At any rate, the manuscript in question shows Muslim angels drinking wine in Paradise. This brings us to illustrations of the angel Jibril in relationship to other prophets, the subject matter of this next section of this chapter.

Jibril, Art and Some Other Prophets

In addition to the many depictions of Jibril bringing Al-Qur'an to the Prophet Muhammad, and the angel transporting Muhammad on his steed Buraq during the Night Journey, another common theme in Islamic art is the angel Jibril bringing revelations to many of the other prophets, or *Anbiya* in Islam. Often, for example, depictions of Ibrahim sacrificing his son may include the *Malak Jibril* bringing the animal for sacrifice in the son's place. In Islamic art, however, that son is most often Ismail, and not Ishaq (Isaac), as in the Hebrew Bible.

Most renderings of Ayyub (Job), Nuh (Noah) and Yunus (Jonah) in Islam often include the angel Jibril bringing revelations to these prophets, as well. When Adam and *Hawa*, or Eve, are depicted being banished from the Garden of Eden, it is often Jibril that brings about the expulsion. One good example of this phenomenon is an eighteenth-century Turkish manuscript owned by the University Library in Jerusalem. Adam and Eve, with haloes around their heads, are expelled by the *Malak Jibril*, who is accompanied by three other angels.[544]

Another prophet that frequently is shown with angels in Islamic art is *Yusuf*, or Joseph. Most often, it is an angel that saves Yusuf from the well. One good example of this is a manuscript owned by the British Library. The manuscript is called the *Garden of the Happy*, which was completed by an artist named Fuduli around 1600. Yusuf sits in the well, supported by the *Malak Jibril*. Indeed, the prophet sits on the angel's lap.[545]

Other depictions of angels and prophets can be seen in Islamic art throughout the fourteenth to eighteenth centuries. Many other Biblical and Qur'anic tales also include artistic representations. One of the finest depictions of a Biblical tale in Muslim art is a manuscript that shows a delegation of angels sent by the Queen of Sheba to King Sulayman (Solomon). This manuscript that contains the image in question is owned by the Catherine and Ralph Benkaim Collection in Los Angeles, California. The depiction shows Sulayman saving the Queen and, afterward, she sends a delegation of *Mala'ika* to thank the King.[546]

Another image that shows Sulayman receiving the Queen of Sheba is from a sixteenth-century Persian manuscript that also is owned by the Benkaim Collection. The miniature shows the visit of the Queen to the King after she has renounced idolatry and has accepted Allah and Sulayman as His Prophet. In the center of the image, the Queen is being carried toward the King by a Black Jinn.[547]

Another image of Solomon and his Vizier, Asaf, shows Asaf holding a scroll bearing the words, "In the name of Allah, the Compassionate and the Merciful," while in a lower register an angel, most likely Jibril, his wings spread wide behind him, observes the scene.

Images of the Angel Mika'il in Islamic Art

The single reference to the angel Mika'il in Al-Qur'an, which comes at Surah 2:98, has generated a variety of legends about this angel. Many of these tales refer to the relationship between the angel Michael and the Jews. In one of these narratives, Muhammad is questioned by Jews about his prophetic mission, and he answers these questions quite satisfactorily.

But when Muhammad says that Jibril is the bearer of his revelation, the Jews attack Jibril as a spirit of destruction and foe of Mika'il.[548]

There is also extant a variety of images of the *Malak Mika'il* in Muslim art, mostly in the Modern period. A double-page frontispiece of a manuscript owned by the Topkapi Palace Library in Istanbul, for example, shows the Prophet Muhammad, a flamed halo obscuring his face, seated on a minbar inside a building that may be a residence or a Mosque. Horses, with attendants, wait outside the building. A gaggle of people inside a room includes four soldiers wearing battle helmets.

Their leader kneels at the foot of the minbar. He points to a severed head on a platter. The text that accompanies the image was written by a man named Naysaburi. He tells us that the angel is *Mika'il*, who has flung Abu Jahl from his horse, and Abd Allah Ibn Mas'ud "killed him and presents his head to Muhammad."[549]

Other legends associated with the angel *Mika'il* in Islamic art is the story that the angel was so shocked when he visited *Jahannam* (Hell), that he vowed to never laugh again. Other Islamic narratives suggest that the *Mala'kayn*, Jibril and Mika'il, were the first to follow the command of Allah to bow down to Adam. Mika'il and Jibril are also credited with purifying the heart of Muhammad before his Night Journey from Mecca to Jerusalem and his subsequent assumption to *Jannah* (Heaven). Mika'il is also remembered in Islamic lore as aiding the Muslim Army in the earliest military campaigns in Islamic history.

An image of *Malak Mika'il* and *Malak Jibril* prostrating themselves before Adam can be seen in a sixteenth-century manuscript also owned by the Topkapi Palace Library. Folio 11a of the manuscript shows Adam enthroned, while Michael and Jibril, and four other angels prostrate themselves before Adam. The other angels may be the other Muslim archangel. The angel to the lower left is most likely Mika'il, while the one on the right is Jibril.[550]

A third image of *Malak Mika'il* again shows him accompanied by three other archangels bowing to Adam. The manuscript is owned by the Getty Museum in Los Angeles.[551] The angel Michael appears on the bottom right of the illustration. Like the other *mala'ika*, he wears a gold crown. He is dressed in blue with a green sash. His red and blue wings are behind his head.

The angel Mika'il is also frequently shown in a variety of manuscripts that depict the expulsion of Adam and Eve from Paradise. One fine example of this is a text owned by the Staatsbibliothek in Berlin. Mika'il stands, sword in hand, a bevy of other angels stand behind him, while in front, the human pair has been thrust out.[552] Another example of the same theme is from a set of eleven miniatures called the *Hadiqat al-Su'ada*, owned by the Turk ve Islam Eserleri Museum in Istanbul. Folio 8a repeats the theme of the archangels Mika'il rejecting Adam and Hawa from the garden.[553]

Angel Images in Islamic Art: Seventeenth to Nineteenth Centuries

In the seventeenth to the nineteenth centuries, most of the images of the *Mala'ika* in Islamic iconography came from Turkey. The themes of these depictions, for the most part, are the same as those we have seen in earlier ages: Muhammad and Jibril on the Night Journey, the angel Jibril bringing the revelation of Al-Qur'an to the Prophet Muhammad, and angels aiding the early Muslim Army in times of war. But there are also a few new themes, particularly in eighteenth – and nineteenth-century Turkey, as we shall see.

A seventeenth-century Turkish image shows Muhammad flying over the city of Mecca, during the *Mi'raj*. The prophet sits atop a crowned Buraq. They are surrounded by Jibril and seven other *Mala'ika*. Beneath them, on a lower register, the Kaaba can be seen, as well as the ancient city of Mecca.[554] Another eighteenth-century Turkish scene also has both Heavenly and Earthly scenes. Below, Muhammad is presented to the monk Abd al-Muttailib and the inhabitants of Mecca, while in the upper register, a male figure and two Houris inspect the Earthly scene. This manuscript is supposedly a copy of an eighth-century original. It is owned by the Topkapi Palace Library. The two Houris in the illustration both have large wings and female faces. Between the two is a male figure, perhaps a saint or holy man, who has large wings that stretch across the entire scene.[555]

Another eighteenth-century Turkish rendition of angels is from the same manuscript mentioned above. The *Malak Jibril* inspires Muhammad in a mosque in Medina. The multi-colored angel wears a gold crown and carries a book, presumably Al-Qur'an. The angel is standing, and his wings are in layers of feathers. The Prophet Muhammad stands to the right, dressed in Eastern garb. He has a blazing halo around his head. Muhammad's face is obscured in this image, as it often is in this period.[556]

The angel Jibril appearing to the Prophet Muhammad on the *Mount al-Noor*, or the Mountain of Light, where the prophet is said to have received his first revelation, is an image from another eighteenth-century Turkish manuscript. Muhammad is kneeling in the center of the composition, while Jibril hovers above. The angel wears a gold crown and has a very large pair of wings. Mount al-Noor is a hill near the city of Mecca.[557]

One final nineteenth-century Persian image of angels comes from a miniature in a manuscript owned by the New York Public Library. The Prophet Muhammad is on his steed Buraq being carried to Paradise from the Kaaba below. This image comes from a book by Italian writer Giuli Ferrario published between 1823 and 1838. The original book was entitled, *Il Costume antico e modern storia del governo*, or "Ancient and Modern Stories and Costumes."[558]

Robert Hillenbrand gives a description of what he believes are the most important texts of Muslim art during the Ottoman period. Hillenbrand writes:

> The arts of the book in Ottoman times drew their initial inspiration predominantly from those in Iran under the Tirmurids, and their rivals, Turcoman Aqqoyunlu in the latter 15th century. In some of the associated specialties—for example, in most Qur'anic illuminations and in the illustrations of romance verse—they did not progress significantly beyond this heritage. But for the most part, they struck out on their own. In the field of book-painting, for instance, entire cycles of religious images were devised, almost for the first time in Islamic Art. This involved the creation of nearly hundreds of new images. The *Anbiyaname* ("The Book of the Prophets") of 1558, whose image of the founder of Islam, with a white veil and gigantic, flame halo, sometimes attain a visionary intensity. Illustrated guides to Jerusalem, and to the Holy cities of Arabia, entitled *Futuh al-Harmamain*, became popular during the 16th century.[559]

Professor Hillenbrand highlights the *Book of the Prophets* and popular illustrated guides to Arabia and the Holy Land. But by far, the most significant Muslim text with renderings of angels is the Turkish epic the *Siyer-i-Nebi*.

Angel Illustrations in the *Siyer-i-Nebi*

The *Siyer-i-Nebi* is a Turkish epic about the life of Muhammad and his family completed around 1388 and written by Mustafa, son of Yusuf of Erzurum, a noted Sufi Dervish. It was written for a commission Mustafa received from Sultan Berkuk, the Mamluk ruler in Cairo at the time. After the death of Berkuk, Ottoman ruler Murad, the Second, who ruled from 1574–1595, ordered the work to be illustrated. In due time it was illustrated by Lutfi Abdullah, a man in charge of a manuscript workshop at the Royal Palace in Istanbul.

The illustrations for the *Siyer-i-Nebi* were not completed, however, until the ruler of Murad's successor, Mehmed, the Third. Lufti Abdullah completed the illustrations that included 814 miniatures in six volumes, were finally completed on January 16, 1595. The *Siyer-i-Nebi* is written in Turkish on delicate, finished *aharli* paper, with thirteen lines of black ink on a page of large *Naskhi* script. The text is written with gilded edges in black ink. Proper names in the manuscript are written in red ink.

The areas between the lines of the manuscript are filled with gilding whose edges are outlined in black ink. The six volumes of the *Siyer-i-Nebi*, or "Life of the Prophet," tells the tale of the birth and life of the Prophet Muhammad, as well as the history of his family and that of the early portion of the Islamic faith. The sixth volume ends with the death of the prophet. The copy of volume IV owned by the Topkapi Palace Library in Istanbul is a copy of the original. This volume has 545 folios, including 193 miniatures. Whenever there is an illustration on a page, it is usually between the top two or the bottom two lines.

The volumes have a brown leather binding that are adorned with oval medallions with palmette pendants and corner pieces. The fourth volume begins with the birth of Muhammad's daughter, Fatima, and goes on to describe her marriage to Ali. This is followed by descriptions of the battles at Badr and Uhad, and the death of the prophet's uncle. The Topkapi Library owns Volumes I, II, and VI of the original *Siyer-i-Nebi*. Volume III is owned by the New York Public Library, while Volume IV is owned by the Chester Beatty Library in Dublin, Ireland.

Twenty miniatures extracted from Volume IV are in private hands. These illustrations have changed owners several times since their appearance in an auction in a Paris gallery in 1984. Many of the images of the *Siyer-i-Nebi* are of individual angels in the Islamic tradition. In one of these, in the presence of Saint Ayse, the *Malak Jibril* brings the word of Al-Qur'an to the Prophet Muhammad. Muhammad sits to the right on a prayer rug, a blazing halo around his head. The crowned angel kneels on the left, also on a prayer rug, gesturing with his left hand toward Muhammad.[560]

Another image of angels in the *Siyer-i-Nebi* is a rendering of the Prophet Muhammad at the Battle of Badr. The prophet stands to the right, blazing halo around his head; his troops spread out below before him. An angel—most likely Jibril—hovers above the soldiers, while he stretches his right hand toward the prophet.[561] Another image of Prophet Muhammad in the *Siyer-i-Nebi* shows the infant prophet at his birth. Muhammad and his mother are surrounded by angels.[562]

Another angel image comes from Volume II that was produced in 1595. The Prophet Muhammad sits on Mount Hira, together with the *Malak Jibril*, as well as a host of other *mala'ika*. This is ostensibly the site of Jibril bringing the first revelation of Al-Qur'an to the prophet. The angel approaches the prophet, holding the revelation in his left hand. This pair is on the left of the rendering. They are accompanied on the right by five other celestial beings, either angels or Jinn.[563]

Another angelic image in the *Siyer-i-Nebi* shows a group of *Mala'ika* coming to the aid of the Muslim Army at the Battle of Uhud. This image was made by Mustafa Ibn Vali in 1594 for Sultan Murad, the Third. It is one of the miniatures that was removed from Volume IV. It was last sold at Sotheby's in 2001 and is now in private hands.[564] In another image from the *Siyer-i-Nebi*, Muhammad advances on the city of Mecca, accompanied by Jibril, Mika'il, Israfil and Azrael, the principal archangels in Islam. The Muslim Army prepares for the conquering of the city from the Quraysh Tribe.[565]

Perhaps the most interesting of these angel images from the *Siyer-i-Nebi* comes from Volume II. Muhammad is on Mount Hira accompanied by all of the archangels. The prophet is on the left. He is seated, a blazing halo around his head. His face is obscured. Over his left shoulder is the *Malak Jibril*. In front of the prophet stand the four other archangels. One of the angel's wings are flat behind his back, while those of the other three are stretched out and pointing upward.[566] This brings us to a variety of other angels depicted in Muslim art.

Other Depictions of Islamic Angels

In addition to the angels mentioned above, there also are extant a number of other renderings of Islamic celestial beings. One is a sixteenth-century image of the angel Azrael, the Angel of Death. He is a handsome figure shown from the shoulders up. His left wing stretched, is next to his head. The Farsi text that accompanies the image tells us:

> Earth, that is the Seventh Earth, and his head is in the High Firmament, which is the highest of all the firmaments, and the face of Azrael. He stands before the Protected Tablet, and he has closed humanity's mouth, and his command, according to the number of people who die, and all these people are before his two eyes. He does not take any creature's life unless his provisions have been exhausted and the hour of his death has come.[567]

The *Protected Tablet*, of course, is a reference to the book on which are written the deeds of all human beings that will be read at the End of Time. The Farsi text of this image continues:

> And it has been related from Ash'ab Ibn Aslam who spoke of the monarch of death, and said, "Why are you engaged upon this when you are not yet to be here? One is in the East, and the other one in the West, or is it in a country of warfare flairs up between the two armies?" Azrael, Allah's praise be upon him, said, "I summon the souls of all animals and human beings."[568]

Another image of the archangel Israfil is from an Iraqi miniature from a manuscript entitled, *'Aja'ib al-Makhluqat*, or *The Wonders of Creation*. It was completed by an artist named Al-Qazwini. The manuscript in question is owned by the Free Gallery of Art in Washington, DC. The angel has his *Sur*, or trumpet, to his lips, waiting for Allah to give him the command to blow. Israfil is dressed in a blue and green tunic, his green and orange wings spread behind him.[569] In another contemporary image of Israfil is done in the giclee process, whereby older images are transformed into contemporary ones. In this sixteenth-century rendering, Israfil holds his *Sur* to his lips. He wears a white crown. His legs are spread at the base, and he wears a sash around his waist.[570]

Other more modern images of Islamic angels can be seen in Russia and England. In the former, Mikhail Vrubel (1856–1910), a Russian Symbolist painter, completed a painting entitled *Six-Winged Seraph: Azrael*. It is an oil on canvas creation completed in 1904. The painting is owned by the Russian National Museum in Moscow. In the image, Azrael, the Angel of Death, holds a dagger in his right hand and a lamp in his left. He appears on the ready to claim someone's soul. The piece is multi-colored with lots of light and dominated by blue tones.[571]

Two other modern paintings of the Angel of Death can be seen in the work of pre-Raphaelite artist Evelyn De Morgan (1855–1919). Her *Angel of Death*, completed in 1890, shows the angel carrying a harvesting instrument in her right hand while comforting a young man before her with her left.[572] A second painting of De Morgan's is entitled, *The Field of the Slain*, that also features the angel Azrael. In the painting, the angels gather up souls in a black cape with her right hand, while the left hand clutches a skull. Her feathery, dark wings are spread behind her.[573]

Neither Vrubel nor De Morgan were Muslims, but they both borrowed some of the names and themes from Islamic art to use in their own creations. Finally, another contemporary image of *Malak Jibril* was painted by Amaya Kouryuun. In the painting, the angel Jibril appears as a female figure. She stands, dressed in a blue and white dress. His hair is tinted green. She has enormous, white wings spread behind her.[574]

Angels and Islamic Carpets

In addition to the angel images discussed above in Muslim painting, there also has been a long tradition of putting *mala'ika* on carpets in Islamic lands. Muslims long have regarded the carpet with special esteem and admiration. For the traditional Bedouin tribes of Arabia, Persia and Anatolia, the carpet has been at the center of Islamic life, often employed, over the centuries, as tent sheltering from the Sun, as well as sand storms. In fact, in Surah 88 of the Muslim Holy Book, Al-Qur'an, the carpet is counted among the riches promised to believers in Paradise. This text relates about Judgment Day:

> Other faces that Day will be joyful, pleased with their
> striving. In a High Garden, where they will hear no words
> of vanity. Therein will be a bubbling stream. Therein will
> be Thrones of Dignity. Raised on high, goblets placed at
> the ready, and cushions set in rows. And rich carpets all
> spread out. Do they not look at camels and how they
> are made? And at the sky, and how it is raised high?
> And at the Mountains, and how they are fixed firm?
> And at the Earth and how it is spread out?[575]

The Arabic word for "carpet" in the passage quoted above is
zulia, whose plural form is *Zawali*. The Holy Book promises that at
the Day of Judgment, a host of pleasures shall be enjoyed by those who
believe in Allah and His Prophet, Muhammad. Among those pleasures
are bubbling streams, couches set in rows, Thrones of Dignity, and
exquisite *Zawali*.

The earliest evidence for Islamic carpets are fragments found at Al-
Fustat, or "Old Cairo." The oldest of these belong to the ninth century,
while most date from the thirteenth to the fifteenth centuries. Based
on the knots and decorative designs on these carpets, these Egyptian
carpet fragments may be divided into two types. The first are carpets
with a single knot and geometric designs similar to modern Andalusian
carpets in Spain from the fifteenth century—particularly in Toledo.[576]

The other category of Islamic carpets often incorporates stylized
animals and battle scenes, like Anatolian animal designs from the
fourteenth and fifteenth centuries. Among this second variety can
sometimes be found angels decorated on these carpets. One example is
a sixteenth-century Persian court carpet. The main subject matter is a
battle scene of dragons and phoenixes pursued by fifty-eight huntsmen.
On the border of this carpet, which is owned by the Austrian Museum
of Art and Industry, are a pair of Jinn.[577]

In a second Persian carpet from the first half of the seventeenth
century, there is a central panel that shows a crowned Jinni, surrounded
by twelve other Jinn. On the borders of this same carpet, two sits on His
throne, while on either side is an angel with outstretched wings. This

carpet is owned by the Residenz Museum in Munich.[578]

One Ushaq rug from the late sixteenth century, or early seventeenth century, incorporates angels on its borders.[579] Similarly, in the late nineteenth century, Persian carpets from Azerbijan often show large medallions in the midst of carpets that often include images of angels. Many of these carpets began to appear in Europe in the sixteenth century, particularly in England, Italy, Germany and France. One of the ways these *Zawayli* began to appear in painting is in the Renaissance masters. Indeed, carpets can be seen in Oriental scenes by painters such as Van Eyck, Hand Memlic, Lorenzo Lotto, and Hans Holbein, both the Senior and the Junior. This brings us to one final section of this seventh chapter, images of the Peacock Angel.

Images of the Peacock Angel

A final collection of angel images for this chapter can be found in a Kurdish people known as the Yazidi or Yezidi. These people are Kurdish speaking and mostly live in and around Mosul in northern Iraq. There are also traditional Yazidi communities in Armenia, Turkey, the Caucasus and Syria. The sacred books of the Yazidi are the *Kiteba Cilwe*, or "Book of Revelation," and the *Mishefa Res*, or "Black Book." The two most important features of Yazidi beliefs for our purposes are first, a preoccupation with ritual purity, and secondly, a belief in reincarnation or transmigration of souls. This latter belief has led some scholars to posit an Indian origin of the Yazidi. Although the Yazidi are not Muslims, they nevertheless share with Islam a number of beliefs. Among these are the exercise of five daily prayers, at the same times as those in Islam.

Another belief that the Yazidi share with Islam is the notion of a sacred city to which prayer is oriented and to which a pilgrimage must be made once in a lifetime. The sacred city of the Yazidi is Lalish, just north of Mosul. The tomb of the religion's founder, Sex Adi, is also there.

Members of the Yazidi also are required to attend a yearly festival called "The Feast of the Assembly," which is celebrated for a week in late September and early October.

The Yazidi are important for our purposes in this seventh chapter because of a figure called the *Tawsi Melek*, or "Peacock Angel," who is the most important of the deities of the Yazidi people. The Yazidi, like many Muslims, believe that they are following the oldest religion on Earth. They believe that the Peacock Angel is the Creator God and the Ruler of the Universe.

Beyond the *Tawsi Melek*, however, there is a Supreme Deity. He created the Peacock Angel out of light, in the form of a seven-rayed rainbow. These seven rays also stand for the seven great angels, including the *Tawsi Melek*. Since their creation, these seven angels have been identified with the seven days of the week. The Peacock Angel's day is Sunday.[580]

Very little has been written in English on the Yazidi people. R. H. W. Empsom's *The Cult of the Peacock Angel*, with a commentary by Sir Richard Carnac Temple, remains the standard work in English on the Yazidi.[581] This volume contains a number of representations and photographs of the Peacock Angel. The frontispiece shows the figure of a steel angel, originally in three pieces, but now a complete creation.[582]

Other images of the Peacock Angel can be found in various Yazidi shrines, like the Temple at Dahadia in northern Kurdistan. The image in question is Persian in origin and was presented to the British Museum by Mr. Imre Schwaiger of Calcutta in 1912.[583] Although the Yazidi are not Muslims, their art often involves the depiction of the *Tawsi Melek*. These Yazidi images provide another avenue on the question of angel iconography in the Middle East, and thus deserves a mention here.

Conclusions

We began Chapter Seven with a thumbnail sketch of the history of Islamic art from the Abbasid Caliphate in the seventh and eighth centuries, to the Persian and Turkish Empires in the fourteenth to eighteenth centuries. We have seen in this history that, even early on, certain events in the life of Muhammad, as well as in the history of Islam, have been conducive in being represented in Islamic art. As we have shown, among these central events were the birth of Muhammad, the angel Jibril bringing the revelation of Al-Qur'an to the prophet, the prophet and his steed Buraq on the Night Journey, and angels assisting the Muslim armies in various early battles of the faith.

In subsequent sections of this chapter, we described and discussed the many ways that angels in the Islamic tradition have been shown in Muslim art, from the ninth to the twelfth centuries. As we have shown, this art was dominated by a classic work by Rashid Al-Din's called the *Jami'al-Tawarikh*. In the third section of this chapter, we described and discussed the depictions of angels in Islamic iconography from the thirteenth to the fifteenth centuries.

In this period, Al-Din's text continued to be very popular, as was the late fourteenth century *Siyer-i-Nebi*, produced by Mustafa Ibn Vali. In fact, this work of six volumes is so important, we have given it its own section in this chapter.

What we saw in these depictions of angels in the *Siyer-i-Nebi*, for the most part, were the same themes that dominated earlier periods—Jibril bringing Al-Qur'an, the Night Journey and angels in battle. In another section of this chapter, we explored and discussed the uses of Islamic angels in the nineteenth and twentieth centuries. We also explored a few non-Muslims whose art employs the *Mala'ika*, including one Russian painter and one English artist. We ended this chapter with an analysis of the art of the Yazidi people and their representations of the *Tawsi Melek*, or Peacock Angel. We shall now turn our attention to another race of Celestial and Earthly beings, the Jinn (singular, *Jinni*).

Chapter Eight:
The Nature and Roles of the Jinn in Islam

The Jinn are a third form of sentient life alongside humans and angels. They are created from smokeless fire as opposed to the angels from light and humans from clay.

—C. T. R. Hewer, *Understanding Islam*

Islam makes a distinction between angels and another category of supernatural beings called *Jinn* [singular, *Jinni*], from which the English word Genie is derived.

—John Kaltner, *Islam: What Non-Muslims Should Know*

May We fashion from fermented, clay dried tingly hard, as We fashioned the Jinn before from intense, radiant heat.

—The Holy Qur'an 15:26–27 (Author's translation)

Introduction

The major goal in this chapter is to explore the nature and functions of a class of sentient beings known as the *Jinn*, in the Islamic faith. Evidence from Arabian history, including archeological evidence found in northwestern Arabia, indicate that the Arabs before Islam believed in a class of beings known as the *Ginnaye*, an obvious cognate to the words *Jinn*, and the singular *Jinni*. Indeed, an Aramaic inscription from Beth Fasi'el, near the city of Palmyra, pays tribute to these *Ginnaye*.

As we have noted, the Arabic name for the anglicized Genies in Islam is the *Jinni*, or *Djinni*. These are supernatural creatures in Islamic and Arabian folklore, as well as the subject of intense discussion in Muslim literature and scholarship in the mythologies of Arabia, Persia, Egypt, Syria, Turkey and North Africa. Some Muslim accounts suggest that the Jinn were on the Earth before the appearance of human beings. Some say as much as two thousand years before the creation of Adam.

The Jinn originally were said to be in possession of a lofty place in the Heavens, somewhere just below the angels. They are said to be made from a "smokeless fire," or *marijin min nur*, in Arabic; but after Allah made Adam and his wife *Hawa* (Eve), the Jinn, under their proud and willful leader, Iblis, he refused to bow down to Adam, after having been commanded to do so by Allah Himself. For this grievous offense, the Jinn were cast out of Paradise, some becoming wicked Jinn, while others became believers in Islam.

When the Jinn came to the Earth, as the tradition has it, they lived in the Kaf Mountains that supposedly encircle the Earth. The Jinn, along with Allah, the angels, and human beings, is one of the four sentient classes of beings in existence. Like humans, the Jinn can be good or evil, and like them, they possess free will and are accountable for their actions. The Jinn frequently are mentioned in the Muslim Holy Book, Al-Qur'an. In fact, *Surat al-Jinn*, the 72nd Surah of Al-Qur'an, is dedicated to the nature and activities of the Jinn.

In traditional Islam, there are three different kinds of Jinn. The first are called *Ghul*, from which comes the English word Ghoul. They are treacherous spirits capable of changing shapes. The second type of Jinn are known as the *Ifrit*. They are the diabolical, evil Jinn. The third kind of Jinn are called *Si'la*. They also are treacherous spirits of variable forms. Although the Jinn can see human beings, human beings cannot see them. As indicated earlier, many Jinn are capable of assuming either human or animal forms. They are said to dwell in various inanimate objects like stones, trees and the ruins of buildings. The Jinn possess the bodily needs of human beings and thus can be killed. Nevertheless, they are free from all physical restraints.

In Islam, the Jinn are understood in two different senses. First, they are the opposite of the word *ins* in Arabic, which means something has a "physical form." The Jinn are spiritual beings. They cannot be perceived by sensory organs. Secondly, the Jinn are intelligent beings, much like humans and angels; but unlike the angels, the Jinn possess free will and are held morally responsible for their actions, while angels are not.

Some Muslim traditions describe a fourth race of Jinn that are called the *Marid*. The *Marid* are often described as the most powerful kind of Jinn, having particularly great powers. The Marid are also said to be proud and arrogant. It is thought they have the ability to grant wishes to people, often when humans are at battle, or in prison. The *Marid* are also said to be the kind of Jinn that brings sickness and disease to humans. This is evidence by the Semitic root MRD, from which we get the Arabic verb "to be sick."

D. B. MacDonald, in an article on the Jinn in the *Encyclopedia of Islam*, suggests that "The Djinn divide naturally under three headings, though these necessarily shade into one another."[584] The first heading of MacDonald's are the "pre-Islamic Arabia where the nymphs and satyrs of the desert."[585] The second heading for MacDonald is the role of the Djinn in "official Islam."[586] The third variety of Djinn for MacDonald refers to "The role of the Djinn in magic."[587]

As we have suggested earlier in this introduction, our principal job in this eighth chapter is to explore and discuss the nature and uses in Islam of this category of sentient creatures known as the Jinn. We will begin the chapter by speaking of the etymology of the words *Jinn* and *Jinni*, in Islam.

Etymology of Jinni and Jinn

The Arabic words *Jinni* and *Jinn* come from the Arabic verb *Jinna*, the verb "to be angry," as well as the verb "to be possessed." Other philologists suggest the word Jinn is derived from the Arabic *idjtinan*, which means "to hide" or "to be hidden." Others argue for a borrowing from the Greek, *Genus*, or the Latin, *Genius*. Still, other scholars argue that the Arabic Jinn comes from a Syriac or Aramaic source. At any rate, the Arabic singular is *Jinni*, or *Djinni*, and the plural is *Jinn* or *Djinn*. In modern Turkish, the Jinn are called *Cin*, for the singular, and *Ecinni*, for the plural form.[588]

From the same Semitic root, JNN, we also derive other Arabic terms, including *junan*, or "madness;" *Majnun*, or "Mad Man;" *Jannah*, the Arabic word for "Heaven;" *Jin*, the word for "sex" and "gender;" *junna*, the verb "to be angry;" *Janun*, an Arabic word for "Demon;" *jan jan*, the "breast bone;" and *junni*, a word that designates a "south wind."

In pre-Islamic Arabia, the Jinn were nymphs and satyrs of the desert, not unlike the *Eumenides* in Greek mythology. The Jinn represented an aspect of life that remained unknown to humans. By the time of Muhammad, the Jinn already were passing into a vague, impersonal existence, like minor gods. Indeed, the Arabs of Mecca saw a kinship (*nasab*) between the Jinn and Allah, as suggested by the Holy Book's Surah 37:158. This ayat, or verse, reveals:

> They link Him [Allah] with Jinn by lineage, yet the Jinn
> must know that they will be brought before Him.[589]

This is clearly a reference to the fact that the Jinn will be brought before Allah on the Day of Doom or Judgment Day. Since like humans, they are morally accountable for their actions, the Jinn are also subject to Paradise or damnation, depending, of course, on the individual's deeds.

In some Muslim traditions, the Jinn are said to have lived on the Earth, particularly in the desert, long before human beings came along. Some say the Jinn were created by Allah and then sent to Earth some two thousand years before Adam and Eve. This transition can most clearly be seen through the Jinn and their relationship to magic. The Jinn are said to appear to humans in many different forms, most often as animals. More specifically, they are said to appear as black cats without any lighter markings, as a goat, black dogs, hens with chicks, as a buffalo, as a fox, a snake, and sometimes even as human beings.

In the second section of this chapter, we will describe and discuss the major places in the Muslim Holy Book, where the Jinn appear. The places of the Jinn in traditional Hadith literature is the subject matter of the third section of this chapter. In section four, we will examine the relationship between the Jinn and Prophet Sulayman, or Solomon. Other sections of Chapter Eight are dedicated to a comparison of Jinn to other creatures—human and angelic, and the places where Richard Burton, in his *One Thousand and One Nights*, discusses the Jinn. We will end this chapter, by supplying a chart that shows the comparisons and contrasts of what Muslims say about the Jinn compared to angels (*Mala'ika*) and humans, or *El jins el besheri* in Arabic.

Before we move to these sections, however, it might be well to say a little more about the nature of the Jinn. Thomas Lippman, in his book *Understanding Islam,* gives us a short summary of the nature of the Jinn in Islam. Lippman writes:

> God created the earth, the heavens, the elements, men, angels, and Jinn. The Jinn are mysterious creatures, invisible to man, defined by the Islamic scholar Fazlur Rahman in his *Islam* as, "An invisible order of creature, parallel to man, but said to be created from a fiery substance, a kind of duplicate of man which is, in general, more prone to evil and from which the Devil is said to have sprung."[590]

Lippman adds, "The Koran says that God created the Jinn, but tells us little about them. They seem to be spirit creatures, whose impact on the lives of men is only tangential."[591] Ron Geaves, in his work *Key Words in Islam*, gives us this for his entry on the "Jinn:"

> A supernatural life form that Allah created from fire as opposed to humankind who were created from earth. Tradition states that Muhammad was sent to preach to them and some became Muslims. It is even stated that Muhammad first believed that he was under attack by Jinn when He received the first revelations of Al-Qur'an. There are many imams who are taught how to exorcize bad Jinn during their training at the Dar Al-Ulum, or religious schools. In village traditions, Jinn are often blamed for mental and physical illnesses and misfortunes.[592]

Scholar Ruqalyyah Waris Maqsood, in her book *Teach Yourself Islam*, adds to our understanding of the nature of the Jinn:

Jinn are also non-physical beings, and they can either be good or bad, having free will like humans. They are thought to inhabit unclean places, and can often confuse or frighten human beings by involving themselves in their lives and homes. Occasionally, they attempt to possess human bodies and have to be exorcised. They are not always malevolent, however, and Surah 72 mention Jinn that were converted to Islam.[593]

John Kaltner, an American scholar, in his book *Islam: What Non-Muslims Should Know*, speaks of the distinction between angels and Jinn. He writes:

Islam makes a distinction between angels and another category of supernatural beings called "Jinn" (singular, *Jinni*), from which the English word Genie is derived. The relationship between the two groups is not completely clear. In Pre-Islamic times, the Jinn were spirits found in the desert and other places on Earth that are hostile to human beings. In Islamic thought, they have the capacity to interact with humans in ways that can both help and harm them.[594]

A Hadith from At-Tahawi (843–945) speaks of three different kinds of Jinn: A type that has wings and can fly through the air, a type that looks like snakes or dogs, and a type that stops for a rest and then resumes its journey.[595]

Other Muslim scholars also describe three kinds of Jinn. The first is called *Ghul*, from which we get the English word "Ghoul." They are spirits associated with graveyards. They have the ability to change their shape and form, and they dislike the daytime. A second variety of Jinn are called *Si'ia* who appear in many forms like snakes, black cats and black dogs. The most destructive form of Jinn are the third variety. They are known as the *Ifrit*. Their primary job is to test the moral characters of human beings.

Both Abu Buhaqi (fifteenth-century Syrian interpreter) and Al-Tabarani (873–970) confirm the three basic varieties of Jinn, but they give them different names. For them, the first type of Jinn are called *Amir*, who live with people. The second kind are known as the *Shayatin*, or Devils. They are the wicked Jinn. The third variety of Jinn, according to Buhaqi and Al-Tabarani, are the *Ifrit*. They are the strongest and most powerful kind of Jinn.[596] Both scholars also tell us that the way of life of the Jinn is much like that of human life. For example, the Jinn are morally accountable for their actions, just as humans should be, because the Jinn have free will, like humans, while angels do not.

All three varieties of Jinn are associated with magic in Islam. The evil Jinn have a tendency to enter human beings through six orifices (nostrils, ears, anus and mouth). Sometimes they go straight to the head, making people mad or delirious. Small Islamic traditions credit sneezing, coughing, hiccups and yawning to the Jinn. Some say the good Jinn do not bother people, but the evil ones do. The good spirits or Jinn are often called *Hafazah*, who only accompany believers when they are pure. The opening of Surah 72 speaks of the Jinn, who have converted to Islam. The text tells us:

> Say, "I have been informed that a number of Jinn had listened and then said, 'We have heard the wondrous Qur'an which guides to the right path and we have come to believe in it; and we shall not associate anyone with the Lord.'"[597]

The Muslim Holy Book, Al-Qur'an, at Surah 46:29, also speaks of a company of Jinn who "listened to Al-Qur'an." They arrived as it was recited, and they uttered, "Be silent!" because of their admiration for the truth.[598] With these clear understandings of the Jinn, we may now proceed to many of the other passages in Al-Qur'an, where the Jinn are discussed, followed by a section on the Jinn in classical Hadith literature.

The Jinn in Al-Qur'an

The Islamic category of the Jinn is described and discussed in twenty-two different Surahs, or chapters, in forty-four *ayats*, or verses of the Holy Book. Surah 55:15 speaks directly of the creation of the Jinn, "And We created the Jinn from the white, hot flame of fire."[599] The same judgment is made at 15:26–27:

Men, We fashioned from fermented clay, dried tingling
hard, as We fashioned Jinn before from intense, radiant
heat.[600]

Al-Qur'an's 7:12 also speaks of the Jinn being made from *Nar*,
or fire. Other passages that confirm the creation from "smokeless fire
can be seen at Surah 55:74. A second set of Qur'anic verses on the
Jinn speak specifically of the Jinn's power to whisper (*waswas*), and
therefore, to deceive human beings. One example of this phenomenon
can be seen in the final Surah of the Holy Book. It reveals:

1. Say, "I seek refuge with the Lord of men.
2. The King of men.
3. The God of men.
4. From the evil of him who breathes temptations into the
   minds of men.
5. Who suggest evil thoughts to the hearts of men.
6. From among the Jinn and the men."[601]

The Qur'an's Surah six, ayat 128, speaks of the Jinn misleading
humans. It tells us, "And on the day when We will gather them all
together and say, 'Oh you assembly of Jinn, many did you mislead
men.'"[602] In the same Surah, at verse 112, we are given this:

And so We have appointed for every Prophet enemies—
devils among mankind and Jinn, inspiring one another
with adorned speech as a delusion or by way of
deception.[603]

Although Al-Qur'an tells us that some Jinn are deceivers, human
beings, nevertheless, seek refuge from the Jinn. The Holy Book's 72:6–
7 tells us:

And verily, there were many among mankind who took
shelter with the masculine among the Jinn, but they
[the Jinn] increased them [mankind] in sin and disbelief.
And they thought as you thought, that Allah will not
send any Messenger to either Mankind or to Jinn.[604]

Surah 72 is named after the Jinn, and it makes a number of

observations about their nature. Verses five and six tell us "that neither men nor Jinn can tell a lie about the Almighty Allah." Verses one to four of Surah 72, speak of "A number of Jinn who has listened to Al-Qur'an," and then exclaimed, "We have heard the wondrous Qur'an." Surah 72:14–15 confirm that there are both good and evil Jinn. The text says:

> Some of us had come to submission, and some of us
> are iniquitous. Those who have submitted have taken
> the right course; but those who are iniquitous will be
> fuel for Hell.[605]

Surah six, ayat 100, suggests that some people "ascribe to Allah partners with the Jinn."[606] Verse 128 of the same Surah tells us that Allah will gather together men and Jinn on Judgment Day and say, "Oh you assembly of Jinn, you made great use of human beings."[607] Surah 7:38 speaks of "past generations of men and Jinn."[608] And Surah 46:18–19 tell us this about the Jinn: There are those on whom the sentence of Allah would be justified as on communities of men and Jinn before them. They will surely perish. Each will have a position in accordance with his deeds, and no wrong will be done to them.[609]

These four passages in the Holy Book of Islam (6:100, 6:128, 7:38 and 46:18–19), point to three similarities that the Jinn share with humans—they possess free will, they are capable of making moral decisions, and they will be judged at the End of Time on the moral quality of those decisions. The Holy Book's 55:33 speaks more about this capacity of the Jinn for morality. It informs us:

> Oh Society of Jinn and Men, cross the bounds of the
> Heavens and the Earth if you have the ability, then pass
> them beyond them, but you cannot unless you have
> acquired the Law.[610]

This passage suggests that only those believers who have accepted the Muslim *Fiqh*, or *Shariah*, or Muslim Law, can enter the life to come. But it leaves open the question of whether men or Jinn can, in fact, "pass over the boundaries of the Heavens and the Earth."[611] Surah 55:56 implies that both men and Jinn can deflower the Houris, or the comely maidens of Paradise, and ayat 74 of the same Surah makes the same claim.[612] This point about the kinship of humans and Jinn is also made in a number of passages in Al-Qur'an that many humans and Jinn are destined for *Jahannam*, or Hell. Among these ayats are 6:130–131, 11:119–120, 37:157–158, and 7:179.

The latter of these passages tells us:

> And surely, We have created many of the Jinn and Mankind for Hell. They have hearts where they understood not; they have eyes where they don't see; and they have ears but they do not hear the Truth; they are like cattle, nay even more astray, these people are heedless ones.[613]

Perhaps the most important place in Al-Qur'an to understand the nature and roles of the Jinn is Surah 51:56–57 that informs us, "I have not created the Jinn and men but to worship Me. I want no sustenance from them, nor do we want them to feed Us."[614] In the Islamic faith, the Jinn, like human beings, is simply another class of sentient creatures, and their principal aim is to worship Allah. Surah 55:44–45 tell us something of the Jinni's nature, as well as its destiny:

Undeflowered by man nor Jinn before them—
How many favors before your Lord
Will then both of you deny?[615]

This brings us to several places in traditional Islamic Hadith literature where the nature and functions of the Jinn are discussed at some length. As we shall see, much of these Ahadith confirm what we already have learned about the Jinn.

The Jinn in Hadith Literature

Most of the traditional collectors of Hadith in the Islamic tradition speak of the Jinn. In fact, even some non-traditional scholars like Yusuf Ibn Abdul Barr, an eleventh-century Sunni scholar, in his book, *The World of Jinn and Devils*, tells us these five things about the Jinn:

1. If one is mentioning the Jinn purely of themselves, they are called Jinni.
2. If one mentions the Jinn that live among humans, they are

called *Aamar*.

3. If one mentions those who antagonize the young, they are called *Arwaah*.

4. If one mentions those that are evil, they are called *Shaytan*, for the singular and *Shayatin*, for the plural.

5. If they cause even more harm and become strong, they are called *Ifrit*.[616]

A Hadith from Sahih Muslim tells us that "Every human being has a Jinn attached to him." He says, "There is none among you to whom a Jinn is not attached. They [the Companions] said, "Allah's Apostle be with you," whereupon he said, "Allah help me against them, so that I am safe."[617]

A Hadith from Abu Bukhari tells us what to do with our possessions when the Jinn might be around. He relates:

Cover your utensils, tie your water skins, close your doors, and keep your children close to you at night, since the Jinn spread out at such times and may snatch your things away. When you go to bed, don't put out the light, or a mischief doer may carry away the wick of your candle and burn the dwellers of your house.[618]

In another Hadith from Sahih Muslim, he tells us that the prophet said, "The Jinn sometimes intervene between me and my prayers and my reciting of Al-Qur'an, and this confounds me."[619] Al-Tirmidhi, in one of his Hadith, informs us about the Jinn:

The screen between the eyes of the Jinn and the private parts of the sons of Adam as one of them enters the privy is that he should say, "In the name of Allah, I seek protection in You from unclean spirits, both male and female."[620]

Another Hadith from At Tirmidhi tells us, "Don't clean yourselves with dung or with bones, for this is the food of your brothers, among the Jinn."[621] A third Hadith from Al-Tirmidhi informs us:

> The Prophet used to seek protection against the Jinn and the Evil Eye. Until Surah *Al-Falaq* and *An-Nas* were revealed. After they were revealed, he stuck to them and discarded everything besides them.[622]

Al-Falaq is the 113th Surah of Al-Qur'an, and *An Nas* is the 114th and final Surah of the Muslim Holy Book. Together, they are sometimes called "*al-Mu'awwidhatsyn*," or "The Surahs of Refuge," in that they both deal with the same theme, forming a kind of pair. Both Surahs 113 and 114 are Meccan chapters, and they both ask for protection from various evils like the darkness of the night, witches and the Evil Eye.

The 113th Surah makes a reference to the "Evil Eye." This is the name for a sickness or misfortune, with or without intentions by someone who is envious, jealous or covets, among men and Jinn. The Evil Eye can affect children, adults and even livestock. The most vulnerable to the Evil Eye are the young, the wealthy and the beautiful, for these people are most often envied.

A Hadith from Abu Dawood also speaks of the Jinn, particularly those who over-take the bodies of snakes. Dawood tells us:

> Muhammad Ibn Abu Yahya said that his father told him that he and a Companion went to visit Abu Sa'id al-Khudri to pay a sick visit to him. He said, "Then we came out from him and we met another Companion of ours. We went ahead and sat in the Mosque. He then came back and told us that he heard Abu Sa'id Al-Khudri say, 'Some snake are Jinn. So whenever anyone sees one in the house, he should give it a warning three times. If it returns after that, you should kill it, for it is a Devil.'"[623]

A similar Hadith from the *Al-Muwatta* tells us, "Shaytan and the Jinn do not lock a door, or untie a knot, nor uncover any vessel."[624]

Another Hadith recorded by Abu Dawood informs us about the Jinn:

> Ali said on the pulpit in the Mosque of Kufah that when Friday comes, the Jinn go to the market with flags, and they involve people in their needs to prevent them

from their Friday worship.[625]

Ibn Taymiyyah Majmu, a thirteenth-century scholar born in Harran, gives another account concerning the Jinn. He tells us:

> The numerous people who have experienced these events all confirm the amazing effectiveness of this verse in warding off the Jinn and breaking their spells. It has a great effect in repelling Devils from humans, from the possessed and from those picked out by the Jinn, such as wrong-doers, people with bad tempers, and those who follow their desires and lusts. Musicians, and those who become ecstatic through whistling and clapping. If these verses are read over them with sincerity to Allah, then the Jinn will leave, and it will put an end to the mirage created by the Jinn. It will also disclose the falseness of those, the brothers of the Jinn, who perform miraculous acts. The Jinn inspire their devotees with some knowledge that the ignorant think are miracles that Allah has granted His pious servants. In fact, they are simply *Shayatin*, or Evil Jinn, who perform acts of deception over their devotees, of those who have earned Allah's wrath and those who have gone astray.[626]

This tradition speaks of a number of attributes of the Jinn, as believed among Muslims. That they often employ mirages and "miraculous" deeds, deceptions and spells in attempting to harm human beings. It also indicates that there are techniques among Muslim scholars to ward off the Jinn. A number of other Ahadith about the Jinn also describe their capacity to turn themselves into animals, like this entry from Sahih Muslim:

> The Jinni may appear in the form of a dog or a black cat as confirmed when the Prophet said, "A black dog is a Demon."[627]

Another Hadith from Ibn Taymiyyah agrees when he writes, "The black dog is a Devil, and the Jinn often appear in its form, since the black dog can bring devilish powers more than any other color."[628]

Another similar Hadith from Sahih Muslim informs us:

> The Jinn can appear in the shape of snakes. Thus the
> Prophet blamed the killing of snakes lest any of them
> be Muslim Jinn.[629]

Abu Al-Bukhari speaks in a Hadith about the Jinni's ability to
transform himself into human form. He relates:

> The Jinni may appear in the form of a human being, like
> when a Devil came to Abu Hurayra in the shape of a
> poor, old man. And Abu Hurayra found the Devil taking
> much food of Charity.[630]

At-Tirmidhi cautions us to, "Say the *Bismallah* when entering
one's home, eating, drinking or when having intercourse. That will
keep the Jinn from entering the house or partaking with a person's food,
drink or sexual activity." He adds:

> Similarly, mentioning the name of Allah before entering
> the toilet, or taking off one's clothes will prevent the
> Jinn from seeing the person naked or from harming
> him. Thus, the Prophet said, "Say the *Bismallah*, when
> entering the toilet."[631]

The Arabic noun *Bismallah*, or *Basmala,* is a word to stand for
the phrase *Bi-smi llahi r-rahmani r-rahim*, which means, "In the Name
of Allah, the Most Gracious and Most Merciful." This is a phrase
recited before each Surah of the Muslim Holy Book, except for the
9th. The phrase is also used in various contexts, including the five daily
prayers. This Arabic phrase is also the opening of the preambles in the
constitutions of many Arab and Islamic countries, including Iran, Iraq,
Egypt, Kuwait, Pakistan, Libya, Afghanistan, Tunisia, the UAE and
Bangladesh, among many others.

Ibn Abbas, the cousin of the Prophet Muhammad and His
companions, tell us that the Jinn were on the Earth two thousand years
before humans and that they started causing much shed of blood. Then
Allah sent a group of *Mala'ika* to banish the Jinn to islands in the far-
away seas.[632] Ninth-century collector of Hadith, Iman Al-Bukhari,

informs us that, "All human beings are accompanied by a *Jinni*, that incites people to try to do evil." He also says that Muhammad was the exception to this practice because the prophet was assigned by Allah only to do the good.[633]

Finally, in a Hadith from Ibn Mas'ud, he gives us a tale about a companion with a Jinn. Abdullah Ibn Mas'ud (594–653) was originally a member of the Zuhra Clan of the Quraysh Tribe and later became one of Muhahammad's *Sabaha*, or companions. He tells us:

> Strength and faith in one's religion are the best ways to keep Jinn from harming humans, so much so that if they were to fight, the one who has the most faith would win. A man from among the Companions to Muhammad met a man from among the Jinn. They wrestled and the man knocked down the *Jinni*. The man said, "You look too small and skinny to me, your forearms look like the front paws of a dog. Do all the Jinn look like this, or only you?" He said, "By the name of Allah, I am strong among them, but let us wrestle again, and if you beat me I will teach you something that will do you good." Then the man responded, "Fine," and then he recited the following: "Allah there is no God save Him, the Alive and the Eternal. Neither slumber nor sleep overtake him. All of the heavens and the Earth belong to Him. No one intercedes with Him, save those of His leave. He knows what is in front of them and what is behind. They accomplish nothing of His Knowledge except what He wills. His Throne rules the Heavens and the Earth, and He is never weary of preserving them. He is Sublime, and the Tremendous.[634]

In conclusion, traditional collectors of Hadith literature suggest that the Jinn have their own communities and kings, much like those of people. Jinn eat, marry, reproduce and die. They possess free will and make moral decisions, which makes them susceptible to salvation or damnation. They are invisible to humans, but the Jinn can perceive people. There are both good and evil Jinn, and they may help, or harm, human beings.

King Sulayman and the Jinn in Islam

Another avenue for understanding the Islamic views of the Jinn is to look carefully at the relationship that Sulayman Ibn Dawood, or "Solomon, Son of David, had with the Jinn. The Muslim Holy Book calls Sulayman a *Malik*, or king, as well as a *Nabi*, or prophet. At Al-Qur'an's 27:16, we are told that Allah gave Sulayman special gifts, including the ability to speak with and understand animals. The previous ayat, 27:15, says that Sulayman remained faithful to Allah throughout his entire life.

The Holy Book of Islam, at Surah 38:55, maintains that King Sulayman was blessed with a level of kingship that "none has possessed after him." At 38:40, we are told that Sulayman fulfilled all of Allah's commandments, and he was promised a "nearness" to Allah in Paradise in the afterlife.[635] Most Arab historians regard Solomon as the greatest king of the world's rulers.

In several places in the Qur'an, the Holy Book speaks of Malik Sulayman's relationship to the Jinn. At Surah 34:12–14, the text tells us that Sulayman was given power over the Jinn and the *Shayatin*, or Devils. Indeed, he utilized the Jinn in his service. The Jinn carried out the king's orders, albeit grudgingly, and they were punished by Allah when they disobeyed. Another verse of the Holy Book, Surah 21:17, tells us that:

> And before Sulayman marshalled his hosts of Jinn, and men, and birds, and they all were in orders and ranks.[636]

Other accounts in Al-Qur'an, at Surah 38:35–39, for example, we are told that Sulayman was given dominion "over the winds." Another account suggests that Sulayman employed the labor of the Jinn in his major building projects, like the construction of the temple in Jerusalem.

Surah 38:55 and 34:14 informs us that the death of Malik Sulayman was a lesson to be learned from. At the Qur'an's 3:81 and 7:157 suggest that Muhammad Ibn Abdullah is mentioned in the Song of Songs, in chapter five, noting the consonant root MHMD and the Hebrew MHMDYM of Song of Songs 5:16, which are translated as "altogether lovely."[637]

Another tale of Sulayman and the Jinn involves the king's Vizier, a man named Asaf, who discovered that jewelry began to go missing from the palace. Sulayman prays for Allah's help. He entreats that the evil Jinn who stole his jewelry should be punished by God. Allah sends the angel *Mika'il* (Michael), who gives the king a gold ring. The angel tells the king to recite the words, "By the power of this ring may these demons [*Shayatin*] be punished," and the jewelry was immediately restored to their rightful owners.[638]

The main sources for these Qur'anic accounts of King Sulayman, of course, is the Hebrew Bible, the Talmud, and various Midrashic narratives about the king. Sulayman's dominion over the animal kingdom is derived from First Kings 5:13 that tells us, "He spoke of beasts and of fowl, and of creeping things, and of fish."[639] The tradition that Sulayman has control over supernatural powers was derived from Midrashic exegesis on passages like First Chronicles 29:23 that informs us:

> Therefore, Solomon sat on the throne of the Lord as King in place of his father, David. He prospered, and all of Israel obeyed him.[640]

The Muslim Holy Book implies that Malik Sulayman harnessed the powers of the Jinn for his ambitious building projects. Surah 34:14 alludes to a tradition regarding Sulayman's death.

According to Al-Qur'an, the king died while leaning against his walking stick; but his demise did not become known until a worm began to gnaw through the stick. Had the enslaved Jinn known this fact, they would not have continued their obedience to the king.

Another version of this tale has it that while leaning on his cane, the king silently died, but did not fall. He remained in that position, and the Jinn, thinking he was still alive while watching them work, kept to their labor. Malik Sulayman eventually falls forty days later. After that, the Jinn, along with humans, regretted that they were not allowed to know more than Allah has allotted them. This brings us to the next section of this eighth chapter, the idea of the Jinn in Richard Burton's *One Thousand and One Nights*.

Richard Burton on the Jinn

As we have indicated earlier in this chapter, the belief in the Jinn was common in Arabia, before and after the advent of Islam. The Jinn also were the inspiration of Arab poets and fortune-tellers. Even the Prophet Muhammad originally feared that his revelations of Al-Qur'an might have been the work of the Jinn. The Jinn, especially in their association with magic, always have been related to the magical arts in North Africa, Syria, Persia and Turkish folklore. At times, the Jinn are also at the center of an immense popular literature, appearing most notably quite frequently in Richard Burton's *One Thousand and One Nights*.[641]

In Volume III of the *Alf Laylah wa Laylah*, or *One Thousand and One Nights*, Burton tells us that there are Jinn who are "of the upper who fly or of the lower who walk the Earth, or of those who dive the Seas."[642] In the same volume, Burton speaks of a *Jinni* who "swears by the seal-ring of Solomon, Son of David."[643] The name of this *Ifrit*, or evil Jinni, is *Dahnash*, the son of *Shamhurish*, also called, "The Flyer."[644]

The very first of Burton's tales, called, "The Story of King Shahryar and His Brother," also gives an account of an *Ifrit*. Burton tells us about the Jinn, "They are generally, though not always, malignant beings, hostile and injurious to mankind.[645] In this tale, a female *Jinni* entices humans and tells them to come down. If they don't, the Jinni says:

> Allah upon you both that you come down forthright, and if you come not, I will rouse upon you my husband, this *Ifrit*, and he shall do to you that you shall die the illest of deaths.[646]

Later, in the same tale, Burton tells us that a female *Ifrit* is called a *Ifritah*, and points out that she "is not necessarily an Evil Spirit."[647] In a later narrative, called, "The Prince and the Ogress," Burton relates that the female version of a *Ghul* is called a *Chullah*. In a note to this narrative, Burton further explains, "Etymologically, a *Ghul* is a calamity, a panic fear, they are evidently the embodiment of horror of the grave and the graveyard.[648]

Richard Burton, in Night seventy-two of his *One Thousand and One Nights*, describes the angels, *Marut* and *Harut*, in a footnote. He says about this *Mala'kayn*, or pair of angels:

> They are two fallen angels who taught men the art of magic. They are mentioned in the Qur'an (chapter two); and the commentators have extensively embroidered the simple text. Popularly, they are supposedly to be hanging by their feet in a well in the territory of Babel; hence, the frequent allusions to "Babylonian Sorcery" in Muslim writings.[649]

Richard Burton adds:

> "And those who would study the Black Arts at headquarters are supposed to go there. They are counterparts of the Egyptian *Jamnes* and *Mambres*, the *Jannes* and *Jambres* of Saint Paul (Second Timothy 3:8).[650]

In early Jewish and Christian traditions, the *Jannes* and *Jambres* are names given to magicians mentioned in the Book of Exodus, at chapter seven, verses ten to twelve. Origen speaks of an ancient book called the *Book of Jannes and Jambres*, that purportedly contained many exploits of these two magicians. Others call the text in question the Apocryphon of Jannes and Jambres, the Magicians, the name of some Greek fragments in a Chester Beatty Papyri in Dublin, Ireland.[651]

In Burton's *One Thousand and One Nights*, the Englishman gives us another footnote on the Jinn. He tells us:

> *Jinni*. The Arab singular (whence, the French "Genie"); fem. *Jinnayah*; the *Div* and *Rakshah* of old Guebre-land and the "Rakshsa" or "Yakshe" of Hinduism. It would be interesting to trace the evident connection, by means of "accidental," or "Jinn" with "Genius," who came to the Romans through the Asiatic Etruscans.[652]

The British scholar Burton continues his analysis:

> We know nothing concerning the Jinn amongst the pre-

> Islamic pagan Arabs. The Muslims made a supernatural
> anthropoid being, created from subtle fire not of earth
> like man, propagating his kind, ruled by mighty kings,
> the last being *Jan Ibn Jan.*[653]

In Hebrew and Arab folklore, *Jan Ibn Jan*, or *Gian Ben Gian*, is the last of the seventy-two Jinn of Malik Sulayman, or Solomon. In Islam, he is the ruler over all the Jinn who labor on the king's building projects. It is said that he was overthrown by Azazael. Jan Ibn Jan also is said, in Islam, to be the builder of the pyramids of Egypt, and his shield was said to be a powerful magical lens that came into the hands of Malik Sulayman, allowing the king to bind demons, or Shayatin.[654]

Richard Burton also informs us that the plural of Jinn is *Jann* and that classes of the *Jinn* include the *Ifrit* (fem. *Ifritah*) and the *Marid* (fem. *Maridah*), who are usually but not always, hostile to human beings.[655] The phenomenon of the Jinn are discussed in many places in Burton's volumes, particularly in the first few volumes. There the Jinn are most often the enemies of humans, usually ought of spite. Roaming the world at night, the Jinn can transport human beings over great distances, as revealed in Night 76. He does this to make humans lose their ways. In Night 48, a Jinni turns a man into a monkey, and into dogs in Nights 5 and 66.[656]

On the other hand, Burton suggests that the Jinn sometimes restore men to their natural form, as in Nights five and thirty-four.[657] A Jinni protects another man who has been duped by another Jinn in Night 47.[658] In Night 78, Burton reveals that Jinn join together to sometimes do the good. A fisherman imprisons a Jinni in a jar in Night 11. This is most likely the origin of the tenth-century beliefs about freeing Jin from a flask, a jar, or a lamp, by rubbing it.

In other places of *The Thousand and One Nights*, a Jinni teaches a man how to free himself from possession by Jinn by means of exorcism. In the First Night, a man eating dates throws away one of the pits, and it strikes his child, killing him. This is also attributed to a Jinni. In Night 538, the prince of the Jinn takes humans to the "Black Country," that belongs to one of the Jinn kings.[659]

In another well-known story in *One Thousand and One Nights,* Burton describes a Jinni who has displeased King Sulayman and was punished by being locked in a bottle and thrown into the Sea. Since the bottle was sealed with Sulayman's seal, the Jinni was helpless to free himself. Many centuries later, a fisherman discovers the bottle and frees the spirit.[660] Another classical reference to a Jinni in Burton's volumes is the story of "Aladdin and His Lamp," in which a Jinni who has been trapped in a lamp is released after Aladdin's mother rubs the lamp.[661] The story of "Sinbad, the Sailor," described in Night twenty-nine, also mentions an evil *Ifrit,* that harasses the sailor in order to turn him toward the dark arts.[662]

Mr. Burton also outlines methods for avoiding the bad Jinn, that are divided into two categories. In regard to the first variety, anyone can accomplish these precautions, but in the worst variety of the evil Jinn, one must consult a specialist. Burton tells us that some of the precautions against the worst of the evil Jinn are that one avoid the places that they frequent like locations in the dark, don't spit or urinate in those places, and always say the *Bismallah,* and "with your permission," when visiting these places.

Richard Burton points out that some traditions about the Jinn in Islam is that they are to be found in ruins of abandoned buildings, graves and graveyards, bathrooms, dung heaps, garbage dumps and cemeteries. In fact, the Prophet Muhammad told his followers to avoid such places, and if one does to recite a *Adhkar,* an Arabic word that means to mention the name of Allah. A Hadith from Anas Ibn Malik, tells us that when the prophet entered a bathroom, he would recite, "Allahumma inni a'udha bika min al-khubuthi wal-khaba'ith." This line may be translated, "Oh Allah, I seek refuge with You from all offensive and wicked things, both bad deeds and evil spirits."[663]

Finally, Burton tells us that serious cases of illness and disease are caused by the bad Jinn, and that Muslims must consult a specialist, who are called *Khodja* or *Sheikh,* or more directly, "people without a religion." Another term, *al-Huddamli,* is sometimes employed in Arabic to describe humans who are patrons or servants of the Jinn, or those who cooperate with them.

The Turkish word for the exorcist is *Cindar*, and the corresponding word in Arabic is *Al-Djindar*.

These same specialists were to be consulted with by those humans who suffer from the curse of the evil eye, or those Muslims who wish to know the future. This brings us to an analysis of the views of Ibn Taymiyyah on the Jinn, perhaps the most famous scholar to write about the Jinn.

Ibn Taymiyyah on the Jinn

Perhaps the most famous Islamic work on the nature and activities of the Jinn is thirteenth-century Turkish scholar Ibn Taymiyyah and his "Essay on the Jinn."[664] Ibn Taymiyyah, in this essay, tells us a number of things about the Jinn, many of which we have seen in our analysis in this eighth chapter. One observation that Ibn Taymiyyah tells us about the Jinn is this:

> The Jinn usually communicate by either vision or voice [*sawt wa yamin*]. The gleaning of hidden information by way of visions and voices have been documented by clairvoyants and mediums. A medium may be defined as a person through whose agency or through whose organism there are received communications ostensibly from deceased human beings or other discarnate or remote entities.[665]

Later, in the same essay, Ibn Taymiyyah informs us:

> The Jinn may take the form of a live picture portraying whatever the sorcerers and fortune-tellers wish to know about. When these deviants see the image of what they sought, they then inform the other human beings about it. Some of them may actually know that the image is actually an illusion, while others may be deluded into believing that they are actually witnessing the real scene.[666]

Ibn Taymiyyah adds:

> Jinn may also make humans hear the voice of those whom they call upon who actually is far away. Such cases are frequent among idolaters, Christians, Jews, and ignorant Muslims who seek refuge in those whom

they consider to be Holy.[667]

Ibn Taymiyyah further observes that when slaves and servants are called by their masters, they are sometimes answered by the Jinn, using the master's voice. Ibn Taymiyyah adds:

> This has happened to many people, some of whom are known to me. The Devil will often respond while taking the form of one sought, whether alive or dead, even if he is actually unaware of who is actually calling him. Those committing *Shirk* [disbelief] in this fashion believe that a person beseeched has actually replied when in fact, it was a *Jinni* who was replying.[668]

The Arabic vocabulary of Ibn Taymiyyah's about the Jinn is filled with references to the words *Sarab* or "Mirage," *Takhayyal* or "Illusion," and *Khayal* or "Vision." Indeed, the Semitic root, KHYL, is the root for many words related to "illusions," "hallucinations," and "visions."

In Ibn Taymiyyah's essay on the Jinn, he also points out that the Jinn often employ oaths, or *yamin*, and incantations when they act against humans, but he also suggests that the Jinn, as well as their leader Iblis, tend not to be very successful among the most pious of believers.[669]

The Hanbali scholar Ibn Taymiyyah puts a great deal of emphasis on the role of deception and deceit in the operations of the bad Jinn. They use voices, visions and sometimes even impersonations in order to trick both believers and non-believers in the Islamic tradition.

Finally, Ibn Taymiyyah also points out that the role of that the *Jinni* plays in hallucinations and optical illusions is very strong, often making humans perceive something that is not actually there. This brings us to two final sections of this chapter, where we will explore the Jinn in Egyptian folklore, and the Jinn in the Sufi tradition, the mystical wing of the Muslim faith.

The Jinn in Egyptian Lore

Today, in the city of Cairo, and probably for many centuries, a host of tales are told concerning the Jinn. When Arabs invaded Egypt in the eighth century, many Egyptians actually attributed the building of the pyramids to the Jinn, as well as other ancient temples, like Karnac, for example. Shooting stars and meteors are also said to be related to the activities of the Jinn in Egypt. They are believed to be darts thrown by the angels at the evil Jinn. When Egyptians see a shooting star, they proclaim, "May Allah transfix the enemy of the faithful."[670]

It is said in Egypt that during the month of Ramadan, the Jinn are confined to prison, and hence, on the eve of the holy month some Egyptian women sprinkle salt upon the floors of their homes while chanting, "In the name of Allah, the Compassionate and the Most Merciful."[671]

It is also believed in some sections of Cairo that each quarter of the city has its own peculiar guardian *Jinni*, called *El Agathodaemon*, that is said to be in the form of a serpent.[672]

It is believed by some people in contemporary Cairo that in the time of the pyramids, the Jinn also built great cities, and that their kind populated these cities before the arrival of human beings. The good Jinn were then in Allah's favor, but if they offended Him or disobeyed Him, Allah sent an army of *Mala'ika* against them. Other Egyptian accounts suggest that the Jinn will remain on the Earth long after humans are no longer here. In earlier Egyptian times, it was common in Cairo that if someone spilled a liquid on the ground, the Egyptian muttered, "*Destoor!!*," which was a begging of the pardon of any *Jinni* that may have occupied that piece of land. This custom is described in the *Arabian Nights,* where a merchant kills a Jinni by throwing aside the stone of a date.[673] In another story in the same collection, a Jinni is represented as approaching a whirlwind of sand and dust and is warded off by a devout Egyptian shouting, "Iron, thou unlucky," for the Jinn are said to have a great dread for this metal. Much more was said about the Jinn in the *Arabian Nights* in an earlier section of this chapter.

Scholar of Islam, Nerina Rustomji, speaks of the pre-Islamic tradition in Arabia concerning the Jinn. She speaks of what she calls the *Kuhhan*, or soothsayers who were said, "to receive Divinely inspired poetry from the gods, or from the Jinn."[674] Ms. Rustomji continues,

"That is from beings of the Desert understood to be composed of vapor and flame," consistent with the Jinn coming from "smokeless fire."[675]

Dr. Rustomji, who teaches at Saint John's University, goes on to add:

The beliefs in deities and in Jinn suggest belief in an unseen world. Yet that world did not necessarily exist inside the realm of time. Instead, life existed on one plane of existence. Each person had a fixed time or *Ajal*. What happens after one *Ajal* is not clear.[676]

A few pages later, in the same book, Rustomji suggests that when it came to the Jinn in pre-Islamic Arabia, they are believed to have been at work within the spatial and temporal realities of the Earth. This helps, perhaps, to explain many of these ancient Near-Eastern beliefs about the Jinn that suggest that they may be harmed in the context of activities with human beings.

The Jinn in the Sufi Tradition

The mystical wing of Islam, the Sufi tradition, also contains a number of traditions regarding the Jinn. A text entitled, *The Stories of Awilya Allah*, for example, suggests that certain of the Jinn have taken initiation rites with certain Sufi masters.[677] Other sources in Sufi literature indicate that at times the Jinn assist the Sufis in transporting people quickly from one place to another. Other Sufi sources suggest that the Jinn may be responsible for some of the ecstatic states that Sufi masters sometimes find themselves in.[678]

Many of these ecstatic states and mystical experiences of Sufi masters can be found in the *Awilya Allah*, as well as in other mystical texts such as the poetry of Rumi, the sixteenth-century *Muhawi*, or his classical *The Light of Tirmuria*.[679] A recent book by American scholar Michael Sells, called *Early Islamic Mysticism*, gives a good account of some of these texts and mystical experiences.[680] Some Sufi historians and scholars suggest that these mystical experiences, as well as certain mental disorders and diseases, are the works of the activities of the Jinn. In fact, in the Sufi tradition, much mental activity—for both good and evil—are interpreted that way.

In the final section of this chapter, we will explore many of the ways the Jinn are similar and distinct from the *Mala'ika*, the angels, as well as similarities and differences in Islam to the *El Jins El Besheri*, or human beings.

Jinn Compared to Angels and Humans

In this final section, we speak of how the Islamic views on the Jinn are like, and not like, how Muslims understand angels and humans. This comparison can be seen in the following table, and the subsequent commentary about it. In this Table, H stands for humans, A for angels, and J for Jinn.

Activity/Role Created Beings

1. Possesses free will: H and J.
2. Makes moral decisions: H and J.
3. Capable of salvation/damnation: H and J.
4. Muhammad was sent to preach to H and J.
5. Appears to humans in various forms: J and A.
6. Sent as messengers of Allah: A.
7. Brings revelations to prophets: A.
8. Practices possession of humans: J.
9. Takes human and animal forms: A and J.
10. Made from clay, light or smoke: H, C, A, L, J, F.
11. Can be avoided with certain methods: J.
12. Can reproduce its own kind: H and J.
13. Is capable of dying: H and J.
14. The capacity to choose Islam as a faith: H and J.

Analysis/Discussion

By looking at the chart above, we can see that there are many ways that the Jinn are similar to human beings. Chief among these are the possession of free will, the ability to make moral choices, the ability to reach salvation or damnation, the capacity to choose Islam as a faith, the ability to reproduce one's own kind, and the capacity to die. Another similarity between humans and Jinn is that in both groups, the Prophet

Muhammad was sent to preach to them. Some Muslims, as well as some Jinn, respond to the faith of Islam in a positive manner.

There is some disagreement among Muslim scholars about whether humans can interbreed with the Jinn.

Additionally, we have examined in this chapter the "Essay on the Jinn" completed by Turkish scholar Ibn Taymiyyah, who, as we have seen, puts much emphases on the illusory capacities of the beings made from "smokeless fire." At the very end of Chapter Eight, we have supplied a chart that summarizes the natures and activities of the Jinn, compared and contrasted to the *Mala'ika*, or angels, and the *El Jins El Besheri*, or human beings. In that comparing and contrasting, we have seen many similarities and a few differences among the three classes of beings.

In the following chapter, we explore and discuss the figure of *Shaytan* or *Iblis* in the history of the Islamic faith. More specifically, we will attempt to show what roles these demonic figures, and their minions, have had in the Muslim faith. Along the way, we shall say more about the demonic in Islam in relation to humans, angels, and to the Jinn. As we shall see, there is at times, some confusion in Islam concerning those basic relationships, particularly contradictory evidence, from Al-Qur'an about the nature of Iblis.

We also can discover from our chart that the Jinn share a number of characteristics with the *Mala'ika* in Islam. Among these are the ability to take on human form, that they were made from something other than clay, and that they are usually invisible to the human.

But there are also some roles/attributes that are peculiar to angels in Islam, like being messengers of Allah and bringing Allah's revelations to human beings. These are roles that are unique to angels. We also have seen in this eighth chapter, that another major difference between humans and the Jinn is that the former has methods by which the latter may be avoided, while the latter does not. This brings us to the major conclusions we have made in this chapter.

Conclusions

In this chapter, we have described and discussed the Islamic category of created beings known as the Jinn, a group of sentient creatures who possess free will and are capable of salvation and damnation. We began the chapter by making some general comments about the etymology of the words *Jinni* and *Jinn*, as well as exploring where in Al-Qur'an these spiritual beings are described and discussed.

We also discussed where the traditional collectors of Hadith in Islam had turned their attention to the Jinn and their activities. We also examined a number of curious places in Islam where King Sulayman is said to have relationships with the Jinn. In that section of this chapter, we saw that Sulayman enlisted the Jinn in his army, as well as their working on some of Malik Sulayman's building projects, such as the temple in Jerusalem.

In another section of this chapter, we described and discussed a number of observations made by Richard Burton in his *A Thousand and One Nights*, where the Jinn are a topic of conversation. We have also shown that Burton makes many of the traditional judgments about the Jinn made in the Qur'an and Hadith literature. We also described some of the peculiarities that contemporary and historical Egyptians have made about the Jinn and their activities.

Additionally, we made some observations about how contemporary and historical Egyptians have made a number of unique observations about the Jinn. We also have examined some observations by Turkish scholar, Ibn Taymiyyah about the Jinn in his "Essay on the Jinn." And in the Final Section of this chapter Eight, we have compared and contrasted the ontological statuses of the Jinn, verses humans and the angels. We also have supplied in this chapter Eight, a Chart that sketches out the basic similarities and differences among the Jinn, the Humans, and the angels.

In the next chapter, we will explore and discuss the figures of *Shaytan* and *Iblis* in the Muslim tradition. More specifically, we will attempt to make some observations about the roles of these figures, as well as of their minions, in Islam to human beings as well as to the angels and the Jinn. As we shall see, there is some confusion in the Qur'an concerning the nature of Iblis, and those relationships. Indeed, as we shall see, the Muslim Holy Book, Al-Qur'an, offers contradictory evidence about the nature of Iblis.[681]

Chapter Nine:
The Role of the Demonic in Islam

He [Shaytan] promises them and entices them, but what the Devil promises is nothing more than illusion.

—The Holy Qur'an 4:120

Shaytan flows through human beings like blood does.

—Sahih Muslim, *Hadith*, Vol. II, Bk. 22, #5405

Good dreams come from Allah, and bad dreams come from Shaytan.

—Abu Qataba, *Hadith*, Vol. IV, Bk. 54, no. 513

Introduction

A number of the world's religious traditions have chosen to personify evil. Zoroastrianism, the ancient Persian religion, for example, gives the god of evil the name, Angra Mainya. In the Old and New Testaments, the demonic is known as *ha Satan*, or the Satan. Hinayana Busshism personifies evil as *Mara,* and in Norse mythology, the embodiment of evil was known as *Niddhogg*. This latter figure, according to Arthur Cotterell, in his book, *Norse Mythology*, is a dragon living under one of the three roots at the base of a cosmic tree called *Yggdrasil*.[682]

The Buddhist idea of *Mara* is thought to be a personification of the distractions that the world provides. Indeed, the traditional bad guys of the Buddhists, in their Pali Canon, are "dominated by the single figure of *Mara*, and there are many long passages devoted to this Evil One."[683] In traditional Judaism, *ha Satan* is associated both with the demonic, as well as the *yetzer ha ra*, or evil imagination or evil inclination.[684] And in the New Testament, the demonic goes by many names, including the Devil, Satan, the Evil One, Beelzebub, Belial, Samael and many others.

In Hinduism, both the gods Kali and Bhairrava, another name for Shiva, take on demonic qualities at times. A figure known as *Rakshasa* is another mythological creature of Hindu mythology. *Chemosh* was a Moabite demon; *Culsu* was the Etruscan figure of the devil; in Slavic Mythology, *Drekavac* is the name of a demon; and in some Native American tribes, a figure called *Dzoavits* serves a similar function.

Japanese mythology has a demon called *Jikininki* and another named *Oni. Lempo* is the Finnish devil; *Leyak*is is a demon in Indonesia, and their mythology has another devil named *Pocong*, and a third called *O Takata*. For both the Sumerians and the Akkadians, a figure named *Namtar* was a demon. And finally, Hungarian mythology speaks of a figure called *Ordog*, who is an embodiment of evil. From all of this, we may conclude that many, if not most, of the world's religious traditions, have personified evil, turned it into a bad god or some other spiritual entity.

The main purpose of this ninth chapter of this study of angels in Islam is to explore the concept of the demonic in the Islamic faith. As we shall see in this chapter, there are two separate names in Islam to designate the demonic. The first is *Iblis*, and the other is *Shaytan*.

In the opening section of this chapter, we shall explore the possible origins of these two Arabic terms, as well as where they appear in the Muslim Holy Book, Al-Qur'an. Additionally, we shall discuss Arabic vocabulary and transliteration associated with demonic figures in the Islamic faith.

In the second section of Chapter Nine, we shall explore and discuss a number of places in the works of the traditional collectors of Hadith literature, where either Iblis or Shaytan are discussed. In section three of this chapter, we will make some observations about the demonic in Islam in other Muslim sources, including traditional Islamic philosophy, as well as some observations from a number of Sufi scholars, the mystical wing of the Islamic faith.

We will also allude to certain Muslim theologians, who have made observations about the demonic in Islam. In this chapter, we also will explore the roles that Iblis, Shaytan and the Shayatin, the plural form of Shaytan, have played in the lives of many of the principal prophets in the Islamic faith.

In another section, we shall explore the question about the nature of the figure of Iblis. Is he a *Malak*, or "angel," or is he a *Jinni*, or a member of the "Jinn?" As we shall see, this has sometimes become a controversial question in the history of Islam. In fact, Al-Qur'an provides contradictory evidence about the matter, as we shall see later in this chapter.

As in the preceding chapters, we also shall end this chapter by cataloging the major conclusions we have made in it about the Islamic understandings of the demonic. We move first, then, to the etymology of terms about the demonic in the Muslim faith, as well as classical Arabic vocabulary related to these figures. Finally, we also will compare and contrast Islamic views about the demonic to the other classes of creatures we have introduced in earlier chapters.

The Origins of the Demonic in Islam: History and Etymology

As mentioned earlier in this chapter, there are two principal names or personifications for the demonic in Islam, Iblis and Shaytan. The former appears eleven times in Al-Qur'an, while the latter appears, along with its plural form, *Shayatin*, some eighty-eight times in the Holy Book. The plural form of the Arabic noun, Iblis, is *Abalis*, but it does not appear in Al-Qur'an, and only rarely in Hadith literature.

There are a number of theories regarding the origins of the word *Iblis*. Some say the word derives from the triconsonantal Semitic root BLS that has a broad meaning of words related to "grief" and "despair" in Semitic languages. One typical Arabic verb from this root is the word *balasa* that means, "He despaired."[685] Other Arabic words for "despair" and "grief" are also predicated of both Iblis and Shaytan. The words *yas wa mayus*, for example, are also terms for "despair." The triconsonantal Semitic root HZN is also another source for the Arabic language related to "grief." And "mourning," like *hazan*, "to mourn;" the word *Faqid*, or "mourner;" the words *huzin* and *shekwa*, are two other words for "grief;" and the verb *hazana* means either "to be grieved" or "to be sad."

A second theory about the origins of the word Iblis is that it is nothing more than a contraction of the ancient, classical Greek term, *Diablos*, a word for "devil." Or possibly, the Latin *Diablus*. There is no consensus among scholars, however, about the root of this term.

The word Iblis may be related to the Sanskrit *Devi* or *Deva*, which also expressed the idea of the demonic in ancient India. The word Diablo in Spanish is the term for the "devil." There is also an American submarine named the *USS Diablo*, and Lamborghini makes a sports car named the "Diablo."

A third theory about the origins of the word *Iblis* is that early Islam was influenced by either Zoroastrianism of Manicheanism's beliefs about gods.[686] These traditions found the universe to be bifurcated between good and evil, with one God being responsible for the good and the other for evil. In Zoroastrianism, the good God's name was *Ahura Mazda*, while the evil God was Angra Mainya.[687]

A fourth theory about the origins of the demonic in Islam is the suggestion that demons come from the Persian epic *Shahnamen*. In this work, there is a figure called the *Div-E-Sapid*. He is a White Demon, in fact, the chieftain of the *Divs*, or Demons. The White Div is a nasty monster, with horns like a cow and protruding teeth. Posters from the Iranian Revolution sometimes depicted Jimmy Carter, or Uncle Sam, as White Divs. The English word devil may have arisen from the Farsi *Div*, and in turn from the Sanskrit, *Devi*.

A fifth and final theory about the origin of the demonic in the Muslim faith comes from the *Tafsir* of Islamic philosopher Allah Ibn Abbas (619–687), uncle of the Prophet Muhammad.

Ibn Abbas suggested that the figure of Iblis came from the pre-Islamic period in Arabia, in which there was a belief in a God-Creator of evil known as Iblis. In Islam, that period is known as *Jahaliyyah,* or the "Period of Ignorance," in the early Muslim faith. The word *Jahaliyyah* is employed to designate those in Arabia who did not know about Monotheism or were "ignorant" of it. In more modern times, thinkers like Abu Al-Ala Mawdudi (1903–1979) have suggested that

Islam, in the face of modernity and the west, is engaged in a new period of Jahaliyyah.[688]

At any rate, the Arabic name Shaytan most likely derived from the ancient Hebrew *ha Satan*, a term that means "enemy," "adversary" or "opponent." The word Satan comes from the triconsonantal Semitic root STN that is generally associated with words related to opposition, temptation and the demonic. At any rate, the English word Satan also is most likely from the Hebrew Bible idea of *ha Satan*.

There is also a well-established Arabic vocabulary that is associated with the figures of Iblis and Shaytan. Among the verbs often associated with the demonic in Islam are *ishteka* and *shikiya* or "accuse" and "accusation;" *tam* and *tamma'* or "avarice" and "avaricious;" *fhish* and *ghashashash*, usually rendered as "deceit" and "deceitful;" the Arabic expression *ma beyyen el haqiqa*, that means "misrepresent;" and the words *qallad wa Qashmara* that refer the verb "to mock" and to "mockery."

Other Arabic verbs associated with the demonic in Islam include *ghashnash* or "to trick," *'akkas* or the verb "to thwart," and the Arabic terms *jedheb* and *tajriba*, which are usually translated as "to tempt" and "temptation." The verb "to sheme" in Arabic usually is transliterated as *debber*, and the words *boq* and *boqa* are best translated as "steal" and "stealing."

The Arabic nouns most often associated with *Iblis* and *Shaytan*, include the following:

1. *Ghishhish* cheat
2. *Tadlis* fraud
3. *Matrud* outcast
4. *Manfi* outlaw
5. *Desses* plotter
6. *Kedheb* liar
7. *Majnun* lunatic
8. *Hila harbiya* strategist
9. *Yatim* orphan
10. *Faqid* mourner

There is some disagreement over what Muslim scholars think the sin of Iblis is. Some say it is *tekebbur* or "pride." Others argue for *hasad* or "jealousy." Still, others say Iblis' sin is *'asi itali'* or "disobedience." Some scholars suggest the sin of Iblis is *za'al*, or "anger." And other thinkers regard the sin of Iblis as good, old fashioned *Hubris*, in the classical Greek vocabulary.

This Arabic word-study is consistent with the Islamic judgment that the main tool of Iblis or Shaytan is their "whispering" or *waswas* of evil ideas in the ears of humans. They hope that humans will join them in *Jahannam* or "Hell," if they give in to the temptations. The activities of Iblis are spoken of in the language of persuasion, as many of the Arabic words discussed above have indicated. This Arabic word-study also will be important in the final section of this chapter on the demonic in Islam, where we will explore the places in the Muslim Holy Book where Iblis and Shaytan appear.

The Demonic in Al-Qur'an

As mentioned earlier, the word *Iblis* appears eleven times in Al-Qur'an that are contained in seven different narratives about the figure in the Muslim Holy Book. These come at *Surah 2:*34, 7:11–18, 15:31–32, 17:61–64, 18:50, 20:116 and 38:74–75. Each of these seven narratives are connected in one way or another to the same story in Islam. This narrative has several parts. Among these are:

1. Allah creates Adam and asks him to demonstrate his great knowledge to the angels. That knowledge consisted of Allah allowing Adam to know the names of all of His creatures.
2. Since Adam's knowledge is so great, Allah tells the angels to fall down and pay homage to Adam.
3. All the angels comply except Iblis, who refuses to bow down to Adam.
4. Iblis refuses because he is made of "Fire," while Adam is made of clay or earth.
5. Because of his refusal, Iblis is cursed.
6. Iblis requests a reprieve until the Day of Reckoning,

and Allah grants it.

7. In the meantime, Iblis attempts to mislead humans in any way they can.

8. Allah informs Iblis that he will have no authority over His *Ibad* or "Servants," those who follow Allah. Allah tells Iblis, "As for my servants, you shall have no authority over them."

9. Iblis is granted his reprieve.

10. Iblis' status is to be reevaluated at the Resurrection of the Dead.

Each of these ten aspects of this narrative pertains to some portion of Iblis' refusal to bow down to Adam. In the process, the Muslim Holy Book employs the name Iblis eleven times.

The other references to Iblis in Al-Qur'an pertain to his nature, and whether he is a Malak, or angel, or a Jinni, one of the Jinn. Scholar Hasan Basra, for example, answers the identity question about Iblis by saying he is one of the Jinn. He observes about Iblis, "He was not an angel, even for the time of an eye-wink. He is the origin of the Jinn, as Adam is the origin of people."[689] Much more will be said about the identity of Iblis in a later section of this chapter.

The Arabic term, *Shaytan*, and its plural form, *Shayatin*, are used eighty-eight times in Al-Qur'an. Many of the mentions of the terms speak of particular attributes of the demonic in Islam. At the Holy Book's 4:120, for example, it informs us:

> Whatever the promises he [Shaytan] makes, whatever desires he enkindles, and whatever the hopes Shaytan arouses in them, they are no more than simply delusions.[690]

Al-Qur'an's 23:97–98 tells us that another attribute of Shaytan is that, "My Lord, I take refuge in you to keep from the whisperion [*waswas*] of the Shayatin.[691] In the final surah of Al-Qur'an, for example, at 114:1–6, the Holy Book employs the plural noun form of "whisperers," at 114:4, and the verb, "to whisper" at 114:5. The latter *ayat*, or verse, tells us that Shaytan "whispers into the chests [or hearts] of human beings." In early Islam, as in ancient Judaism, the seat of the self was thought to be the heart, as well as the organ of thought.

In several places, Al-Qur'an reveals a third attribute of *Shaytan*. Two examples of this attribute can be seen at the Holy Book's 2:169 and 6:142. The latter of these passages advise us: "Do not walk in the footsteps of Shaytan, who is surely your declared enemy."[692]

The Muslim Holy Book at 2:168 also tells us not to "follow in the footsteps of Shaytan, for he is your acknowledged enemy,"[693] and the same judgment can be found at Al Qur'an's 2:208, as well. We find the same admonishment at the Holy Book's 24:21 because he who follows those footsteps will be "enticed by what is shameful and forbidden."[694] Al-Qur'an's 17:64 tells us that, "The promises of Shaytan are nothing but deceit."[695] The Holy Book's 35:6–7 again tells that:

> Shaytan is an enemy to you, so treat him as an enemy.
> He only invites his followers so that they may become
> companions of the Blazing Fire.[696]

Several other passages of Al-Qur'an also emphasize that Shaytan is the enemy of any who believes in Islam, such as 2:208 and 6:142. Other verses of Al-Qur'an give us information about the demonic in Islam. Surah 24:21 tells us that Shanytan "advocates Evil and Vice."[697] Surah 7, ayat 179 appears to suggest that the Shayatin have powers "similar to a hypnotist."[698] And Surah 17, ayat 62 suggests that on the Day of the Resurrection, Iblis or Shaytan will be in control of "most people, save but a few."[699] Finally, Surah four, ayat 120 indicates that the only thing that Iblis really promises human beings is nothing more than *takhayyal*, the Arabic word for "illusion."[700]

Indeed, another Arabic verb that is often predicated of Iblis and Shaytan is the word *ghashash*, the classical Arabic verb "to deceive." This verb is employed at the Holy Book's 6:112–114 and 15:14–15, for example. In the former, the verb is used in the present tense, while in the latter, it is in the past tense, in reference to the demonic.

The Islamic Holy Book in several places highlights that the demonic is characterized by *takhayyal*, or illusion and *ghish*, or "deception." Among these passages are 6:22–24, 7:30, 18:103–104 and 43:37. Many of these verses indicate that Shaytan is committed to "straying from the Will of Allah. Both 7:30 and 18:104 is that verb in the Arabic text.

Five other attributes of Shaytan are suggested by Al-Qur'an. First, at 17:65, 15:40–42, 16:99–100 and 38:82–83 point out that no devil can have power over the faithful in Islam. The Shayatin can influence human beings, but not the most devout ones, or those truly devoted to Allah and His Holy Book.

Secondly, at Surah 3:175, we learn that "Only the Shayatin can make men fear their friends." Allah says, "But fear them not, but fear Me if you are true believers."[701] Thirdly, the Holy Book's 14:22 reveals that all of Shaytan's promises are "false promises," what today we might call "fake news." Fourthly, at Surah seven, ayats 200 and 201, we are told that if Shaytan whispers (*waswas*) in your ear, it is best to seek the help of Allah. And finally, in ayat 27 in the same Surah (seven), we are told that the Shayatin were made to be *Auliya' wa hafahd*, or protectors and helpers, for the *Kafarim*, or "non-believers." The verb *sa'ad* in classical Arabic is transitive. It means "to help." When used as a noun, it is usually *musa'ada*.[702]

From this discussion of the demonic in Al-Qur'an, we have made the following conclusions. First, that after Allah made Adam, Iblis refused to bow down to him because the human was made of clay, while he was made of fire. Second, the coaxing of Shaytan may be nothing more than delusion. Third, that Iblis whispers temptations into the ears and hearts of humans. Fourth, the Holy Book advises to not walk in the steps of Shaytan. Fifth, Shaytan is nothing more than a *Aduw*, the classical Arabic word for "enemy." The plural of this noun is Adwan.

And finally, when Shaytan is depicted as a whisperer or temptor, he is called *Ash-Shaytan*. The plural of the verb *waswas*, "to whisper" is *yuwaswas*, and the noun form is *Waswasa*. This brings us to the places in Hadith literature, where Iblis and Shaytan are discussed at some length.

Iblis and Shaytan in Hadith Literature

Many of the major collectors of Hadith speak of the roles of Iblis and Shaytan in their traditions. One of the most interesting features about the demonic in Hadith literature is that most of the traditions speak of the many harms that Iblis/Shaytan and the Shayatin may bring to human beings. Other traditions about the demonic in Hadith are pieces of advice about how to behave in the face of Iblis. Sahih Muslim, for example, tells us, "Do not pray [*salat*] at the rising of the Sun, for the Sun rises 'between the horns [*quran*] of Shaytan.'"[703]

Hadith number 2174 in Sahih Muslim's volume 1 of *Hadith*, narrated by Ibn Malik, tells us that:

> Shaytan flows through the bodies of human beings like blood does.[704]

Abu Muslim at volume 2, Book 22, number 5405, repeats the narrative of Iblis circulating in the human body like blood. This tradition is also employed as an epigram for this chapter. Other ahadih, the plural form, about the demonic and everyday life, includes Abu Hurayra's contention that yawning, or *tathawab*, comes from Shaytan. He also says that:

> Allah likes sneezing [*ya'tas*], but does not like yawning [*tathawab*].[705]

Abu Hurayra says the same thing in a Hadith from the same volume and book, but number 509. He also makes the same judgment at Volume 8, Book 73, numbers 242 and 245.[706] Abu Bukhari tells us that, "Oversleeping is caused by Shaytan residing in one's nose at night, at hadith number 238. Sahih Muslim also confirms that same tradition at Volume three, number 238.[707]

Abu Bukhari's Volume IV, Book 54, from Hadith 491 until number 516, all speak of the role that Shaytan plays in Islam. Among these is the claim that "Afflictions come out of the side of Shaytan's head."[708] Au Hurayra also speaks in his traditions of the many goings-on of Shaytan. At Volume IV, Book 55, number 641, for example, he tells us, "Babies cry at birth because Shaytan visits them in the womb."[709] Abu Hurayra also tells us:

> During sleep [*nom*] Shaytan begins to tie knots in the backs of the heads of humans, so that they might become confused [*qalabalough*].[710]

In another tradition from Volume II, Book 22, number 301, Abu Hurayra tells us that:

> Shaytan came in front of me and he tried to interrupt my prayers [salat], but instead Allah gave me the strength to choke him.[711]

In another Hadith from Volume IV, Book 54, number 522, Abu Hurayra observes, "When a Cock [dik] crows, it is because he saw an angel," and when a donkey [hamar] brays, it is because he has seen a Shaytan.[712] In another tradition from Ibn Abbas, narrated by Abu Dawood, they praise Allah because He "has reduced the role of Shaytan to mere whispers [waswas]."[713] Another tradition from Abu Qaraba tells us that, "Good dreams [ahlam] come from Allah, while nightmares come from Shaytan."[714]

Traditional Muslim collectors of Hadith also have commented copiously in Iblis. Ibn Abbas, for example, tells us that Iblis' "former name was Azazil."[715] Sahih Muslim tells us that, "The Throne of Iblis is upon the ocean, and he sends his representatives to test human beings and to sow the seeds of derision."[716] The classical Arabic word for "test" is imtihan, or its plural form Yomtahin. Sahih Muslim repeats this tradition at Volume III, Book 22, number 2925.[717] Al-Qayyim tells us this about Iblis in his Hadith:

> When Iblis and his warriors go to battle, they do not rejoice from anything more than a believer who killed another believer.; a man who died in a state of unbelief; or heart that is in fear of poverty.[718]

There are also extant several traditions that say that Iblis met the Prophet Muhammad, and they engaged in conversation, where Muhammad asks a question, and Iblis gives the answer. One thinker who tells this tale is Ismail Haqqat, a seventeenth-century Turkish scholar.[719] Philosopher Ibn Taymiyyah, in his famous *Fatawa al-Kubra*, argues against the authenticity of these Ahadith that claim that Iblis and Muhammad have met.[720] This brings us to the next, and central, section of this chapter—a discussion of the nature of Iblis.

The Nature of Iblis

At first blush, the Qur'an seems to offer contradictory evidence about the nature of Iblis. The issue is whether Iblis is an angel (*malak*) or a *Jinni*, one of the Jinn. Several passages of the Holy Book, such as 2:34, 20:116 and 38:71–74, all suggest that Allah ordered the angels (*mala'ika*) to prostrate themselves before Adam. And all complied, "except Iblis." This would seem to suggest that Iblis is an angel.

Yet, in another portion of the Muslim Holy Book, at Surah 18:50, the text reveals:

> When We said to the angels, "Bow down before Adam
> in adoration, and all bowed down, except Iblis.[721]

So far, so good. But the same ayat continues to tell us, "He was one of the Jinn and rebelled against the Lord's commands; and yet you take him and his offspring as friends, instead of Me, even though in reality, they are your enemies. How sad a substitute for the Evil-Doers."[722] This passage clearly indicates that Iblis is not an angel, but rather a Jinni, one of the Jinn.

Some Muslim scholars have attempted to solve this apparent contradiction the same way that Rashad Khalifa, Egyptian-American scholar, has done. Khalifa translates the beginning of 18:50 this way:

> We said to the angels, "Fall prostrate before Adam."
> And they fell prostrate, except Iblis. He became a Jinn,
> for he disobeyed the order of his Lord.[723]

Mr. Kalifa's translation appears to presuppose that Iblis was originally an angel before he became a Jinn. Other Muslim scholars, like Al-Tabari, for example, claim that there is a "special angelic tribe called the Jinn."[724] This same view also was held by Ibn Abbas, Musa Ibn Harun al-Hamadani, and Abu Al-Azhar al-Mubarak.[725] Contemporary Qur'anic translator, Muhammad Asad, also agrees with this view that the Jinn are angels. Indeed, in a footnote to Surah 18:50, Asad tells us, "This denotes in this instance, the angels."[726]

Although these solutions to solving the paradox of the nature of Iblis are ingenious, they are clearly unsatisfactory for a number of reasons. First, in a number of places in Al-Qur'an, angels are always said to follow the Will of Allah. See Surah sixteen, ayats forty-nine and fifty, for example. Iblis seems not to do that, so he could not be an angel. Secondly, the Holy Book, at 21:19–20 tells us that angels "glorify the praises of Allah, night and day." Iblis appears not to do that, as well. Thirdly, in several places of the Holy Book, Iblis tells us that he was made from fire (15:27), and Adam was made from clay or soil. But the *Mala'ika* were made from *Nur*, or light. If Iblis was made from fire (*Hareeq*), then that may be different from light. Indeed, Ibn Abbas tells us:

> All angels were created from Light, except this one angel [meaning Iblis].[727]

If that is true, and Iblis was made from *Nur*, then is/was no angel. In fact, Al-Qur'an at Surah 55:15 and 15:27, tell us that it was a special kind of fire, which in classical Arabic is called "smokeless fire." In one of his Hadith, Sahih Muslim puts the matter this way:

> The angels were created from Light, the Jinn were created from smokeless Fire, and Adam was created from that which has been described to you [meaning "clay"].[728]

Fourthly, Iblis was given the task of persuading humans to do evil things, while the angels were assigned the job of always following the Will of Allah, as well as assisting human beings. These seem to be very different reasons for being.

Fifthly, the Holy Book often points out that since the angels can do nothing but follow the Will of Allah, the *Mala'ika* do not possess free will. Iblis, on the other hand, seems to be operating as a free agent, independent of Allah. If that is true, then Iblis may be said to possess free will, and therefore he could not be an angel.

Iblis' refusal to bow down to Adam is an indication that he possesses free will, and so he could not be numbered among the *Mala'ika*, for they always follow the Will of Allah, no matter what. Finally, the Holy Book at Surah seven, ayat 179, informs us that Allah said, "We have created many of the Jinn and humans for *Jahannam* (Hell)". A similar judgment is at 55:39. Nothing in the Holy Book, however, indicates that any of the angels were created for damnation. So again, Iblis is no angel.

The bottom-line conclusion about the nature of Iblis should be obvious. Iblis was created as a Jinni, which is one of the Jinn. So, we must agree with Hasan Basra, noted Bukhara Jurist in the eighth century. He observes, "Iblis is not an angel, but the Father of the Jinn, as Adam is the Father of people."[729] This is the philosophical position held by many well-respected Islamic scholars, both Sunni and Shiite. Ibn Kathir, for example, in his *Tafsir*, asserts this about the nature of Iblis:

> Although Iblis was not an angel, he was trying to imitate
> an angel's behavior and deeds, and this is why he was
> included in the command to bow down to Adam.[730]

Other notable Islamic scholars who considered Iblis to be a Jinni were Ja'far Al-Sadiq, Ibn Kathir, and Al-Munajjid. Scholars of Islam who believed was the first of the Jinn include Zayid Ibn Ali Hasan Al-Basri, and philosopher Ibn Arabi.[731] On the other hand, Islamic thinkers who maintained that Iblis is numbered among the angels, include Ibn Abbas, Al-Tabari, Musa Ibn Harun Al-Hamdani, Abu Al-Azhar al-Mubarak, and contemporary Qur'anic translator Muhammad Asad.

Each of these latter scholars all maintain that the Jinn are/were a "special tribe" of the Mala'ika, as indicated earlier.

In our analysis, we clearly have sided with the "Iblis as Jinni" school. This brings us to the perspectives of a number of Islamic philosophers on Iblis and Shaytan, the topic of the next section of this chapter of this study of angels in Islam.

Iblis and Shaytan in Islamic Philosophy

Among the many philosophical views of Iblis and Shaytan in Islamic philosophy, a number of Sufi philosophers and Sufi theologians developed contradictory understandings of the demonic. One of these Sufi teachers we have in mind is Mansur Al-Hallaj (858–922), Persian mystic, poet and teacher of Sufism. Al-Hallaj is most famous for his monistic or pantheistic proclamation, "I am the Truth." Other interpreters, however, say that what the mystic meant was nothing more than the distinguishing of the ego.[732]

Over the centuries, countless Islamic philosophers and theologians, across different sects and legal schools, have taken, for the most part, a dim view of Iblis or Shaytan's place in Allah's Creation. Islamic philosophy, however, has not been unanimous in their presentations of Iblis/Shaytan's role in Islam. In addition to Husayn Al-Hallaj introduced above, the famed Sufi poet, Rumi, also had an unorthodox view of Iblis. The Hanbali Jurist, Ibn Taymiyyah, also had a view of the demonic outside the normal Islamic understanding of the figures in Islam.

The understanding of Al-Hallaj centers on the period before Shaytan's exile from the grace of Allah, and Al-Qur'an's 7:11 to 15. Al-Hallaj sketches out his view in his literary work, *Kitab Al-Tawasin*.[733] Al-Hallaj also uses poetry to further explain his views on the role of Iblis. Al-Hallaj suggests that when Iblis was told to bow down and worship Adam, Iblis answered this way to Allah:

> When Iblis was told to lay prostrate before Adam, he addressed the truthful Allah, "You have the lofty honor of prostration, and only by You may it be lifted. So, should I prostrate myself for him? By ordering me to lay prostrate, I will be prevented from Prostrating myself to You."[734]

In Al-Hallaj's view, Iblis is a classical, tragic figure, complete with his tragic flaw, pride. Iblis is also seen that way by Abd Al-Karim Al-Jili, fourteenth-century Indian Muslim mystic. Indeed, Al-Jili says of Iblis, "One day he will return to his place in Paradise on the Day of the Resurrection."[735] Thus, Al-Jili, too, thought that Iblis' sin was pride, and he was a classic tragic figure in the Aristotelean sense.[736]

Husayn Ibn Mansur Al-Hallaj often employed a pedagogical technique of the Sufi mystics that suggest that things exist because of their opposites. One cannot have light without darkness or cold without warmth. The life of Iblis is also described by Al-Hallaj as a combination of opposites. In the heavens, Iblis preached to the angels, while on Earth, he teaches people the ways of evil. In his book, *Taflis Iblis*, Al-Hallaj also sees Iblis and Muhammad as integral characters in the unfolding of Allah's Divine Plan, the philosopher's major response to the problem of evil.[737]

Indeed, for Al-Hallaj, both Iblis and Muhammad are instruments whose obedience to Allah is unswerving, despite the ordeals that each suffers Iblis was told to bow, and Muhammad was told to look. But neither obeyed. This fidelity to the Will of Allah links the Jinn (Iblis) to humanity (Muhammad). Neither strayed from his appointed path. Al-Ghazali (1056–1111), a great Muslim philosopher, wrote an essay entitled, "Shaytan's Ways to the Heart." For the most part, he borrowed many of the ideas of Al-Hallaj on Iblis. He also, for example, thought that Iblis' tragic flaw was *tekebbur*, or "pride" in Arabic. Al-Ghazali tells us about this:

> The story of Iblis has been related to you not as a mere fable, but so that you might understand the outcome of Pride. For it was Pride that compelled him to say, "I am better than him."[738]

The Persian philosopher, mystic and poet Rumi also makes a number of observations about Iblis/Shaytan in his *Mathnawi*, particularly Book II, Sections 2706 to 2743. There Rumi says of Shaytan, "I cannot overcome him, since he is the temptation and calamity of every noble and every lowly person."[739] At Section 2713, Rumi has Shaytan say, "Every man who is suspicious does not listen to the truth, every if there are a hundred signs and proofs of it."

At Section 2720, Rumi tells us about humans, "You curse Shaytan who is innocent, since you don't see that the cunning deceit [*ghish*] is from you." In Section 2730, Rumi has Shaytan observe, "Oh thinkers of fantasies full of suspicions, how do you know the difference between lies and the truth? (*yikdhab wa Haqq*). Rumi also relates about Iblis:

> The disease of Iblis was 'I am better than him,' and this same sickness resides In every human soul.[740]

Finally, Rumi also tells the tale of Iblis leading Umar, the Second Caliph of Islam, into a Mosque that contained one man at prayer, and another sleeping soundly. Iblis says, "I will destroy the man who prays because he is in the ecstasy of the love of Allah, while the sleeping man is only in oblivion."[741] In this narrative from the mystical poet Rumi he puts emphasis on many of the Sufi views of Iblis, including his tragic circumstances, his great love for Allah, and the mystical unison of the opposites of good and evil. Of course, one might expect the man in prayer would be commended, while the sleeping man is rebuked. In fact, however, in typical mystical Sufism, the poet has them do just the opposite.

Other Islamic philosophers who say much about Iblis/Shaytan include Ibn Taymiyyah, Ibn Kathir and Al-Tabari. The latter, in his work, *Al-Hilyah* suggests that Iblis has five sons. Their names are:

1. Thabir, who makes people imitate Jahiliyyah.
2. Al-Anwar, who encourages zina, or improper sexual relations.
3. Musawwat, who persuades people to tell lies.
4. Daism, who makes husbands angry at their wives.
5. Zulunbur, who sows temptations in the buying and selling at the *Souk*, or marketplace.[742]

Ibn Kathir (1300–1373), a highly influential Sunni philosopher of the Shaf'I School, tells us in his *Al-Bidayah was-Nihayah*, that, "Iblis cried loudly four times. First, when Allah declared him cursed (*mau'un*). Second, when he was thrown out of heaven. Third, when the Prophet Muhammad was born. And finally, when Surah Al-Fatiha was revealed." The Al-Fatiha is the first Surah of the Muslim Holy Book. It means, "The Opening." Its seven ayats, or verses, are a prayer that asks for guidance and mercy from Allah. Some see the Fatiha as a way of "opening hearts of the non-believers," (vol. 1, no. 166).[743]

Iraqi-born Ibn Taymiyyah (1263–1328), was one of the most forceful and accomplished Islamic philosophers and theologians in the Middle Ages. He was a member of the Pietist School of *Fiqh*, or "Religious Law," that was founded by Ibn Hanbul. Ibn Taymiyyah is important for our purposes because he was the author of the work, *The Devil's Deceptions*, and another piece of writing known as the *Essay on the Jinn*.[744] In these two works, Ibn Taymiyyah makes copious remarks about Iblis, Shaytan, and the Shayatin, as well as the Jinn. In the latter essay, Ibn Taymiyyah tells us that "Iblis whispered to Adam with four matters in mind. The first is how he whispered to Adam and Hawa, or Eve. The second is about the enmity between the Jinn and humans. The third is about the relationship of Iblis and he Jinn to magic. And the last is about the relationship of the Jinn to the angels.[745] About each of these four issues, Ibn Taymiyyah makes a number of key observations.

In *The Devil's Deceptions*, Ibn Taymiyyah tells us, "The biggest enemy of humankind is Shaytan because our father Adam and mother, Hawa, were removed by him from Paradise. He adds, "It also was him who made false promises and lured humans, making them follow their desires [*irada*] and disobey [*asiyin*.] Allah. Whereby, they were really oppressing themselves because disobedience to Allah is self-oppression."[746] Ibn Taymiyyah also tells us that since "the day that Allah expelled Shaytan from Paradise, he and his offspring have been coming up with plots [*daysayis*] and tricks [*hiyal*], to lead the offspring of Adam astray." "Shaytan," Ibn Taymiyyah tells us, "is a tool or a test where a person's level of self-trust and self-control is known by Shaytan. This is how Shaytan always calls people to disobedience toward Allah; and he works hard to get more and more people to come with him to Hell Fire."[747]

In *The Devil's Deceptions*, Ibn Taymiyyah likens the actions of Iblis to a thief (*harami*) in the night. He observes, "Iblis is like a bandit. Every time a person wants to travel towards Allah, Iblis tries to intercept him."[748] One chapter of this work is entitled "The Cure from the Arrows of Iblis." In this chapter, Ibn Taymiyyah provides three pieces of advice for those who have been hit by the arrows of Iblis, or those who wish to avoid him. First, get married or find a slave-woman. Second, remain constant in one's five daily prayers. And finally, remove oneself from any place or person who has deeply affected him. Ibn Taymiyyah concludes this chapter by observing:

> Distance leads to abandonment, and as much as the thought of something is reduced, its effects on the heart [*qalm*], also will be weakened. So, one should implement these steps, and he should improve with the resultant changes that occur in his condition.[749]

A final Islamic philosopher who has written about Iblis and Shaytan is Imam Ibn Jawzi (1126–1200). Ibn Jawzi was a Sunni Muslim Jurist, theologian and philosopher of the Hanbali School. Ibn

Jawzi was also the author of a work called *Tablis Iblis*, also translate *The Devil's Deceptions*. In this work, Ibn Jawzi makes a number of observations about Iblis/Shaytan, including his observation that Iblis "does his damage through *waswas*," or "whispering," and that Iblis is to be numbered among the Jinn.[750]

The Demonic and the Prophets of Islam

There are a variety of narratives in the Islamic faith, where the demonic has some relations with the prophets of Islam. Among these Muslim prophets are Adam; Musa; Sulayman; Yahya, or John the Baptist; Idris; Nuh, or Noah; and Nabi Ayyub, or Prophet Job.

Already, we have said much about the interplay between Adam and Shaytan. It was Shaytan who enticed Adam and Eve to eat from the forbidden tree. It was the refusal of Iblis to bow down to Adam that was the cause of the fall and curse of Iblis, and it was Iblis who proclaimed his desire to mislead the sons of Adam.

One tradition about Prophet Musa (Moses) in the Islamic tradition in regard to Iblis/Shaytan is that it is said that Shaytan approached Nabi Musa and said, "You are a Prophet of the Lord and I am one of his sinners. I desire to repent before Him. So, could you ask Him to accept my repentance? [*toba*]" Musa agreed and prayed for Iblis, whereupon Allah said:

> Oh Musa, I shall accept your intercession for him. Tell him to prostrate before Adam's grave in order for me to accept his repentance.[751]

Upon hearing this, Iblis said, "I did not prostrate before Adam while he was alive. How can I prostrate before his grave when he is dead? I shall never do such a thing." The Iblis said to Musa, "Since you now have obliged me, I will now give you three pieces of advice, so that you don't face damnation. First, when you are in a state of anger, I am inside your heart and my eyes are inside your eyes. Second, in a state of Jihad [battle], I cause soldiers to bring their wives and children to mind, so they lose track of the battle. And third, never sit close to a comely woman, for I will whisper temptations into the ears of both of you.[752]

Another tradition about Iblis and Prophet Musa comes from a Persian psychiatrist and writer of Sufi mysticism, Javad Nurbakhsh (1926–2008). Dr. Nurbakhsh also was the Chief Minister of the Nimatullahi Sufi Order. He tells us about Iblis and Musa:

> Encountering Iblis on the slopes of Mount Sinai, Musa hailed him and asked, "Oh Iblis, why do you not prostrate yourself before Adam?" Then Iblis replied, "Heaven has forbidden that anyone worship anything but Allah...This command was a Test."[753]

This tradition displays a few features about Iblis that often are found in Sufi literature. First, Iblis is shown in dialogue with a luminary from Islam. Second, Iblis recognizes that only Allah should be worshipped. For him, bowing down to Adam would constitute a form of disrespect to Allah.

Shaytan also gives three pieces of advice to Nabi Nugh, or Prophet Noah. They come in lieu of the prophet's time in his ark. Shaytan is reported to have said:

> Now in reciprocation of your good deeds, I shall give you three pieces of advice. First never exhibit arrogance [muttekebbir], for it was because of this vice that I did not prostrate before Adam. Secondly, stay away from greed [tamma], for this is why Adam consumed the wheat [hanta], and was deprived of Paradise. Thirdly, distance yourself from envy [hasad], for it is because of this vice that Cain killed Abel, and eventually perished because of Divine Punishment [Qisas].[754]

The mention of "wheat" in the above tradition is connected to an Islamic view that the forbidden fruit was wheat. In classical Hebrew, the word for wheat is *khitah*, which may be a pun on the word *khet* that means "sin." This view can first be seen in a comment by Rabbi Yehuda in the Talmud, at *Berachot*, 40a and *Sanhedrin*, 70a. A number of later Muslim scholars also adopted this view. The Arabic word for "wheat" *hanta* may have come from the Hebrew Khetor Khetah.

Another Islamic narrative tells of Iblis and Prophet Yahya Ibn

Zakariyyah. Yahya is the Arabic name for John the Baptist, of the New Testament. Nabi Yahya approached Iblis, who is carrying numerous ropes [*hanta*] in his hands. The prophet asks, "Why are you holding those ropes in your hands?" Shaytan replied:

> These ropes [*hibal*] are the various attachments, inclinations, and lusts that I have found in the children of Adam.[755]

Then Yahya asks, "Is one of these ropes for me too?" Then Iblis answered, "Yes, when you overeat, you experience a weightiness and it is for this reason that you become disinclined with respect to doing your prayers, to *Dhikr*, and supplication. To this, Nabi Yahya responded, "Never shall I eat my fill again." To which Iblis answered, "And I shall never advise someone again."[756]

The Arabic word Dhikr in the quotation above is a form of devotion among those in the Sufi tradition. In a state of *Dhikr*, the worshipper is absorbed in the rhythmic repetition of the name of Allah, or His attributes. The plural form of the noun is *Zikirs*.

Several narratives about Nabi Idris, or Enoch, appear in the Holy Book of Islam. Some of these can be found at Surah 19:56, 21:85–86, and at Surah Maryam, ayats 56 and 57. In a narrative from Persian philosopher Ishaq Al-Isfarayini, he observes:

> Shaytan came to Prophet Idris, who was sewing. Every time he put a stitch in, he would say, "Allah is free of imperfections." And every time he pulled it out, he would utter, *Al-Humdullah*, or "praise and thanks to Allah."[757]

Then Shaytan brought a peel to Idris, and he asked, "Could Allah fit the universe inside this peel [*gishir*]? Then the Prophet Idris poked the eye of Shaytan with a needle, and this is how he became one-eyed [*a-war*]. Indeed, there are many traditions in Islam that suggest that both Shaytan and the Antichrist [*at-Dajjal*] are one-eyed.[758]

There are also extant a significant number of traditions and tales concerning Nabi Ayyub, or "Prophet Job," and his relationship with

Shaytan. For the most part, the Islamic views on Job closely follows the narrative in the Hebrew Bible, or Old Testament, with a number of significant differences. We will speak of seven of those differences here. First, the Old Testament book says nothing of Job's lineage, while Islam says he was "The son of Amwas, the son of Aaes, the son of Ishaq, who was the son of Ibrahim [Abraham]."[759]

Secondly, the Old Testament implies that Job's faith in God becomes stronger as Satan is given more and more permission to take away Job's possessions (his house, animals, children, etc.). In the Islamic tradition, Nabi Ayyub becomes more and more thankful. Thirdly, in the Hebrew Book of Job, there are restrictions placed on Satan in regard to Job. In Islam, Shaytan is told he cannot touch Ayyub's heart, eyes, tongue, and ears.[760] In another version, Allah tells Shaytan, "You have been given power over Ayyub's body, but not his *aquil*, or power of reasoning."

A fourth difference of the Islamic view of Job to that of the figure in the Hebrew Bible is the nature of Job's disease. Ibn Asaker says of the illness, "It lasted a long time until his visitors became disgusted with him. His friends kept away from him. No one gave him sympathy but his wife.[761] Nothing like this appears in the Hebrew Book. A fifth difference between the two traditions has to do with the way the patriarch/prophet is depicted in iconography. In the Judeo-Christian tradition, Job is portrayed with sores over his entire body. Whereas, in Islam, he is shown as a much younger man whose sores already have been healed. Nabi Ayyub is always shown with smooth skin in Muslim iconography.

A sixth difference the two traditions have about Job is how long he suffered. The Old Testament book says nothing about this issue, while the Islamic tradition offers many answers to the question. According to some Muslim thinkers, Ayyub's suffering last eighteen years, and according to others, it was only seven years. This latter view is the more prevalent one.

Finally, the Islamic view of Nabi Ayyub, Shaytan is said to be angry for Ayyub's following the ways of Allah, and he becomes increasingly angry as the book goes on. The Hebrew Book, of course, says nothing about the anger of Job nor that of Satan, as well.[762]

A number of traditions exist in the history of Islam about Nabi Sulayman, Iblis-Shaytan, and the Jinn discussed earlier in Chapter Eight. One is related to the king's death. Sulayman was seated on his throne, holding his staff, while overseeing the Jinn at the same time. Indeed, the king died in this position, and, for the longest time, no one noticed it. The Jinn continued in their toils, but none the wiser about the state of Sulayman.

Many days later, or so the story goes, a hungry ant began nibbling at the king's staff. He continued to do so until it fell from the king's hand, and Sulayman fell to the ground. His people hurried to him, realizing that he had died some time before, and the Jinn did not perceive the situation. Had they known the status of the king, they would not have continued to work, for they believed Sulayman still was alive.

We close this chapter here because Iblis is/was to be numbered among the Jinn, as we have maintained earlier.

Conclusions

This chapter has been devoted to explanations of the concepts of the demonic in the Islamic faith. We began the chapter with a short section on the possible historical and etymological origins of the Arabic terms *Iblis, Shaytan* and the *Shayatin*. In this opening section, we also supplied a transliterated Arabic vocabulary of verbs, nouns and adjectives, often associated with the demonic in the Islamic faith.

This was followed by a second section devoted to the many places in the Muslim Holy Book, Al-Qur'an, where these Arabic terms are employed. Indeed, from this second section of this chapter, we enumerated a number of attributes of the demonic, as expressed in the Holy Book of Islam.

The places in many of the major collectors of Hadith, where the demonic is commented upon, has been the topic of the third section of Chapter Nine. There we explored some traditions on the demonic from Sahih Muslim, Aby Hurayra, Aby Bukhari, as well as another half a dozen collectors of Hadith. What we have discovered in this section are the many schemes, tricks and strategies that Iblis, Shaytan and the Shayatin have employed against humanity.

In section four of this chapter, we have conducted an inquiry into the nature of Iblis. Is/was he a Jinn or an angel. The final conclusion we have come to in section four of this chapter is that Iblis is, indeed, a Jinni, despite what appears to be contradictory evidence on this question in Al-Qur'an. Ideas about the demonic among Muslim philosophers was the subject matter of section five of this chapter. There, we have explored comments about the demonic from Al-Tabari, Al-Ghazali, Ibn Abbas, Ibn Taymiyyah and Ibn Kathir, among a host of other Islamic philosophers and theologians. For the most part, as we have seen, these comments mirrored those of the demonic to be found in Hadith literature.

In the sixth and final section of Chapter Nine, we explored the many relationships between Iblis/Shaytan and the Islamic *Anbiya,* or "prophets." Indeed, in this sixth section, we have discussed narratives concerning Adam, Sulayman, Idris, Ayyub, Yahya, Musa, Ibrahim, and Nuh, among others of the Muslim prophets. Again, we have seen in this material that these traditions have tended to concentrate on a very few issues: to wit, the techniques of the cunning of the demonic the superiority of the moral status of the prophets in relation to Iblis/Shaytan, and a discussion of the nature and influences of the demonic in Islam.

Chapter Ten:
Major Conclusions of this Study

They do not disobey Allah's commands that they receive; they do precisely what they are commanded at all times.

—The Holy Qur'an 66:6 (Author's translation)

The Prophet believes in what has been revealed to him by his Lord and so do the faithful. Each one believes in Allah, and His angels, His books and the Prophets, and we make no distinctions among the apostles. For they say, "We hear and obey, and we seek Your forgiveness, Oh Lord.

—The Holy Qur'an 2:285 (Author's translation)

The Angelology of Islam is very extensive and has been treated only partially by Western scholars, although it holds such an important place in the belief of popular Islam.

—Samuel M. Zwemer, "The Worship of Adam by Angels" (1937)

Introduction

The major goal of this chapter is to describe and to discuss the most important ideas about angels in the Islamic faith from the previous chapters. In that sense, this chapter should be seen as a summary or a highlight reel of what has come before it in this study of the *Mala'ika*, or angels.

Along the way, in this tenth chapter, we also will review what conclusions we have made in this study on Allah's other creatures in Islam—the *Houris,* the *Jinn,* and the two figures of the demonic in the Muslim faith—*Shaytan wa Iblis*, or "Satan and Iblis." We also will make conclusions about how these other creatures of Allah are related to the *Mala'ika*. It is best to see the organization of this study as having five parts. Part one consists of the introduction and Chapter One on the nature and functions of angels.

Part two of this study, Chapters Two and Three, are devoted to archangels in Islam; the former chapter to the angel Jibril, the most important angel in Islam, and the latter chapter to the other archangel.

Part three, Chapters Four and Five, deal with angels associated with death, or *Mawt*, in Islam, and with the Houris. Part four consists in chapters on the guardian and recording angels and angels in Islamic art, Chapters Six and Seven. Finally, part five of this study, Chapters Eight and Nine, deal with sentient creatures in Islam, other than the *Mala'ika*. In that regard, Chapter Eight is devoted to an explication of the Jinn; and Chapter Nine to the roles of the demonic in the Islamic faith.

We begin, then, by discussing the first part of this study, the introduction and the nature of the angels in Islam.

Part One: Introduction and the Nature of Angels in Islam

In the introduction of this work, we sketched out what was to come in the next nine chapters of this study on angels in Islam. In that introduction, we have provided a primer on the entire work.

The principal goal of Chapter One was to provide a basic description of what we know about the ontological status of the category of the *Mala'ika* in the Islamic faith. We began the chapter by describing the basic Arabic vocabulary in regards to angels in the Muslim faith, including the words *Malak*, *Mala'ika* and *Malakayn*, or "angel," "angels" (plural form), and "angels" (dual form). We also indicated in the opening of Chapter One the Semitic root MLK, the source for these words in Arabic. We also indicated other classical Arabic words from the same tri-consonantal root, like *malak*, or "king" or "messenger," and *Malik*, or "king."

We then have pointed out in the opening chapter of this study that belief in angels is one of the six principal "Articles of Faith" in Islam, as indicated by the second epigram of this chapter. Those six beliefs were/are:

1. Belief in Allah and His Oneness
2. His Angels
3. His Prophets
4. His Revealed Books
5. The Afterlife
6. And Destiny and Divine Decree[763]

The remainder of Chapter One has been taken up with a discussion of the nature and extent of the category of the *Mala'ika* in Islam. To that end, we have shown where the language about angels in Islam shows up in the Muslim Holy Book, Al-Qur'an. Altogether, we have shown that the Arabic words, *Malak, Mala'ika* and *Malakayn* appear in the Holy Book about one hundred times.[764]

About the nature of the angels in Islam, we have shown in Chapter One that the *Mala'ika* are spiritual, non-material beings who put the commands of Allah into actions in the world. They have no wills of their own, unlike humans and the Jinn, and they act as intermediaries between Allah and the world. Since angels in Islam are not physical beings, they cannot be seen by human beings. The *Anbiya*, or "Prophets in Islam," do have the capacity to experience the angels. Some Muslim scholars maintain, however, that this "seeing" of the angels by the prophets of the faith is a "seeing with a spiritual, or mind's eye, as in dreams and visions."

We also have shown in Chapter One of this study that the *Mala'ika* perform two different kinds of functions, a function in the physical world, and a function in the spiritual world. In the former realm, the angels are governed by the laws of nature. In the spiritual realm, the angels communicate Allah's revelations to the prophets, as well as other righteous people. In this capacity, the *Mala'ika* bring comfort and strength to the hearts of true believers; and also inspire noble thoughts in the minds of people.

In the same way that light is needed as a medium for the eyes to see, and air is necessary to carry sounds to our ears, similarly, human beings have a capacity to activate our spiritual understanding. The angels are that agency for humans. They bring Allah's messages to the "inner" eyes and "inner" ears of righteous people. The angels in Islam also cast good and noble thought into the hearts of humans, but it is only the righteous, who, because of their highly developed spiritual senses, that they may be able to perceive the workings of the *Mala'ika*.

The Muslim Holy Book, Al-Qur'an, tells us that humans have been given by Allah the ability to acquire knowledge of all things in the universe. The Holy Book also reveals that the angels, who put Allah's laws into action in the world, submit to humans because of their great knowledge. In other words, people can use their knowledge of the laws of nature to control the world. So Al-Qur'an disclosed many centuries ago that humans can make the greatest progress in the sciences and technologies, because of the angels—the agents who put Allah's laws into action in the running of the world.

We also have shown in the opening chapter that every belief in Islam requires the Muslim to do something positive and productive. The Holy Book tells us to follow our good impulses and to reject the bad ones. Al-Qur'an also suggests that there are "devils," or *Shayatin*, that attempt to put low, selfish thoughts in the hearts and minds of humans. Even though they exist, however, the Holy Book does not require a Muslim to believe in devils, and, in fact, to disbelieve in them. The belief in the *Mala'ika*, on the other hand, is something that is required of all Muslims. In fact, as we have shown, it is one of the "Six Articles of Faith."

The belief in angels, then, is one of the issues of the *Ghaib*, or "Unseen World." The angels, as we have shown in Chapter One, are entities that possess intelligence and comprehension, and are honorable servants of Allah. They are totally subservient to Allah, and they never exhibit insubordination to Him. The Mala'ika have been assigned important and greatly varied responsibilities from Allah.

One group of angels hold up the *Arsh*, or "Throne," of Allah. Another group seizes the souls of people at death. Another group of *Mala'ika* is vigilant in the recording of the deeds of humans, and another group of angels protects humans from perils and from untoward incidents.

Some Muslim angels have been given the responsibility for punishing and chastising the rebellious and recalcitrant nations on Earth, and other angels have been assigned to aid believers during battle. And, most importantly, some of the *Mala'ika* bring down the revelations and the Divine Books of the Muslim faith. The angels are perpetually engaged in the glorifying of Allah. As the Muslim Holy Book tells us at Surah 42:5:

> And the angels sing the praises of their Lord, and they
> ask for forgiveness for those who are on the Earth.[765]

We have shown in the opening chapter of this study that angels are made from light. They do only what Allah tells them to do, and they cannot ever disobey, because, unlike humans and the Jinn, they have no free will. The Islamic angels pray, worship and glorify Allah all the time.

In another section of Chapter One, we provided an analysis of the concept of the *Ruh al-Qudus*, or "Holy Spirit," in Islam. In that analysis, we have shown that there are two principal theories concerning the nature of the "Holy Spirit" in the Islamic faith. The first of these is to maintain that the angel *Jibril*, who brought Al-Qur'an to Prophet Muhammad, is identical with the *Ruh al-Qudus*.

The second theory we have put forth about the Holy Spirit in Islam is that he functions much like the idea of the Holy Spirit of the New Testament.

As indicated by this, we did not mean that the Muslim faith believes in the Trinity. Clearly, there are explicit indications against the idea of the Christian Trinity in Al-Qur'an. Some of these come at 4:171, 5:73 and 5:116. The first of these tells us:

> So believe in Allah and His apostles and do not call Him
> Trinity. Abstain from this for your own good, for Allah is
> the only One God.[766]

Surah five, ayat 73 concurs. It reveals:

> Disbelievers are those who surely say, "Allah is the third
> of the Trinity. But there is no God other than Allah; and
> if they do not desist from saying what they say, then

they are in a state of disbelief; and for this they will suffer painful punishment.

The Muslim Holy Book again returns to the issue of the Trinity in Islam, when it reveals at 5:116:

And when Allah will ask, "Oh Jesus, son of Mary, did you say to human beings, 'Worship me and my mother as two deities apart from Allah,' Jesus will answer, 'Halleluja! Could I say what I knew I had no right to say?' For you know what is in your heart, but I know not what you have. You alone know the secrets of the unknown."

Although it is clear that Al-Qur'an is against the idea of the Christian Trinity, nevertheless, there is some indication that the constructors of the Holy Book, at Surah 5:116, believed that the Trinity consists of God, Jesus and Mary, the mother of Jesus. In that sense, the makers of Al-Qur'an did not fully understand what the concept means. The text in question reveals:

Beware of the Day when Allah will say, "Oh Jesus, son of Mary, did you say to the people, 'Take me and my mother as deities?'"[767]

This would seem to indicate that the Trinity, in this *ayat*, or verse, consists of God, Jesus, or *Isa*, and Mary, or *Maryam*.

Additionally, in the first chapter of this study of angels in Islam, we also introduced several places in Hadith literature where the *Mala'ika* is the subject matter of the traditions. We have shown that many of the major collectors of Hadith, such as Sahih Muslim, Abu Bukhari, and Abu Hurayra, each described several traditions about the angels. For the most part, this material reflects what we know of angels from Al-Qur'an.

A number of other writers of Ahadith, the plural form, also have commented on the nature and activities of the *Mala'ika*. Among these thinkers and scholars, we mentioned Arab scholar Sa'd Ibn Abi Waqqas (595–674), Yemini scholar Mu'aadh Ibn Rifaa'ah Al-Zuraqqi, and Al-Hakim Al-Tabarani (839–923), Persian philosopher and theologian.

Other issues raised in the opening chapter of this study are the contrast of *Nur*, or light, and *Zulamat*, or darkness in the Islamic faith, as well as light and darkness related to believers and hypocrites in Islam. At the Holy Book's 57:12, for example, some hypocrites ask, "to borrow some of the Light of Allah."

We also have shown in Chapter One that the angels were created before both the Jinn and human beings, and because Adam knew the names of Allah's other creatures, the angels were asked to bow down to Adam. It is sometimes the case, as well, as we have shown in the first chapter, that angels are sometimes mistaken for human beings. Among these incidents include Muhammad thinking Malak Jibril was a man in Surah 95 and a number of women believing that the man Yusuf was really an angel.

Additionally, we have shown in the first chapter that angels bear the Ark of the Covenant in Islam, in addition to eight *Mala'ika* carrying the *Arsh*, or "Throne," of Allah. We also outlined in Chapter One that angels do not eat, neither do they get bored or weary, nor do they get tired. We also have shown that there are no fallen angels in Islam.

In the first chapter, we have shown that there are nineteen *Mala'ika* who are "Keepers of the Gates of Hell," which is confirmed by Surah forty, *ayats* 49 and 50. These nineteen minions of Malik also are discussed, as we have shown, in the Ahadith of Sahih Muslim and Abu Hurayra.

Additionally, we described and discussed the many uses of the word *Ruh*, or "Spirit," in the Islamic faith, including *Ruhana* and *Ruhina*, which both mean "Our Spirit;" the *Ruh al-Qudus*, or "Holy Spirit;" and the *Ruhul Amin*, or "Honest Spirit." Each of these Arabic names have been employed in Al-Qur'an to express different kinds of holiness.

Also stated in Chapter One, the Arabic word *Ruh*, or "Spirit," in Al-Qur'an is employed over fifty times in the Muslim Holy Book. Among those passages are 2:87 and 253, 5:110, 15:29, 16:2 and 102, 17:85, 19:16–17, 21:91, 26:193, 32:9, 38:72, 40:15, and Surah 66:12.

We ended Chapter One with the major conclusions we have made in it. This brings us to a summary of the second part of this study, an analysis of the archangels in the Islamic faith, the subject matter of Chapters Two and Three.

Part Two: Archangels in Islam: Chapters Two and Three

Both Chapters Two and Three of this study pertain to the category of the *Mala'ika* known as "archangel." In the former chapter, we described and discussed the most important *Malak* in the Islamic faith, angel Jibril, the angel who brought the revelations of Al-Qur'an to the Prophet Muhammad in the seventh century, over a period of twenty-three years.

We began Chapter Two with a discussion of the sources of the ideas associated with the angel Jibril, the most important *Malak* in the Islamic faith. There we have mentioned precursors of Jibril from the Old Testament figure of the angel Gabriel, such as Daniel 8:16 and 9:21, as well as the same figure in post-canonical times in early Judaism, such as the Books of Enoch. This was followed by a section in Chapter Two on the places in the New Testament, where the angel Gabriel appears. Such as the first chapter of the Gospel of Luke, verses 19–36.

In the next section of Chapter Two, we explored many of the places in the Muslim Holy Book, where angel Jibril appears. In that analysis, we have shown that Jibril only appears by name in two places of the Qur'an, at Surah 2:97–98 and 66:4, and in both of those they are mentioned in the context of the *Mala'kayn*, or dual form of angels in Arabic. We then engaged in a discussion of whether the *Ruh Allah*, or the "Spirit of God," is an aspect of the divine or one of the angels synonymous with Jibril. Again, in Chapter Two, as in Chapter One, we also supplied another discussion of whether the "Holy Spirit," or *Ruh al-Qudus* in Arabic, was another name for Jibril, or not. In Chapter Two, we have argued against that view, chiefly because of a Hadith from Sahih Muslim and Surah 78:38–39 from the Holy Book of Islam, that tells us:

> The day the Spirit takes its stand, with the angels arranged in rows, none will speak except those permitted by Ar-Rahman and says what is right.

The name "Ar-Rahman" is the name of the fifty-fifth surah of Al-Qur'an. The word is also one of the ninety-nine names for Allah in Islam. It means "He Who is Beneficent," or "One Who Brings Benefits." This was followed in Chapter Two with a discussion of many of the places in Hadith literature where the Malak Jibril is discussed. There we have spoken of what has come to be known as the "Jibril Hadith," as well as a number of places in traditional Ahadith where the angel Jibril is a subject for discussion. After examining aHadith from Bukhari, Sahih Muslim, and Abu Hurayra, among others, we also discussed other traditions from scholars like Persian scholar Al-Hasan Al-Kisai (737–805), the founder of the Kufi School of Arabic Grammar in the eighth century.[768]

In another section of Chapter Two, we discussed the places in Al-Qur'an where the angel Jibril is said to have appeared, *fi surato hi*, or "in his natural state." or "as he was created." These episodes appear in the Muslim Holy Book at Surah 81:23, 34:16, 53:14 and 16, and 56:28. This was followed in Chapter Two by a discussion of the "Lote Tree," a tree beyond which no creature may pass. We also examined the places in Hadith literature where the "Lote Tree" appears.[769]

The *Sidrat-Al-Muntaha*, as we have shown, is a tree in Islam that marks the end of the Seventh Heaven, the boundary beyond which no creature of Allah can pass. We also indicated in Chapter Two that beyond the Lote Tree is the *Arsh*, or "Throne," of Allah.[770] We ended Chapter Two, as we have with all the chapters of this study, with a summary of the major conclusions made in that chapter.

In Chapter Two of this study, we have also shown that the angel Jibril is numbered among the *Muqaribin*. They are the angels who are closest to Allah, or literally, who "may approach" the Almighty Allah. In fact, Jibril appears to be the only malak who may venture beyond the Lote Tree discussed earlier.

In the second chapter, we described and discussed the five moral requirements, or "Pillars of Islam," that each believer of the faith must fulfill. Additionally, we indicated that it was Malak Jibril that brought the waters of the Zam Zam to the Holy City of Mecca; and it was he who saved the lives of Ismail and his mother, Hajar, in the desert. We also discussed the incidents in Islam where the angel Jibril is said to have appeared in *fi surati hi*, or in his "natural form." And we indicated in Chapter Two what Islam has to say about the *Kidhb Anbiya*, or "False Prophets," such as at Surah 33:36, for example.

In Chapter Two, we stated where in the Muslim Holy Book,

the angel Jibril was said to have brought revelations to many of the other prophets in Islam. To Idrus, or Jonah, at 19:56-57; to Zakarias, at Surah 3:33–37; to Ibrahim, at 21:91, to cite three examples of this phenomenon. In Chapter Three, we examined and discussed the other archangel, besides Jibril, in the Islamic faith. With the help of scholarship from thirteenth-century Spanish scholar Ibn Arabi, Kurdish scholar Al-Sharani, as well as contemporary scholars of Islam, including Kenneth Cragg, C. T. R. Hewer, and John Kalter, we introduced and discussed the nature and activities of the archangels in Islam. In our analysis, we have shown that in addition to the angel Jibril, the Muslim faith also recognizes three other archangels. Their Arabic names, as we have shown, are *Mika'il, Isra'fil*, and *Azrael* or *Isra'il*. Although there are no explicit references to archangels in the Hebrew Bible and Al-Qur'an, there are a variety of other ancient Hebrew expressions related to a class of angels with high status. Some of these Hebrew expressions include the *Melek Elohim,* the *Melek Adonai*, the *Bene ha-Elohim*, and the *Qodesim* or the "Messenger of God," the "angel of the Lord," the "Sons of God," and the "Holy Ones."[771]

In a separate section of Chapter Three, we explored the Hebrew expressions mentioned above, as well as other possible precursors for the idea of archangels in the Islamic faith. We also have shown in Chapter Three the many places in Al-Qur'an and in Hadith literature where the three principal archangels, besides Malak Jibril, appear.

Subsequently, in Chapter Three, we provided individual sections on angel *Mika'il*, angel *Isra'fil*, and the *Malak Al-Mawt* or the Angel of Death. For each of these heavenly beings, we have provided an analysis of where these angels appear in Al-Qur'an, as well as in the major collectors of Hadith literature.

In addition, we explored the places in Islam of a collection of other angels mentioned by name in the Holy Book. These include the *Qiramun Qatabin,* or the "Honorable Scribes."[772] After examining the etymological origin of the words *Qiramun* and *Qatibin*, we also explored the *Malakayn, Harut* and *Marut*, who tested the ancient Jews in Babylon; and Munqar and Maqir, a pair of angels in the Islamic faith who interrogate the soul while in the grave to determine their places in the Afterlife.[773]

We also examined the roles of a number of other prominent angels in Islam, including the "Angels of the Mountains," the *Al-Qarraubiyyum*, or the "Cherubim," and another category of *Mala'ika* in Islam, who are responsible for the conceptions of human beings in the womb.[774]

In two final sections of Chapter Three, we explored the roles of the *Mala'ika* that are associated with the *Arsh wa Qursi*, or "Throne and Foot-Stool," of Allah. After exploring passages in Al-Qur'an about the Throne of Allah, we introduced the Arabic expression, *Al-Firdaws*, a word that means "Paradise."[775] We then explored where the word appears in Hadith literature in a tradition from Sahih Muslim and another from Ibn Kathir. We also introduced subsequent Ahadith from Ibn Al-Qayyim, on the *Arsh* of Allah.[776]

We also have explored in Chapter Three the major Muslim interpretations of Surah 2:98, the origins and meaning of the word *Kafarim*, and it KFR Semitic root, and that some Muslim traditions indicate that the angel Mika'il has not laughed since "Allah created Hell." Additionally, in this chapter, we discussed the Arabic word *Harf*, and its plural form *Ahruf*, to indicate the seven "stages" in which the Holy Qur'an was brought to the Prophet Muhammad.

In Chapter Three, we also indicated that Malak Mika'il, along with the angel Jibril, were the first to bow down to Adam when the *Mala'ika* were ordered to do so by Allah. Additionally, we have indicated that the angel Mika'il in Islam visited other prophets with messages from Allah, including bringing a gold ring to *Nabi Sulayman*, or Prophet Solomon, for example. The only two times the word *Mala'kayn*, the dual Arabic word for angels, is used in Al-Qur'an, it is in relationship to *Malak Jibril wa Malak Mika'il*, or angel Jibril and angel Mika'il.

Finally, at the close of Chapter Three, in the next to last section, we introduced a final archangel in Islam known as *Seraphiel*. The angel, as we have shown, is mentioned in the Third Book of Enoch, where he is described as being "as tall as the Seventh Heaven."[777] Scholar Henry Corbin suggests that Malak Seraphiel has a Zoroastrian origin and that Seraphiel entered Judaism during the Persian period.[778] In some views of Muslim eschatology, the angel Seraphiel is said to be the leader of the *Mala'ika*, who carry the *Arsh*, or "Throne" of Allah.[779] In fact, in Islamic eschatology, a number of other angels are also mentioned as performing this task. Among these, as we have shown, are:

1. Kerubiel
2. Radweriel
3. Orphanniel
4. Chayyliel[780]

In the closing section of Chapter Three and the end of section two of this study, we explored the idea of an angel hierarchy of Christianity, and the corresponding question of whether there is such a thing in Islam. The short answer to that query is no. Unlike the analysis of Thomas Aquinas, who describes nine choirs of angels, there is no corresponding hierarchy for the *Mala'ila* in Islam.[781] While there is clear evidence in Al-Qur'an that Malak Jibril and the other archangels are higher in rank in the Muslim Holy Book, there is no indication there of a hierarchy of the *Mala'ika*.

This brings us to the third section of this conclusive chapter, a summary of angels associated with death in Islam, as well as an analysis of the Houris, traditionally the buxom maidens of Paradise in Islam.

Part Three: Death Angels and the Houris: Chapters Four and Five

In Chapter Four of this study on angels in Islam, we have examined a variety of angels that are associated with *Mawt*, or "Death," in the Muslim faith. In addition to *Azrael* or *Israil*, the *Malak Al-Mawt*, or "Angel of Death*, we also described the nature and functions of two other sets of *Mala'kayn*—*Malik wa Ridwan*, Malik and Ridwan, or *Rizwan*, and *Munqar wa Naqir*, or Munqar and Naqir, the angels responsible for interrogating souls in the grave in Islam.

Malik, as we have shown, is the angel who rules *Jahanam*, or "Hell*, while Ridwan is the Malak responsible for the Gates of *Jannah*, Heaven in the Muslim faith. After these introductory remarks on angels associated with death in Islam, we then provided a section in Chapter Four devoted entirely to the Angel of Death. We began this section by describing some of the precursors of the idea of the *Malak Al-*

Mawt in Islam, including a number of cognates for the word *mawt* in other Semitic languages, such as Syriac, Aramaic and Akkadian, for examples.

We also pointed out in Chapter Four that the Hebrew Bible has an angel known as the *Malach al-Mavet*, or "Angel of Death," and that the Gospel of Luke at 16:19–23 may be a narrative that makes reference to the Angel of Death. We have also shown that references to the Angel of Death appear in a number of books of the Old Testament, including Job 33:22–23, Psalm 89:45 and Ecclesiastes 8:4.[782] The two verses from the Book of Job are representative of what the Hebrew Bible says of the Angel of Death. They tell us:

> His soul draws near the Pit,
>
> And his life to those who bring death.
>
> If there be for him an angel [Author's translation].

In Chapter Four, we explored a number of references to the Angel of Death that may also be found in several passages of the Babylonian Talmud, as we have shown.[783] Most of these reiterate what the Biblical text says about the phenomenon.

After exploring this material in Chapter Four, we then provided a separate section of the chapter where references to the *Malak Al-Mawt* may be found in Al-Qur'an and in Hadith literature. Among the passages we explored in Al-Qur'an are Surah 6:93, 25:22–26, 32:11–12 and 70:4.

Among the collectors of Hadith who have commented on the Angel of Death in Islam, we examined Hadith from Yemini, Anwar Awlaki, Ibn Abbas and Muhammad Kubani.[784] In another section of Chapter Four, we continued our discussion by quoting several additional Ahadith related to the Angel of Death. Much of this material was provided by Ukrainian convert Dov Noy (1920–2013).[785] Among the scholars cited by Professor Noy, we have explicated Sulayman Al-Jamal, Ibn Abi Hatim, Hasan Al-Basri, Ibn Abbas, Al-Kabbani and Al-Tabarani.[786]

In a subsequent section of Chapter Four, we explored the nature and activities of angels Ridwan and Malik. In that section, we relied

on the scholarship of Richard Burton, Abbas Ibn Tamin, Abu Bukhari
and Tariq Ibn Zayid to explicate the *mala'kayn, Malik wa Ridwan*, or
Malik and Ridwan. In that section of the chapter, we also introduced
a few passages in Al-Qur'an where these two angels appear, including
74:26–30, 96:14–18 and 71:25.[787]

We also examined in Chapter Four several places in Al-Qur'an
and Hadith literature where the Angel of Death appears to some of the
Islamic prophets, such as *Nabi Musa* or "Prophet Moses," and *Nabi
Ibrahaim* or "Prophet Abraham. Chapter Four also contains discussions
of two other phenomena of the Muslim faith. To wit, the *Lawhi Al-
Mafuz* and the practice of *Wudu*. The former idea is the notion of the
"Preserved Tablet" on which Allah writes the history of all human
beings. The latter concept refers to the idea of ablution, either "full" or
"dry" in the Islamic faith.

In Chapter Four, we examined a Hadith found in the collection
of Ibn Abbas about a warrior known as Dede Korkut. This Hadith in
question, as we have seen, is a kind of microcosm, or small model,
for most of the beliefs of the Muslim faith. We also included another
discussion of the idea of *Al-Barzakh*, the intermediary state where souls
reside between death and resurrection.

In another section of Chapter Four, we explicated and discussed
the roles of *Munqar wa Naqir* or "Munqar and Naqir." In that section,
we also have written of a number of Muslim scholars who have
described the activities of these two angels when interrogating the souls
of the dead in the grave. Among these scholars were Al-Munuzi, Imam
Ahmad, philosopher Ibn Taymiyyah, and a Hadith from fourteenth-
century Syrian scholar Ibn Al-Qayyim.[788]

We also examined a number of other Ahadith on Munqar and
Naqir, including Ahmad Ibn Al-Qasim, Ibn Abi Hatim, Hasan Al-
Albani, Abu Hurayra and At-Tirmidhi. At the end of the same section in
Chapter Four, we explored the nature and meaning of the Arabic word
Barzakh, a word that means a "space" or a "partition" between two
things. There we quoted Al-Qur'an's 35:22 that employs that term.[789]
The subject matter of another section on angels associated with death in
Islam, we have examined and explicated the Malak, *Ruman,* a celestial
being who appears to have been an associate of Munqar and Naqir. In

fact, we argued in that section that Ruman's treatment of the dead is far stricter than that of the *Malak Al-Mawt*. Fourteenth-century Sufi thinker Al-Qazwini, and contemporary scholars Jane Smith and Y. Y. Haddad agree with that assessment.[790] As with the other chapters in this study of angels in Islam, we also provided a summary of the major conclusions from Chapter Four.

The class of beings known as the *Houris* was the subject matter of Chapter Five of this work. We began this chapter by exploring the vocabulary and etymology of the words *Hur*, *Huriyah*, *houri* and *houris*. This was followed by an explication of the passages in Al-Qur'an, where the *Houris* appear. Among these passages were 2:25, 37:40–48, 38:52, 44:54, 52:20 and many others.[791] This was followed by a summary of many of the places in Hadith literature where the *Houris* are discussed, including traditions from Abu Bukhari, Sahih Muslim and Shiite text *Omn al-Kitab*.[792]

We have also shown in Chapter Five that the *Houris* may be given additional tasks besides the fulfilling of sexual desire in the Afterlife, but Al-Qur'an, as well as Hadith literature, say nothing of what those jobs may be.

In another section of Chapter Five, we addressed the issue of whether seventy-two *Houris*, or "Virgins," are guaranteed to those who are Martyrs, or *Shuhadan*, to the faith. We have pointed out that this claim is not in Al-Qur'an, but it is discussed in a number of ahadith, including one from Ibn Kathir, another of Al-Tirmidhi, and a third from and contemporary activist Muhammad Abu Wardeh.[793] We also examined in Chapter Five the traditional view in Islam on the practice of suicide, or *Aintihar* in Arabic. In the following section of Chapter Five, we examined a passage in Surah 78:33–34 that mentioned "swelling" or "round" breasts. We have examined various translations of these lines, pointing out the deep level of dissimilarity there is about the meaning of these ayats, or verses. Another section of Chapter Five has been devoted to the role that the *Houris* may have played on the battlefield, particularly at places like Badr, Uhud, and the Battle of the Ditch.[794]

In a subsequent section of the fifth chapter, we examined the claim that in the Afterlife, Maryam, the mother of *Isa*, or "Jesus," is to be numbered among the wives of Muhammad in the Great Beyond. We also have shown that Ibn Kathir has written several Ahadith about this question.[795]

In Chapter Five, we discussed the scholarship of two nineteenth – and twentieth-century Semitic language scholars Alphonse Mingana and German philologist Theodore Nokdeke, who both have suggested, like Christoph Luxenberg, that many words in the early Arabic vocabulary of Islam may have had Syriac, Aramaic or even Hebrew, origins.

Finally, in the most important section of Chapter Five, we described and discussed the recent book written by German scholar Christoph Luxenberg about the nature and extent of the *Houris* called *The Syro-Aramaic Reading of the Koran*, published in Germany in 2004.

In this book, Mr. Luxenberg provides a radically different view of the origins of the concepts related to the *Houris*, suggesting, for example, that Ephrem the Syrian, a Christian hymn writer, may have been one of the sources for language about the Houris. Indeed, he believes that the Syriac language is much more central to the understanding of the "chaste wives" than is classical Arabic.[796]

We followed this in Chapter Five with an explication and discussion of the Luxenberg book, suggesting it should be viewed by scholars in a positive light. Finally, at the close of Chapter Five, we raised the issue of whether contemporary discussions of the *Houris* are to be understood literally (*harfiyan*), or in an allegorical, or *mushabada*, sense. We pointed out, in fact, that this issue has gone on as a question since the ninth century in Islamic philosophy and exegesis.[797]

Many contemporary scholars of Islam have raised the same issue. Often these discussions concentrate on the Arabic word, *Qiyas*, a term that means "metaphor" or "analogy." One major translator who argues for an allegorical interpretation of the Houris is Abdullah Yusuf Ali, who published his translation of Al-Qur'an in April of 2001. Again, at the very end of Chapter Five, we cataloged the major conclusions made in that chapter. This brings us to a summary of part four of this study of angels in Islam.[798]

Part Four: Guardian and Recording Angels and Angels in Art:

Chapters Six and Seven

The three major foci in part four of this study on angels in Islam were guardian angels, recording angels, and the phenomenon of the *Mala'ika* in Islamic art. The first two foci are to be found in Chapter Seven, the third in Chapter Eight. Indeed, the chief goal of Chapter Six has been the descriptions and discussions of two sets of *mala'ika*, the *Qiramun Qitibin* and the hafaza.

As we have shown, the former are those angels who write down the deeds of human beings, both good and evil. The *hafaza*, on the other hand, are protective angels, or what Christians might call "guardian angels." The Semitic root HFZ, or Ha-Fa-Za, is employed forty-four times in Al-Qur'an. Most of these applications refer to agents of protection or assistance. We also introduced in Chapter Six another set of angels called the *Moakibat*, which may have been the pre-Islamic Arabic name for "protective angels."[799]

We began Chapter Six with a discussion of the etymological sources of the Hafaza and the Qiramin Qitibin. Then, we sketched out the sources for protective and recording angels in Islam. Among those sources, we indicated passages from the Old Testament (Ezekiel and Malachai), as well as passages from the Babylonian Talmud and the New Testament. This was followed by the places in Al-Qur'an, and in Hadith literature, where the protective and the recording *Mala'ika* appear.

We also cataloged other Old Testament references that may be precursors to the Islamic idea of recording angels. Among these were Ezekiel 9:3–4, Psalms 56:8 and 69:28, Exodus 32:32, and the Book of Job 37:7, which tells us, "He seals up the hand of every man, that all men will know his work." These Hebrew Bible passages are very much like the Muslim Holy Book's Surah 18:49, that speaks of the "Ledger of Deeds," that will be placed before humans at the Resurrection of the Dead. We also indicated in Chapter Six that the Arabic word *Sijjin* appears to be a synonym for the "preserved tablet," or the "Ledger of Deeds.

We also introduced another tradition in Islam that suggest the names of the two recording angels are *Raqib wa Atid*, or Raqib and Atid. This tradition suggests the former sits on the right shoulder of a person and records only good deeds, while the latter, who sits on the left should, records a person's bad deeds. The names of these two angels do not appear in Al-Qur'an, but they can be found in Hadith literature. Abu Dawood, for example, speaks of Raqib and Atid.

Above all, we have shown that the *Hafaza*, or "protective angels" seem to play the same role as the "guardian angels" in the Roman Catholic Church. To wit, each human being is assigned two or more protective angels to aid and protect them, and generally to keep them from harm.

The practice of *Wudu*, or "Ablution," is again discussed in Chapter Six, as is the idea of *Umrah* and *Al-Hajj*, the minor and major Hajj, to circumambulate the Kaaba in the city of Mecca. In the context of whether certain language in Al-Qur'an is literal or allegorical, we have shown that one interpretation of the *Houris* is that they are to be understood as an allegorical activity of bringing a person's good deeds to Paradise, so they be used later at the Resurrection of the Dead.

Chapter Six of this study also contains a discussion of the relative values of good versus bad moral deeds in Islam. In that section, we have shown that good deeds are worth many multiple times more value than bad deeds, somewhere between ten and eight hundred times more. And all of this was followed by the major conclusions of Chapter Six.

Chapter Seven on Islamic angels was devoted to many of the places in the history of Islamic iconography, where angels appear. We began this chapter with a summary of the history of Islamic art. This history began with the Umayyad period, followed successively by the Abbasid, the Fatimid, and the Ottoman period.

This history was followed by a description and a history of the most important Islamic art form over the centuries—calligraphy. The bulk of the remainder of Chapter Seven has been taken up with angel images in Islamic art from the ninth to twelfth centuries, angel images in Islamic art from the thirteenth to the fifteenth centuries, Islamic art in the sixteenth century, and Islamic art in the modern period: the seventeenth to twentieth centuries.

After this history, we explored separate sections in Chapter Seven devoted to the angel Jibril in Islamic art; the angel Mika'il in Muslim iconography; angel images in the *Siyer-i-Nebi*, or the Turkish "Life of the Prophet," produced at the end of the sixteenth century.[800] We ended with one final section on other depictions of Islamic angels as well as a section on angel images on Islamic carpets. There we made some general observations on the role and history of carpets in Islam, and where angels appear on Muslim carpets; and this was followed, of course, by the major conclusions of Chapter Seven.[801]

In the seventh chapter of this study, we have shown that between the fifteenth and eighteenth centuries, a variety of depictions of the *Houris* were made in Persia, so not all of the depictions in Chapter Seven are those of *Mala'ika*. Another important feature we described in this chapter is the compound at *Qasar'Amra*, a square structure with frescoes of angels and many other aspects of Islam.

Also in Chapter Seven, we have shown that the most important maker of Islamic miniatures in the sixteenth to the eighteenth century was a man named Nakkas Oman. Among his most important illustrations is the volume called the *Epitome of Historical Works* produced in 1583. This text is owned by the Museum of Turkish and Islamic Art in Istanbul. Additionally, we have shown in Chapter Seven that several of the Muslim prophets, besides Muhammad, appear in Islamic depictions of angels, including Ayyub, Nuh, Yunus, Yusuf, Sulayman, and many, many more. Additionally, we have tried to explain that other angels besides Jibril have been rendered in images with the *Anbiya*, or "prophets." In fact, we have given a catalog of other Islamic angels shown with the prophets, including one image of Malak Mika'il owned by the State Library in Berlin.

What we have tried to show in the seventh chapter that artistic depictions of the Mala'ika have been extant since the beginning of the ninth century, and that there are far more angels depicted in Islam in the sixteenth to the eighteenth centuries than at any other time. This brings us to a summary of the final part of this study, a discussion of celestial, ethereal beings other than the *Mala'ika—the Jinn* and the two figures of the demonic in the Islamic faith—*Iblis wa Shaytan*, or Iblis and Shaytan.

Part Five: The Jinn and the Demonic: Chapters Eight and Nine

In Chapter Eight, we described and discussed a class of sentient creatures in Islam known as the Jinn. We began that chapter by pointing out that the idea of the Jinn seems to have existed in Arabia long before the beginning of Islam. Evidence suggests there was a class of beings in Arabia known as the *Ginnaye*, an obvious cognate to the terms, *Jinni*, the singular, and the plural, *Jinn*.[802]

Other ancient accounts in Muslim history suggest that the Jinn were on the Earth long before the appearance of human beings, some say as much as thousands of years before Adam and Hawa (Eve). In these ancient accounts, the Jinn were said to have had a lofty place in the Heavens, somewhere below the angels, but above human beings. This is said to be one of the reasons why Iblis, a Jinni, refused to bow down to Adam, for he was made from fire, while Adam was made from clay or soil.

A variety of different exegetes in the Muslim faith have sketched out the varieties of Jinn. Some say there are three types, the Ghul, the *Ifrit*, and the *Si'la*.[803] Others add a fourth class known as the *Marid*.[804]

In the second section, we explored the etymological backgrounds of the words Jinni and Jinn. There we outlined at least four theories about the origins of these words: The Semitic root JNN, the Greek *Genus*, the Latin *Genius*, and the possibility of an Aramaic or Syriac origins. Additionally, we cataloged a number of other Arabic terms that come from the Semitic JNN root. These include words related to "madness," "sex and gender," the breastbone, and the Arabic word for Heaven, *Jannah*. We also have shown that the role of the Jinn in Islam may be very similar to the roles of the *Eumenides* in classical Greek times.[805]

Additionally, we have shown in the eighth chapter that the Jinn sometimes take on animal or human forms, including the bodies of black cats, rabid dogs, snakes, foxes, buffalo and other forms. In another section, we indicated the places in Al-Qur'an where the Jinn are mentioned or discussed. In fact, Surah 72 is named after the Jinn. Ultimately, we have tried to have shown that the Jinn are like human beings in at least three important ways. First, unlike the angels, they possess free will; second, like humans, they are morally responsible for their behavior; and finally, like humans, are destined for salvation or punishment.

We also have shown in Chapter Eight that the Arabic word, *Idjtinan*, the verb "to hide" in Arabic, may be the best view of the nature and status of the figure Iblis. We have argued in that chapter that Al-Qur'an's 6:100 and 128, 7:38, and 46:18–19, are three passages of the Muslim Holy Book that show the nature of Iblis and the other Jinn. From these passages, we made three conclusions about the Jinn. To wit, that they possess free will, that they are capable of moral decisions and choices, and they are subject to salvation and damnation. We also maintained in Chapter Eight that the best advice for how to deal with the whispering of Iblis comes from early Muslim scholar Abdullah Ibn Mas'ud (594–653). Ibn Mas'ud advises us that "Strength and Faith in Allah" are the best ways to respond to the whisperings of the demonic.

In another section, we explored many of the places in Muslim Hadith literature, where the Jinn are a subject for discussion. Among the Muslim scholars who have commented on the nature and activity of the Jinn were Yusuf Ibn Abdul Barr, eleventh-century Sunni scholar; Sahih Muslim; Abu Bukhari; At-Tirmidhi; Abu Dawood; Ibn Taymiyyah; Ibn Abbas; and Ibn Mas'ud.

In subsequent sections of Chapter Eight, we explored the relationship of the Jinn to King Sulayman, or Solomon. There we have maintained that the Jinn added Solomon in the construction of the temple in Jerusalem; we also explored the many places in Sir Richard Burton's *One Thousand and One Nights*, where the crafty Jinn appear. This was followed by a separate section of Chapter Eight devoted to the views of philosopher Ibn Taymiyyah on the issue at hand. As we have shown, the vocabulary of Ibn Taymiyyah on the Jinn is filled with words related to illusion, mirage and visions.[806]

The Jinn in the Sufi tradition was the subject matter of the final section of Chapter Eight. There we have concentrated on a text known as the *Stories of Awilya Allah*,[807] as well as mystical poet Rumi's *Muhawi*.[808] Finally, at the very end of Chapter Eight, we provided a chart that sketches out the comparative ontological natures of the Jinn, human beings, and the *Mala'ika*, or angels.

Chapter Nine of this study was entirely devoted to the idea of the demonic in Islam. In that chapter, we began by pointing out that many of the world's religious traditions, including the Zoroastrians, the Buddhists, traditional Hinduism, Japanese and Norse mythologies, and the Sumerians, Akkadians, the Finnish and the Hungarians, all have personified the demonic in one way or another.

We also explored several theories about the origins of Iblis and the other Jinn. Altogether, we enumerated five theories about that issue. We then discussed a number of views about the nature of Iblis' sin. Some say it was pride; others jealousy, disobedience, and even anger. Following that analysis, we made ten major conclusions about the narratives on Iblis in the Muslim Holy Book.

We also explored four separate conclusions we reached about the figure of Shaytan. These conclusions were: Shaytan has no control over believers; Shaytan's discourse with humans is all "false promises;" Shaytan is the only being who may make you "hate your friends;" and seek the help of Allah against the *waswas*, or "whisperings" of Shaytan.

These opening comments were followed in Chapter Nine by a discussion of the origins of the demonic in the Islamic faith. There we have discussed the etymological beginnings of the words, *Iblis, Shaytan*, and the *Shayatin*. In subsequent sections of Chapter Nine, we explored the places in Al-Qur'an, and in traditional Muslim Hadith literature, where Iblis and Shaytan are discussed. Among the traditional Hadith collectors who have commented on the demonic in Islam are Sahih Muslim, Abu Hurayra, Abu Bukhari, and philosopher, Ibn Taymiyyah.

At the close of Chapter Nine, we explored the question of the ontological status of Iblis. Is he a *Mala'ika* or simply one of the Jinn? After making several arguments concerning our view of this question, we finally concluded that Iblis is, indeed, one of the Jinn. In fact, most likely, the leader of the Jinn.[809]

In addition, we made some comments about how the demonic and the figures of Iblis and Shaytan have been addressed in the history of Islamic philosophy.[810] Among the Muslim philosophers who have commented on these phenomena are Mansur Al-Hallaj, Abd Al-Karim Al-Jili, poet Rumi, Ibn Kathir and Al-Tabari.[811] Finally, in another section of Chapter Ten, we described and discussed what relationships there might have been between the Islamic prophets and Iblis, Shaytan and the Shayatin.

In that regard, we have seen that several traditions in Islam are extant that speak of the encounters of the *Anbiya*, or "prophets," with the demonic. More specifically, we have shown Adam, Musa, Sulayman, Yahya, Idris, Nuh, and Nabi Ayyub, or Prophet Job, to all have had encounters with Iblis or Shaytan.

Arabic-English Glossary

Adhab al-Qabir torment of the grave
Aduw enemy
Adwan plural for enemy
Ahadith plural of Hadith
Ahl Al-Kitab people of the Book
Ahruf stages of revelation, plural of *haruf*
Allah God
Amir kind of Jinn
Anbiya prophets
Aqsa Dome of the Rock
Arqan ad-din five pillars of faith
Arsh throne of Allah
Asaf Solomon's Vizier
Atib recording angel
Ayat sign, or verse in Al-Qur'an
Ayyub Job
Azrael Angel of Death
Bai'a pledge
Bail Al-Ma'amur House of Heaven
Baysayis plot
Barzakh space or partition
Bi to
Buraq Mount of Muhammad during Miraj
Da'if weak
Dajjal Antichrist
Desses potter
Dharba storm
Dif crow
Diyana Articles of Faith
Dhu al-Fiqar sword of holy man
Dhikr solemn prayer
Falaq Surah 113

Faqid mourner
fi surati hi natural state
Fiqh Islamic law
Fijr dawn prayer
Firdaws Paradise
Ghish illusion
Ghishish cheat
Ghoul ghoul
Ghusl full ablution
Gishor peel
Hadith Muslim tradition of sayings of Muhammad
Hafahd helper
Hafaza to protect
Hafiz one who memorizes Al-Qur'an at an early age
Hafizi have guarded
Hafazin guardians
Hajj pilgrimage to Mecca
Hanta wheat
Hasad jealousy
Hila harbiya strategist
Hiyal trick
Hamar donkey
Hoqq truth
Hawa Eve
Haydor lion
Houris maidens in Paradise
Hur singular of Houris
Hur'in white-eyed
Iblis Muslim demon

Ifrit kind of Jinn

Iqra! Recite!

Imam faith

imtihan test

sa Jesus

Isha night prayer

Ishaaq horizon prayer

Islam submission

Isra night journey

Isra'fil Raphael

Itali'I disobedience

Jabal mountain

Jannah Paradise

Janon demon

Jahannam Hell

Jaww matir it is raining

Jibril Gabriel

Jihad striving for Allah

Jin sex/gender

Jin el besheri human beings

Jin jin breastbone

Jinn spirit creatures

Jinni singular of Jinn

Junna to be angry

Junni south wind

Ka'baah cube shrine in Mecca

Kafir non-believer

Kafirim plural of Kafir

Kashkoi diary

Kawthar abundance

Kechen liar

Kidhb Anbiya false prophets

Kitab book

Kitabat recording angels in early Arabia

Kufic style of calligraphy

Lawh-e-Mafoozp preserved tablet

Lut Lot
Madhab school of thought
Maghrib sunset prayer
Mahguz have guarded
Majnun insanity
Mokabat protective angels in early Arabia
Malak angel
Mala'al-la heavenly hosts
Malak Al-Mawt Angel of Death
Malakayn angels (dual form)
Mala'ika angels
Mka'il Michael
Malik King, or gatekeeper of Hell
Malik Shu'ara King of Poets
Maqasid intentions
Maqam Ibrahim place of Abraham
Maryam Mary, mother of Isa
Masjid Al-Musilman Articles of Faith
Marwa mountain in Arabia
Matir rain
Matrud outcaste
Mau'an curse
Milik ul-Tujjar King of merchants
Minfi outlaw
Miraj Night Journey
Min from
Momin soul
Munqar interrogating
Mu'awwidastayya Surahs of Refuge (113 and 114)
Muqarrabin angels who approach, or are closest to Allah
Nabi prophet
Nafs soul
Nahl bees
Nakir interrogating angel
Nar fire
Nas surah 114

Nuh Noah
Nur light
Qabir grave
Qadar kismet, determines
Qalam pen
Qaba qawayini two bow-lengths
Qariyyabim cherubim
Qasar place in Paradise for Khadijah
Qasar Amri ancient site near Amman
Qaus cubit
Qiramun Qatabin angels on shoulders
Qur'an Muslim Holy Book
Quraysh tribe in arabia
Qursi chair or footstool
Rahman merciful
Ramadan month of fasting
Raqib recording angel
Rasala verb, "to send a message"
Rasul messenger
Rasul Karim noble spirit
Rawwahnahum We shall let them rest
Ridwan/Rizwan Gatekeeper of Heaven
Ruh spirit/breath
Ruh al-Amin faithful spirit/honest spirit
Ruh al-Qudus Holy Spirit
Ruhana Our Spirit
Rusul plural of Rasal
Sa' movement back and forth between mountains
Sabiqu closest to Allah
Safa mountain in Arabia
Sahaba companions of Muhammad
Sakinah inspired peace
Salat prayer; obligation to pray
Shadid al-Quwwah Terrible Power (attribute of Allah)
Shahadah Confession of Faith
Shahid Martyr

Sheikh leader or hoy man
Shariah Islamic law
Shayatin Devils
Shaytan Muslim demon
Sidrat al-muntaha Lote Tree
Si'a kind of jinn
Sidrah Lote Tree
Sijjin deep pit or book of deeds
Sirat'antor thirsty sword
Sulayman Solomon
Sur trumpet of Isra'fil
Tadlis fraud
Tafhiyyal illusion
Tafsir commentary on Al-Qur'an
Takhat throne
Tawhid/tahwid Oneness of Allah
Tothawab yawn
Tawrah Torah
Tekebbur pride
Yahya John the Baptist
Yatim orphan
Yikdhab falsehood
Yom Arafah Day of Sacrifice
Yomtihin plural of test
Yusuf Joseph
Wa conjunction "and"
Waswas whispering
Win where
Wudu ablution
Ya'tas sneeze
Yom Ashura Day of Remembrance (Shiite)
Yom al-Qiyamah Day of Judgment
Yuhafidh guards *Za'al* anger *Zabur* Psalms
Zacharyis Zecharias
Zahra bright blooming *Zakat* obligation of charity
Zam zam stream in Mecca

Zawil plural of carpet
Zawwaznaham we shall wed them
Zikirs plural of Dhikr
Zuhr mid-day prayer
Zulamat darkness
Zulia carpet

Unless otherwise stated all Arabic translations in this chapter are those of the author of this study. We also have relied extensively on Ahmed Ali's translation of *The Holy Qur'an* (Princeton University Press, 2000).

Endnotes

1   Christoph Luxenberg, *The Syro-Aramaic Reading of the Koran* (New York: Prometheus Books, 2007).

2   Rashid Al-Din, *Jami'al Tawaeikh* (Istanbul: Miras-e-Maktoob, 2013).

3   Zeren Taninda, *Siyer-E-Nebi* (Istanbul: Hurriyet Foundation, 1984).

4   Bernard Lewis, *Islam and the West* (Oxford: Oxford University Press, 1993), p. 66.

5   The Holy Qur'an 2:177. Unless otherwise stated all Arabic translations in Chapter Two are those of the author of this study. We also have relied extensively on Ahmed Ali's translation (Princeton: Princeton University Press, 2000).

6   Ibid., 2:185.

7   Sahih Muslim, *Hadith* (Lahore: Shiekh Muhammad Ashraf, 1976), vol. 1, p. 128.

8   The Holy Qur'an 4:136.

9   Ibid., 74:31.

10   Ibid., p. 106.

11   Muslim, vol. 2, p. 98.

12   Ahmed Ibn Hanbal, *Ahmed Ibn Hanbal and the Mihna* (London: Kessinger Publishing, 2008), p. 54.

13   Quoted in the *Hadith of Abu Bukhari* (Lahore: Forgotten Books, 2008), vol. 2, p. 613.

14   Alama Fassi, *Hadith* (Lahore: Forgotten Books, 2008), p. 494.

15   Abu Sheikh, quoted in *Al-Nawai's Forty Hadith* (Lahore: Islamic Text Society, 1997), Hadith number 11.

16   The Holy Qur'an 5:15–16.

17   Ibid., 24:35–36.

18   Ibid., 57:12–14.

19   Ibid., 57:13.

20   Ibid., 2:30.
21   Al-Wahani's *Forty Hadiths*, number 12.
22   The Holy Qur'an 2:30–34.
23   Ibid., 4:117–120.
24   Ibid.
25   Ibid., 35:1.
26   The Throne, or *Arsh* of Allah, is discussed in a number of passages in Al-Qur'an. Among these are: 9:129, 11:7, 12:100, 13:2, 17:42, 20:5, 21:22, 23:116, 27:23 and 26, 39:75, 40:7, 57:4, 69:17, and 71:21.
27   Abu Bukhari, *Hadith*, vol. 3, no. 1172.
28   The Holy Qur'an 82:10–11.
29   Bukhari, *Hadith.*
30   Ibid.
31   Ibid.
32   The Holy Qur'an 12:31.
33   Ibid., 37:6–8.
34   Ibid., 38:69.
35   Ibid., 8:9–10.
36   Ibid., 8:17.
37   Sa'd ibn Abi Waqqas, *Hadith.*
38   The Holy Qur'an 3:123–125.
39   Mu'aadh ibn Rifaa'ah al-Zuraaqi, *Hadith.*
40   Ibid.
41   The Holy Qur'an 3:152.
42   Ibid., 77:38.
43   Ibid., 25:25–26.
44   Ibid., 9:129.
45   Ibid., 11:37 and 23:27.
46   Sahih Muslim, *Hadith* (Lahore: Sheikh Muhammad Ashraf, 1976), p. 131. Also see: Abu Bukhari, *Book of Muslim Morals and Manners* (London: Al-Sadawi Publications, 1997), p. 19.
47   Ibid.
48   Ibid.
49   Kecia Ali and Oliver Leaman, *Islam: Key Concepts* (Oxford: Rutledge, 2008), p. 7.
50   The Holy Qur'an 6:8–9.
51   Ibid., 9:29.
52   Sahih Muslim, *Hadith*, vol. 2, p. 131.

53   The Holy Qur'an 82:10–12.

54   Ibid., 2:102.

55   Abu Hurayra, *Forty Hadith* (London: Muslim Hope, 1998), no. 1229.

56   Abu Dawud, *Hadith*, no. 142.

57   Ibn Kathir, quoted in *Muslim Tradition:Studies in Chronology, Provenance, and Authorship in Early Hadith*. Edited by G. H. A. Juynbull (Cambridge: Cambridge University Press, 2008), p. 193.

58   The Holy Qur'an 74:30–31.

59   Ibid., 40:49–50.

60   Ibid., 13:23–24.

61   Ibid., 39:73.

62   Ibid., 21:27–28.

63   Ibid., 19:17.

64   Ibid.

65   Ibid., 66:12.

66   Ibid., 26:191.

67   Abu Bukhari, *Book of Muslim Morals*, p. 22.

68   Tirmidhi and Abu Dawud, quoted in Abu Hurayra's *Forty Hadith*, nos. 1233 and 1234.

69   The Holy Qur'an 26:191–195.

70   Gospel of Luke 1:26–35.

71   Gospel of Matthew 1:20.

72   Matthew 3:16.

73   The Holy Qur'an 5:73–74.

74   Ibid.

75   Ibid., 19:16–19.

76   Ibid., 58:22.

77   Ibid., 16:102.

78   Ibid., 40:15.

79   Ibid., 5:110.

80   Ibid., 3:59.

81   First Enoch 9:1–2.

82   Ibid., 10:13.

83   Ibid., 20:7 and 40:9.

84   The Holy Qur'an 2:97–98. Unless otherwise stated, all the translations from Hebrew and Arabic in this chapter are those of the author.

85   The Holy Qur'an 16:102.

86   Ibid., 78:38.

87   The Holy Qur'an 53:5.

88   Ali Ibn Umar Baydawi, *Anwar-al-Tan'zil* (1264), p. 78. Nasir Al-Din Baydawi (1226–1286) was born in Fars, a Muslim, Sunni scholar. His most famous work is *Anwar al-Tanzil wa Asrar-al-Ta*n'zil, or *The Lights of Revelation and Secrets of Interpretation.*

89   Ibn Abbas, *Divine Sayings: 101 Hadith Qudsi* (London: Anqa Publishing, 2008), p. 141. Ibn Abbas (619–687) was a companion of the Prophet Muhammad and one of the first converts to the faith.

90   The Holy Qur'an 96:1–5.

91   Ingrid Mattson, *The Story of the Qur'an* (Oxford: Blackwells, 2008), p. 19.

92   Ibid.

93   The Holy Qur'an 53:4–6.

94   Sahih Bukhari, *Hadith*, vol. 1, ch. 1, no. 2. Muhammad Al-Bukhari (810–870) was a Persian scholar and one of the main collectors of Hadith in Sunni Islam.

95   Ibid., vol. 6, ch. 60, no. 380.

96   Kecia Ali and Olive Leaman, *Islam: The Key Concepts* (Oxford: Rutledge, 2008), p. 110.

97   The Holy Qur'an 58:8–12.

98   Ibid.

99   Ibid., 11:69.

100   Sachiko Murata and William Chittick, *Vision of Islam* (London: Paragon House, 1998), p. 243.

101   Ibid.

102   Ibn Abbas, *Divine Sayings*, p. 142.

103   Ibid.

104   Abu Ishaq ash-Shabani, quoted in Ahmed Ibn Hanbal, *A Biography of the Imam* (London: Kessinger Books, 2008), p. 134. Abu Shabani (720–790) was an Andalusian, Sunni scholar and Exegete of Al-Qur'an.

105   Al-Kisai, *Hadith Al-Kisai and Supplications of Kumail* (Lahore: Khurasan Book Center, 2001), p. 139. Al-Kisai, who died in 804, was one of the principal Shiite collectors of Hadith.

106   Ibid.

107   The Holy Qur'an 3:46.

108   Ibid., 34:16.

109   Ibid., 53:14 and 16.

110   Frederick Colby, *Narrating Muhammad's Night Journey* (New York: SUNY Press, 2008), p. 95.

111 George Sale, *Al-Qur'an* (London: Macmillan, 2016), p. 323. George Sale (1687–1736) was a Kent-born Englishman and translator of the first great English version of Al-Qur'an, which was published in London in 1734.

112 Ibid.

113 Ibid.

114 Ibn Abbas, *Divine Sayings*, p. 141.

115 Hisham Ibn Urwah, *Hadith* (New York: Xlibris, 2014), p. 17. Urwah (667–772) was an Arab companion to the Prophet Muhammad and the teacher of Ibn Abbas Ibin.

116 Ibid.

117 The Holy Qur'an 74:21.

118 Abu Bukhari, *Hadith*, vol. 1, no. 5417.

119 Ibid.

120 Ibid.

121 Ali and Leaman, p. 68.

122 Ibid.

123 Al-Tabari, quoted in Ram Swarup, *Understanding the Hadith* (New York: Prometheus Books), p. 71. Al-Tabari (839–923) was a Persian historian, exegete of Al-Qur'an, and collector of Hadith.

124 Milton Hatoum, *The Tree of Seventh Heaven* (New York: Atheneum Press, 1994). Also see: Nerina Rustomji, *The Garden and the Fire* (New York: Columbia University Press, 2009), particularly pp. 1–20 and 98–123.

125 Muhammad Asad, *The Message of the Qur'an* (London: The Book Foundation, 2008), p. 77.

126 Al-Tabari, quoted in Ram Swarup, *Understanding the Hadith* (New York: Prometheus Books, 2002), p. 71.

127 The Holy Qur'an 33:36.

128 Nerina Rustomji, *The Garden and the Fire* (New York: Columbia University Press, 2009), p. 111.

129 Ibn Al-Farid, quoted in Mattson, p. 27. Al-Farid (1181–1234) was an Arab poet born in Cairo to Syrian parents.

130 Rustomji, p. 30.

131 Ibid.

132 Ibid.

133 Ibid., pp. 31–32.

134 Ibid.

135 Genesis 5:21.

136 The Holy Qur'an 19:56–57.

137 Stephen Vicchio, *Biblical Figures in the Islamic Faith* (Eugene: Wipf and Stock, 2008), p. 193. The Holy Qur'an 3:33–37.

138 The Holy Qur'an 3:33–37.

139 Ibid.

140 Ibid.

141 Ibid.

142 Ibid.

143 At-Tirmidhi, *Hadith*, quoted in Swarup, p. 72. Abu Tirmidhi (824–892) was one of the six principal collectors of Hadith in Shiite Islam.

144 *Zubdat al-Tawarikh*, Museum of Turkish and Islamic Art, Istanbul.

145 *Zubdat al-Tawarikh*, Chester Beatty Museum, Dublin, Ireland. The *Zubdat*, or "Cream of Histories," is a Turkish manuscript written in a large *Naskhi* script. It was completed between 1574 and 1795. The calligrapher for both the Turkish and Irish copies was Sayyid Loqman Asuri. There also were three painters for both copies. Their names were All-Sayyid Lufti, Molla Kasim or Mullah Qasim, and Ustad Osman. Both copies were completed in their workshop in Istanbul.

146 Ibid.

147 For more on archangels in Islam in general see: Hossein Nasr, *The Heart of Islam* (New York: Harper One, 2004); David Goldman *Islam and the Bible* (Chicago: Moody Publishers, 2004); and Margot Badran, *Feminists, Islam, and the Nation* (Princeton: Princeton University Press, 1996). For Jibril, see: Richard Lawrence, *Gods, Guards, and Guardian Angels* (London: O Books, 2007); D. J. Conway, *Enhance Relationships with Your Spiritual Companions* (London: Llewelyn Publications, 2009); and Gosamer Penwyche, *The World of Angels* (Belair: Fair Winds Press, 2003). For Mika'il, see: Richard Webster, *Michael: Communicating with the Archangels for Guidance* (London: Llewelyn, 2004). For Uriel, see: Richard Webster, *Uriel: Communicating with the Angel of Transformation* (London: Llewelyn, 2005). Unless otherwise stated, all Arabic translations in this chapter are those of the author.

148 Ibn Arabi, quoted in Al-Djahiz, "The Examination of Trade," in *Historians Arab* (London, 1946), pp. 10–11.

149 Ibid.

150 John Kalter, *Islam:What Non-Muslims Should Know* (Minneapolis: Fortress Press, 2003), p. 57.

151 Ziauddin Sardar, *What Do Muslims Believe?* (New York: Walker and Company, 2007), p. 44.

152 Rosemary Guiley, *Encyclopedia of Angels* (New York: Facts on File, 1996), p. 98.

153 Sanhedrin 38b and Avodah Zerah 3b.

154 Ibid.

155 Ibid.

156 J. E. Hanauer, *Folklore of the Holyland* (New York: Dover Books, 2002), p. 183.

157 Anne Rice, *Servants of Bones* (New York: Ballatine Books, 1996).

158 Arthur Miller, *The Creation of the World and Other Business* (London: Dramatist Play Service, 1998).

159 The Holy Qur'an 2:98 (author's translation).

160 Muhammad Asad, *The Message of the Qur'an* (Gibraltor: Dar Al-Andalus, 1984).

161 The Holy Qur'an 2:98 (author's translation).

162 Muhammad Zubayr Siddiqi, *Hadith Literature, Its Origin, Development and Special Features* (London: Islamic Texts Society, 1996), p. 99.

163 Ibid., p. 100.

164 Book of Daniel 10:13–14.

165 First Book of Enoch 20:5 (RSV translation).

166 Siddiqi, *Hadith Literature*, p. 106.

167 Ibid., p. 107.

168 Ibid.

169 Ibid.

170 Al-Tabari, *Commentary on the Qur'an* (Oxford: Oxford University Press, 1987), p. 165.

171 Quoted in Ezzeddin Ibrahim, *Forty Hadiths* (Damascus: Holy Koran Publishing House, 1976), p. 215.

172 Abu Bukhari, *Hadith*, vol. 2, no. 262.

173 Ibid., no. 267.

174 Siddiqi, *Hadith Literature*, p. 79.

175 Ibrahim, *Forty Hadiths*, p. 291.

176 Ibid., p. 94.

177 Ali Al-Kisa'I, *Tales of the Prophets* (London: Twayne Publishers, 1978), p. 348.

178 Ibid.

179 A. J. Weinsinck, "Israfil," *The Encyclopedia of Islam* (Leiden: Brill, 1978), Vol. 4, p. 211.

180 Ibid.

181 Al-Tabari, *Annales*, vol. 1, p. 1248ff. Also see: George Sale, *The Koran: Preliminary Discoursers* (London: Frederick White, 1905).

182 The Holy Qur'an 27:87.

183 Ibid., 36:51.

184 Ibid., 78:18.

185 Ibid., 18:99.

186 Marmaduke Pickthal, *Al-Qur'an* (London: Everyman's Library, 1993).

187 The Holy Qur'an 6:73 (author's translation).

188 Sahih Muslim, *Hadith*, vol. 3, no. 517.

189 Siddiqi, *Hadith Literature*, p. 100.

190 Ibid.

191 Ibrahim, *Forty Hadiths*, p. 180.

192 Ibid.

193 Ibid.

194 Siddiqi, *Hadith Literature*, p. 118.

195 Ibid., p. 191.

196 Abu Al-Bukhari, *Hadith*, vol. 2, no. 277.

197 Siddiqi, *Hadith Literature*, p. 191.

198 Ibid., pp. 192–197 and 266–268.

199 Abu Hurayra, *Hadith*, vol. 1, book 8, no. 122.

200 Ibid., no. 466.

201 Ibid.

202 Sahih Muslim, *Hadith*, vol. 1, book 33, no. 6893.

203 Bukhari, *Hadith*, vol. 2, book 8, no. 269.

204 Ibid., no. 271.

205 Muslim, vol. 1, book 8, no. 6891.

206 Marmaduke Pickthall, translation of Al-Qur'an 69:17.

207 The Holy Qur'an 20:5 (author's translation).

208 Al-Bukhari, vol. 2, book 8, no. 273.

209 Ibid., no. 274.

210 Muslim, vol. 1, book 8, no. 6894.

211 Ibn Kathir, *Hadith*, vol. 4, no. 138.

212 Zayad al-Mad'ad, *Hadith*, vol. 6, no. 581.

213 Sachiko Murata and William Chittick, *The Vision of Islam* (Saint Paul: Paragon Press, 1994), pp. 92–93.

214 Ibid.

215 Gustav Davidson, *A Dictionary of Angels* (New York: Free Press, 1967).

216 Henry Corbin, *Man of Light in Iranian Sufism* (Boston: Shambahala Press, 1979), p. 56.

217 Ibid.

218 Ibid.

219 Thomas Aquinas, *Summa Theologica*, part 1, question 108.

220 Babylonian Talmud, Ned. 49a and Hul. 7b.

221 Babylonian Talmud, M.K. 28a.

222 Gospel of Luke 16:19–23.

223 Gospel of John 13:23.

224 Second Samuel 24:16.

225 Psalm 89:45.

226 Midrash Rabba Koheleth 8:4.

227 Ibid.

228 Ned. 49a.

229 Midrash Tihuma 19b.

230 Derek Eretiz Zuta, sec. 8.

231 Acts of the Apostles 2.

232 Romans 5.

233 Rev. 6.

234 The Holy Qur'an 70:4.

235 Ibid., 32:11–12.

236 Ibid., 25:22–26.

237 Ibid., 55:1–2.

238 Anwar Awlaki, *The Hereafter*.

239 Ibid.

240 The Holy Qur'an 16:32.

241 Ibid., 18:50.

242 Javed Muhammad, *Islam 101* (London: Pyramoid Books, 2003), p. 114.

243 Ibid.

244 Ibid., 114–115.

245 Ibid.

246 Muhammad Hasham Kabbani, *Angels Unveiled* (London: Kazi Books, 1996), p. 294.

247 Ibid., pp. 294–295.

248 Ibid.

249 Ibid., pp. 178–179.

250 Dov Noy, *Folktales in Israel* (Chicago: University of Chicago Press, 1969), p. 178.

251 Ibid.

252 Ibid., p. 115.

253 A. S. Al-Jamal, *Tafsir Al-Jalalylan*.

254 Ibid.

255 Al-Tabarani, *Hadith*, no. 1734.

256 Ibid.

257 Wahb Ibn Munabbah Ramatullah, quoted in *Abi Hatim*, p. 243.

258 Ibid., p. 244.

259 Hasan Al-Basri, quoted in Kabbani, p. 296.

260 Ibid.

261 Sachiko Murata and William Chittick, *The Vision of Islam* (London: Taurus and Company, 2006), p. 228.

262 Ibid.

263 Kabbani, p. 294.

264 Ibid., p. 295.

265 Ulrich Marsolph, *Arabian Nights Encyclopedia* (London: ABC-Clio, 2004), pp. 104–105.

266 At-Tirmidhi, no. 3174.

267 Ibn Al-Qayyim, quoted in Kabbani, p. 296.

268 Richard Burton, *One Thousand and One Nights* (Norwalk, CT: Easton Publishing, 1994), p. 20.

269 Ibid.

270 Ibid., p. 21.

271 Ibid., p. 117.

272 John Renard, *Friends of God* (Los Angeles: University of California Press, 2008), p. 78.

273 Ibid., p. 79.

274 Ibid., p. 80.

275 Ibid.

276 Al-Misaiyab, quoted in Thomas Cleary, *The Wisdom of the Prophets* (London: Shambala Books, 2001), pp. 121–122.

277 Ibid.

278 The Holy Qur'an 48:18 (author's translation).

279 Ibid.

280 Ibid., 14:22.

281 Ibid., 40:49.

282 Ibid.

283 Ibid., 74:26–30.

284 Ibid., 96:14–18.

285 Ibid., 71:25.

286 Ibid., 66:6. Also see: Thomas Aquinas, *Summa Theologica* (Denver: Coyote Canyon Press, 2010), vol. 1, question 88.

287 Ibid.

288 Javad Muhammad, p. 120.

289 Ibid.

290 Ibn Taymiyyah, quoted in Nerina Rustomji, *The Garden and the Fire* (New York: Columbia University Press, 2009), p. 168.

291 Ibid., p 40.

292 Ibid.

293 Quoted in Abi Hatim, p. 419.

294 Ibid.

295 Ibid.

296 Rustomji, p. 170.

297 Ibid.

298 At-Tirmidhi, *Hadith*, no. 3176.

299 Hasan Al-Albani, quoted in Javid Muhammad, p. 127.

300 Abu Hurayra, *Hadith*, vol. 3, ch. 18, no. 447.

301 Ibid., no. 448.

302 The Holy Qur'an 55:20.

303 Ibid., 23:100.

304 Ibid., 25:53.

305 Ibid., 55:19–20.

306 Abdullah Yusuf Ali, The Holy Qur'an (London: Wordsworth Editions, 2001).

307 The Holy Qur'an 35:22.

308 Sayyid Rivzi, *Islam* (New York: Create Space, 2017), p. 31.

309 Ibid.

310 Al-Qazwini, *The Wonders of Creation*. Quoted in V. A. Wright, *A Catalogue of Angels* (Brewster, MA: Paraclete Press, 2006), p. 66.

311 Al-Albani quoted in Javid Muhammad, p. 130.

312 'Izz al-Din Kashani, quoted in Smith and Chittick, p. 43.

313 Al-Qazwini, p. 67.

314 Smith and Chittick, p. 43.

315 Ibid.

316 Ibid.

317 Christoph Luxenberg, *The Syro-Aramaic Reading of the Qur'an* (Berlin: Verlag Han Schiler, 2007) p. 247.

318 Ibid., pp. 247–248.

319 Bernard Lewis and B. E. Churchill, *Islam:The Religion of the People* (Philadelphia: Wharton School Publishing, 2008), p. 251.

320 Ibid., p. 252.

321 Ibn Kathir, *Tafsir Ibn Kathir*. Commentary on Qur'an's 55:56.

322 Anonymous, "Houri," in *New World Dictionary* (London: World Publishing, 1978), p. 680.

323 The Holy Qur'an 37:40–48.

324 Ibid., 44:51–55.

325 Ibid., 52:17–20.

326 Ibid., 55:55–57.

327 Ibid., 55:57–58.

328 Ibid., 56:35–38.

329 Ibid., 52:17.

330 Ibid., 56:17.

331 Ibid., 76:19–20.

332 Malise Ruthven, *Islam in the World* (Oxford: Oxford University Press, 1984), p. 118.

333 Quoted in Lawrence Rosen, *The Anthropology of Justice* (Cambridge: Cambridge University Press, 1989), p. 23.

334 Ruthven, p. 118.

335 Ibid.

336 Ibid., pp. 118–119.

337 Luxenberg, p. 249.

338 Al-Tirmidhi, *Hadith*, vol. 3, no. 234.

339 Mishkat Ul-Massabih, *Al-Hadis* (Damascus: Muslim Books, 1999), p. 172.

340 Al-Tabari, vol. 4, no. 245.

341 Ibid., no. 246.

342 Ibn Maja, *Hadith* (Cairo: Holy Books of Islam, 1956), p. 129.

343 Ibn Kathir, *Hadith* (Damascus: Muslim Books, 1999), p. 130.

344 Ibid.

345 Sahih Bukhari, *Hadith* (Cairo: Holy Books of Islam, 1956), p. 132.

346 Ibid.

347 Sahih Muslim, *Hadith*, vol. 4, no. 257.

348 Ibid.

349 Ibid., no. 256.

350 Omn Al-Kitab, *Hadith* (Cairo: Holy Books of Islam, 1999), p. 132.

351 Ibid.

352 D. B. MacDonald, "Houri," in *Encyclopedia of Islam* (Leiden: Brill, 1978), p. 992.

353 Nerina Rustomji, *The Garden and the Fire* (New York: Columbia University Press, 2008), p. 176.

354   At-Tirmidhi, *Hadith*, vol. 2, p. 138.

355   Ibid.

356   Ibid.

357   Al-Ghazali, *Ihya Uloom Ed-Din* (The Revival of the Religious Sciences), vol. 4.

358   At-Tirmidhi, vol. 2, p. 140.

359   Ibid.

360   Abu Bukhari, *Hadith*, vol. 4, book 55, no. 544.

361   *Hadith Mishkat*, vol. 2, pp. 83–97.

362   Al-Ghazali, *Book of Fear and Hope* (Leiden: Brill, 1965), p. 417.

363   Sahih Muslim, vol. 3, book 40, no. 6793.

364   Abu Bukhari, vol. 4, book 466, no. 306.

365   Ibid., vol. 6, book 402, no. 374.

366   Hadith Mishkat, vol. 2, pp. 83–97.

367   Ibn Kathir, *Tafsir*, commentary on 55:72.

368   Luxenberg, p. 250.

369   Muhammad Abu Wardeh, quoted in Ibn Warraq, "Virgins? What Virgins?" *The Guardian*, January 2, 2001. At the same time *Sixty Minutes* also aired a segment called "Suicide Bombers," in which Mr. Wardeh was interviewed for the segment.

370   Al-Suyuti, *Hadith*, no. 434.

371   Margaret Keffner Nydell, *Understanding Arabs: A Guide for Modern Times* (London: Intercultural Press, 2006), p. 107.

372   Hafiz Salahuddin Yusuf, Riyadhus Salihin: Commentary on Nawawi, ch. 372.

373   The Holy Qur'an, 78:33–34 (author's translation).

374   George Sale, *Al-Qur'an*, translation of 78:33–34.

375   Ibn Kathir, *Tafsir*. Comment on 78:33–34.

376   Abdullah Yusuf Ali, *Al-Qur'an* (Princeton: Princeton University Press, 1984), p. 519.

377   Ibid.

378   Ibid.

379   A. J. Arberry, *Al-Qur'an* (London: Touchstone Books, 1996).

380   Rustomji, p. 176.

381   Ibid.

382   Ibid., pp. 176–177.

383   Ibid.

384   Ibn Kathir, *Qisas*, p. 383.

385   Luxemberg, p. 252.

386 Ibid.

387 Ibid.

388 Luxemberg, p. 253.

389 Marmaduke Pickthal, *Al-Qur'an*. Comment on 44:54.

390 Luxenberg, p. 258.

391 Ahmed Ali, p. 519. Luxenberg, p. 260.

392 Maher Hathout, *In Pursuit of Justice* (Muslim Public Affairs Council, 2006), p. 143.

393 Ibid.

394 Alphonse Mingana, "Syriac Influences on the Style of the Qur'an," http:// answeringislam.org, p. 77.

395 Ibid.

396 Ibid.

397 "What Does the Qur'an Really Say?" CBS News, July 25, 2003.

398 *Jalal al-Din Suyuti*. Translated by Anne Carter (London: NP, 1971).

399 Joan DelPlato, *Multiple Wives and Multiple Pleasures* (Madison: Farleigh Dickenson Press, 2002), p. 207.

400 John Updike, *The Terrorist* (New York: Ballantine Books, 2007), p. 107.

401 Ali and Leaman, p. 487.

402 W. Montgomery Watt, *Free Will and Predestination in Early Islam* (London, 1948) and Richard Bell, *The Origins of Islam in a Christian Context* (Oxford: Routledge, 1968), p. 111.

403 Jacques Jomier, *The Bible and the Qur'an* (San Francisco: Ignatius Press, 1964), p. 38.

404 Ibid.

405 Annemarie Schimmel, *Islam: An Introduction* (Albany: SUNY Press, 1992), p. 59.

406 Ibid.

407 Anonymous, "Hafaza," in *Hastins Encyclopedia of Religion and Ethics*, vol. 4, p. 617.

408 Ezekiel 9:3–4. The version of the Old and New Testaments employed in this chapter is the translations of the Revised Standard Version.

409 Malachai 3:16.

410 Psalm 56:8.

411 Psalm 69:28.

412 Exodus 32:32.

413 Daniel 10:10–21.

414 Book of Job 37:7.

415   Ezekiel 9:4.

416   Abot. III, 20.

417   Ta'an, 11a.

418   Bera., 16a.

419   Second Enoch 23:2.

420   Book of Esther, chapter three.

421   The Holy Qur'an 18:49.

422   Gospel of Matthew 18:10.

423   Gospel of Luke 1:26–38.

424   M. A. Palacios, *Islam and the Divine Comedy* (London: Routledge, 1968), p. 228. Miquel Asin Palacios (1871–1944) was a Spanish scholar of Islam and English literature.

425   The Holy Qur'an 13:11.

426   Ibid., 43:80.

427   Ibid., 50:17–18.

428   Ibid., 80:10–14.

429   Ibid., 83:8–12.

430   Ibid., 83:19–20.

431   Ibid., 84:7–10.

432   Ibid., 36:12.

433   Abu Bukhari, *Hadith*, vol. 4, book 55, no. 544. Bukhari (810–870) was a Persian scholar born in Bukhara. He is one of the major collectors of Sunni Hadith literature.

434   Abu Dawood quoted in Thomas Cleary, *The Wisdom of the Prophets* (Shambala Classics, 2001), p. 230.

435   Ibid., p. 231.

436   Quoted in Cleary, p. 232.

437   Ibid.

438   Ibn Kathir, *Hadith*, p. 100. Ibn Kathir (1300–1373) was an expert on Muslim law and history. He lived during the reign of the Mamluk in Syria.

439   Abu Hurayra, *Hadith*, vol. 4, book 55, no. 534. Abu Hurayra (603–681) was one of the Sahaba, or companions, to the Prophet Muhammad. Because of his affinity to cats, he was known as "The Father of Kittens."

440   Quoted in Cleary, p. 233.

441   Ibid.

442   Ibid.

443   Hurayra, vol. 4, book 55, no. 536.

444   The Holy Qur'an 13:11 (author's translation).

445 Ibn Ansari, quoted in Maqsood, p. 16. Ibn Ansari (616–682), of course, was a member of the Sahaba, or Companions of the Prophet Muhammad, and one of the first converts to the Faith.

446 Hurayra, vol. 4, book 55, no. 537.

447 Maqsood, p. 17.

448 "Hadith Qudsi," quoted in Cleary, p. 235. The Hadith Qudsi was one of the first collections of the sayings and actions of the Prophet Muhammad. It was collected by members of the Sahaba, or Companions of the Prophet Muhammad.

449 The Holy Qur'an 42:26.

450 Ibid., 7:20–21.

451 Ibid., 39:14.

452 Ibid., 40:14–15.

453 Hurayra, vol. 4, book 55, p. 534.

454 Immanuel Kant, *Groundwork of the Metaphysics of Morals* (Cambridge: Cambridge University Press, 2012). Kant (1724–1804) was born in Konigsberg, Prussia, and spent most of his life there. Kant was one of the most influential Western philosophers in Germany and beyond to the present day. Kant proposed that the Holy Will, or proper intentions, were just as important to morality as the universal rules of ethics themselves. He garnered these from what he called the "Categorical Imperative."

455 The Holy Qur'an 11:114 (author's translation).

456 Imam Muslim, quoted in Cleary, p. 235. Abu Muslim (718–755) was one of the major collectors of Hadith literature during the Abbasid Empire.

457 Abu Tharr, quoted in Cleary, p. 233.

458 The Holy Qur'an 5:6.

459 Dawood, quoted in Cleary, p. 233. Abu Dawood, who died in 889 in the city of Basra, was one of the major collectors of Hadith. Altogether he preserved 4,800 traditions.

460 At-Tirmidhi, *Sunan Al-Tirmidhi*, vol. 2, no. 341. At-Tirmidhi (824–892) was a Persian scholar and collector of Hadith. He is also one of the great Medieval scholars of the Islamic faith.

461 Abu Muslim, quoted in M. K. Nydell, *Understanding Arabs* (Intercultural Press, 2006), p. 109.

462 Ibid.

463 Abu Bukhari, *Hadith*, vol. 4, book 55, no. 511.

464 Ibid.

465 Muslim, quoted in Nydell, p110.

466   Bukhari, vol. 4, book 55, no. 511.

467   Al-Tirmidhi, vol. 2, no. 513.

468   Imam Muslim, p. 111.

469   Bukhari, vol. 4, book 55, no. 512.

470   Muslim, p. 110.

471   Bukhari, vol. 4, book 55, no. 529.

472   Al-Sabiq, quoted in Cleary, p. 240. Al-Sabiq Tihami (born 1915) is an Egyptian scholar and collector of Hadith literature.

473   Hurayra, vol. 3, no. 572.

474   Muslim, p. 112.

475   Ibn Hibbon, quoted in Cleary, p. 234. Ibn Hibbon, who died in 965, was a Muslim scholar and historian. He was known as the Sheikh of Khorasan.

476   Bukhari, vol. 4, book 55, no. 531.

477   Abu Muslim, *Aphorisms*, no. 614. The editions of Muslim's *Hadith* and *Aphorisms* used in Chapter Six are those published in Riyadh in 2007 in seven volumes by Dar-us-Salam Publications. This company was established by Abdul Malik Mujahid in the 1990s. They have offices in several other countries, including the UK and the US.

478   Ibid., no. 598.

479   Muslim, p. 111.

480   Ibid.

481   Ibid.

482   Ibid.

483   Ibid.

484   Stephen Vicchio, *Biblical Figures in the Islamic Faith* (Eugene: Wipf and Stock, 2008).

485   Robert Hillenbrand, *Islamic Art and Architecture* (London: Thames and Husdon, 1998), p. 217.

486   Ibid.

487   Ibid., p. 218.

488   Ibid.

489   C. E. Bosworth (trans.), *The History of Al-Tabari*, vol. 13 (Albany: SUNY Press, 1991).

490   Hillenbrand, p. 218.

491   For more on the Baghdad School, see: *Mustahsiriya School* (Baghdad: Department of Antiquities, 1970).

492   *Kelileh va Demneh* (Tehran: Thura Eqval, 2005).

493   Ekrem Ayverdi, *The Tulip in the 18th Century* (Istabul: Kubbewliti, 2006).

494   R. W. Maqsood, *Islam* (London: Hodder Publications, 1993), p. 33.

495   Ibid., p. 34.

496   Katy Kianush, A Brief History of Persian Miniatures, http://bit.ly/2xbjDzg.

497   Ibid.

498   Ibid.

499   Ibid.

500   Ibid.

501   Wijdan Ali, *The Arab Contribution to Islamic Art* (Cairo: American University in Cairo, 1999), p. 262.

502   S. Rappaport, *History of Egypt* (London: Grolier, 1904.), p. 362.

503   Ibid.

504   Ibid.

505   Ibid.

506   "The History of Muhammad," National Library of France, Paris, ca. 1030.

507   *The World in Miniature* (London: Adamany Media, 2001), p. 164.

508   Rashid Al-Din, *The History of the World: A Compendium of Chronicles* (London: Nour Foundation, 1995).

509   Ibid.

510   Ibid.

511   Ibid.

512   *Hamshari* is a daily newspaper in Tehran. The controversy over images of Muhammad occurred in February of 2006.

513   *Muammad and Jibril*, ca. 1360. Topkapi Museum, Istanbul.

514   *Ridwan and Muhammad* (late fourteenth century), Topkapi Museum, Istanbul.

515   *Muhammad on Buraq* (fifteenth century), National Library of France, Paris.

516   Rashid Al-Din, p. 111.

517   *The World in Miniature*, p. 165.

518   Ibid., p. 166.

519   Ibid.

520   *Muhammad Suspended in the Air* (fifteenth century), Nassar Khalili Collection, London.

521   *The World in Miniature*, p. 168.

522   Ibid.

523   Ibid., p. 170.

524   *The Miraj Name* (fifteenth century), National Library of France, Paris. Also see: Nerina Rustomji, *The Garden and the Fire* (New York: Columbia University Press, 2008), p. 141.

525   For more on the *Great Mosque of Damascus*, see: Finbar Barry Flood, ed., *The Great Mosque of Damascus* (Leiden: Brill, 2001).

526   For more on the Qasar Amra Site, see: Kami Khourni, "Qasae Amra," in *Saudi Aramco World* (September–October, 1990).

527   *Night Journey* (fifteenth century), Topkapi Museum, Istanbul.

528   Rustomji, p. 142.

529   Ibid., p. 143.

530   Ibid., p. 145.

531   Ibid., p. 146.

532   Ibid.

533   Ibid.

534   Ibid., p. 68.

535   Zeren Tanindi, *Sier-i-Nebi* (Istanbul: Hurriyet, 1984), p. 67.

536   Ibid.

537   Ibid.

538   *Flying Jibril*, ca. 1595. Topkapi Museum, Istanbul.

539   *The Epitome of Historical Works*, 1583. Museum of Turkish and Islamic Art, Istanbul.

540   Ibid.

541   Ibid.

542   Ibid.

543   Miniature painted in Herat around 1520 by Sultan Muhammad, illustrating a couplet of Hafiz (Harvard Art Museum and the Metropolitan Museum of Art).

544   *Adam and Eve Expelled From the Garden*, University Library of Jerusalem (MS. Ar. 1115).

545   *Yusuf Saved From the Well*, Nenkaim Collection, Los Angeles. (MS. 435).

546   *The Delegation of Angels sent by Queen of Sheba*, Persian Ms. 1570. See: p. 110 of Na'ama Brosh, *Biblical Stories in Islamic Painting* (Jerusalem: Israel Museum, 1991).

547   *Solomon Receiving the Queen of Sheba*, in Brosh, p. 111.

548   *Queen of Sheba and Solomon*, in Brosh, p. 115.

549   MS. H1225, Topkapi Museum (fol. 3b and 4a).

550   MS. H1228, Topkapi Museum (fol. 3b).

551   MS. 85. 237.38. Getty Museum, Los Angeles.

552   MS. Diez A. (fol. 13b). Staatsbibliothek, Berlin.

553   *Hadiqat Al Su'ada* by Faludi, Turk ve Islam Eserleri Museum, Istanbul.

554   *The Miraj*, seventeenth-century Turkish manuscript, University of Jerusalem.

555   *Two Houris*, eighteenth-century Turkish manuscript, Topkapi Museum, Istanbul.

556   *Muhammad Flying Over the City of Mecca*, Turkish manuscript, Topkapi Museum, Istanbul.

557   *The Prophet at Al-Noor*, eighteenth-century Turkish manuscript, Benkiam Collection, Los Angeles.

558   Giulia Ferrario, *Il Costume Antico e Modern Storia del Governo* (Rome, 1837).

559   Hillenbrand, p. 2.

560   "Muhammad at the Battle of Badr," *Siyer-i-Nebi* (Istanbul, 1595), Topkapi Museum.

561   "The Birth of Muhammad," *Siyer-i-Nebi* (Istanbul, 1595), Topkapi Museum.

562   Ibid., p. 198.

563   Ibid.

564   Ibid.

565   Ibid.

566   Ibid.

567   Ibid.

568   Ibid.

569   Ibid.

570   Ibid.

571   Mikhail Vrubel, "Six-Winged Seraphs: Azrael" (1904).

572   Evelyn De Morgan, *Angel of Death* (1890).

573   Evelyn De Morgan, *The Field of the Slain* (1916).

574   Amaya Kouyoon, "The Angel of Death" (2012)..

575   The Holy Qur'an, 88:12–23 (author's translation).

576   Sixteenth-century Persian carpet, Austrian Museum of Art and Industry, Vienna, Austria.

577   Seventeenth-century Persian carpet, Austrian Museum of Art and Indudstry.

578   Sixteenth-century Turkish carpet, Residenz Museum, Munich, Germany.

579   Sixteenth–seventeenth-century Turkish carpet, Berlin Museum.

580   R. H. W. Empson, *The Cult of the Peacock Angel* (London: Ams Pr. Inc., 2009).

581   Ibid.

582   Ibid.

583   Ibid.

584   D. B. MacDonald, "Djinn," *Encyclopedia of Islam*, vol. 2 (Leiden: Brill, 1983), pp. 546–550.

585   Ibid., p. 257.

586   Ibid.

587   Ibid.

588   *Langenscheidt New Stanford Dictionary: Turkish to English* (London: Langenscheidt Publishers, 2005).

589   The Holy Qur'an, 37:158.

590 Thomas Lippman, *Understanding Islam* (New York: Plume Books, n.d.), p. 7.

591 Ibid.

592 Ron Geaves, *Key Words in Islam* (London: Bloomsbury Academics, 2006), p. 60.

593 Ruqalayyah Waris Maqsood, *Teach Yorself Islam* (London: Teach Yourself World Faiths Series, 1996), p. 111.

594 John Kaltner, *Islam: What Non-Muslims Should Know* (Minneapolis: Fortress Press, 2016), p. 81.

595 At Tahawi, *Tahawiyyah* (London: T. M. Kiani, 2012), p. 9.

596 Abu Buhaqi and At-Tabarani, *Hadith* (Louvain: Orientalia Louvaniensia Analecta, 2012), p. 181.

597 The Holy Qur'an 72:1–2.

598 Ibid., 46:29.

599 Ibid., 55:15.

600 Ibid., 15:26–27.

601 Ibid., 114:1–6.

602 Ibid., 6:128.

603 Ibid., 6:112.

604 Ibid., 72:6–7.

605 Ibid., 72:14–15.

606 Ibid., 6:100.

607 Ibid., 6:128.

608 Ibid., 7:38.

609 Ibid., 46:18–19.

610 Ibid., 55:23.

611 Ibid.

612 Ibid., 55:56.

613 Ibid., 7:179.

614 Ibid., 51:56–57.

615 Ibid., 55:44–45.

616 Yuduf Ibn Abdul Barr, *The World of Jinn and Devils* (Karachi: Ur Ulam Books, 1997), p. 199.

617 Abu Muslim, *Hadith* (New York: Create Space, 2017), p. 118.

618 Abu Bukhari, *Hadith*, edited by M. A. Khan (Karachi: Kazi Publications, 1995), p. 834.

619 At Tirmidhi, *Explanation of Hadith by Muhammad At-Tirmidhi* (Karachi: Muktabatulirsand Publications, 2016), p. 21.

620 Ibid.

621 Ibid., p. 23.

622 Ibid.

623 Abu Dawood, *Sunan Abu Dawood* (London: Avenue Islam, 1993), p. 117.

624 *Al-Muwatta* (Islamabad: Islam Digital Services, 2017), p. 1009.

625 Dawood, p. 118.

626 Ibn Taymiyyah, *Essay on the Jinn* (London: International Islamic Publishing House, 1996), p. 61.

627 Muslim, p. 119.

628 Taymiyyah, p. 63.

629 Muslim, p. 120.

630 Bukhari, p. 835.

631 Tirmidhi, p. 22.

632 Ibn Abbas, *Tafsir Ibn Abbas* (Paris: Fons Vitae, 2008), p. 777.

633 Bukhari, p. 839.

634 Ibn Ma'sud, *La Voie et La Loi* (Paris: Actes Sud, 1870), p. 214.

635 The Holy Qur'an 38:40 (author's translation).

636 Ibid., 21:17.

637 Song of Songs, 5:16 (RSV).

638 The Holy Qur'an 27:38–42 (author's translation).

639 First Kings 5:13 (RSV).

640 First Chronicles 29:23 (RSV).

641 Richard Burton, *One Thousand and One Nights* (Norwalk: Easton Press, 1994).

642 Ibid., vol. 3, p. 225.

643 Ibid., vol. 1, p. 11.

644 Ibid.

645 The Holy Qur'an 27:39.

646 Burton, vol. 1, p. 34.

647 Burton, vol. 1, p. 55.

648 Ibid.

649 Ibid., vol. 3, p. 33.

650 Second Timothy 3:8 (RSV).

651 *The Apocryphon of Jannes and Jambres, Magicians*. Gk. inv. 29456 and 25828, Chester Beatty Museum, Dublin.

652 Burton.

653 Ibid., vol. 3, p. 225.

654 See the entry on "Jan Ibn Jan" in *Demopedia Wiki*. Also see: Sabine Baring Gould, *Legends of Old Testament Characters* (New York: Macmillan, 1871), vol. 1, p. 97. Forgotten Books has recently reissued Gould's volumes.

655   Burton, vol. 1, p. 11.

656   Ibid., Night 48.

657   Ibid., Nights 5 and 34.

658   Ibid., Night 47.

659   Ibid., Night 538.

660   Ibid.

661   Ibid., "Alladin and His Lamp."

662   Ibid., "Sinbad, the Sailor."

663   author's translation.

664   See Note 626.

665   Taymiyyah, p. 62.

666   Ibid.

667   Ibid.

668   Ibid., p. 65.

669   Ibid.

670   Al-Toukai, *Red Magic* (Cairo: Ishtar Publications, 2010), p. 117.

671   Ibid.

672   Ibid., p. 118.

673   Ibid., p. 120.

674   Nerina Rustomji, *The Garden and the Fire* (New York: Columbia University Press, 2009), p. 3.

675   Ibid.

676   Ibid., p. 4.

677   "Inspirational Stories From the Lives of the Awilya Allah," www.ummah.com.

678   Ibid.

679   Ibid.

680   Michael Sells, *Early Islamic Mysticism* (Mahwah, New Jersey: Paulist Press, 1995).

681   Compare the Qur'an's 2:34, 15:28–31, 20:116 and 38:71–74 with Surah 18:50.

682   Arthur Cotterell, *Norse Mythology* (London: Anness Publishing, 1999), pp. 9–10. *Nidhogg* is a dragon-serpent who gnaws at the root of the world tree, or *Ydddrasil*, an enormous, mythical tree that connects the nine worlds in Norse mythology. This large tree is attested to in the *Poetic Edda*, a thirteenth-century work on early Norse mythology.

683   Ibid.

684   In classical Hebrew, the word *Satan* means "enemy" or "adversary." Often, it is used with the definite article, *ha*. *Ha Satan* is found thirteen times in the Hebrew Bible, in chapters one and two of Job, and two times in Zechariah

3:1–2. In ancient Hebrew, the *yetzer ha* refers to the "evil imagination" or "evil inclination" of the human heart. The term is drawn from the Hebrew phrase *yetzer lev-ha-adam ra*, or the "imagination of the heart of man is evil" that occurs twice in Genesis at 6:5 and 8:21.

685   The Semitic root BLS is also the source for *ablash* and *yublisu*, the verbs "to give up hope" and "to despair."

686   For more on Zoroastrianism, see: Jenny Ross, *Zoroastrianism: An Introduction* (Delhi: I. B. Taurus, 2011), and John W. Waterhouse, *Zoroastrianism* (London: Book Tree, 2006). For more on Manicheanism, see: Duncan Greeklees, *The Gospel of the Prophet Mani* (London: Book Tree, 2007), and Michel Tardieu, *Manicheanism* (Chicago: University of Illinois Press, 2009).

687   See Ross, pp. 112–119.

688   A. A. Mawdudi, *Islam in the Age of Ignorance* (Cambridge: Cambridge University Press, 1992). Also see: Sayyid Qutb, *Milestones* (Cairo: Mother Mosque Foundation, 1981). A. A. Mawdudi (1903–1979) was a Muslim philosopher, jurist, journalist and imam. Most of his books were written in Urdu. Sayyid Qutb (1906–1966) was a Sunni Muslim author, educator, poet and early leader of the Muslim Brotherhood in Egypt.

689   Hasan Al-Basri (642–728) was a companion of the Prophet Muhammad. He was a brilliant orator. Many of his letters are extant.

690   The Holy Qur'an 4:120 (author's translation).

691   Ibid., 23:97–98.

692   Ibid., 6:142.

693   Ibid., 2:168.

694   Ibid., 24:21.

695   Ibid., 17:64.

696   Ibid., 35:6–7.

697   Ibid., 24:21.

698   Ibid., 7:179.

699   Ibid., 17:62.

700   Ibid., 4:120.

701   Ibid., 3:175.

702   Ibid.

703   Sahih Muslim, *Hadith*, vol. 4, book 2, no. 2174.

704   Ibid.

705   Ibid., vol. 2, book 22, no. 5405.

706   Hurayra, vol. 8, book 73, no. 242.

707   Muslim, vol. 4, Book 2, no. 238.

708   Abu Hurayra, *Hadith*, vol. 4, book 54, no. 491.

709   Hurayra, vol. 4, book 55, no. 641.

710   Ibid.

711   Ibid., vol. 2, book 22, no. 301.

712   Ibid., vol. 4, book 54, no. 522.

713   Ibn Abbas, *Hadith*, no. 431.

714   Abu Qaraba, *Hadith*, vol. 4, book 54, no. 513. Nizam Al-Qaraba was a Moroccan scholar of Shariah and Islamic Fiqh, or Law.

715   Azazil was one of the Jinn who was brought to heaven just after the time when Iblis arrived there. In heaven, Allah instructed Azazil to go to Earth and to fight the non-believers. Afterwards, Azazil was said to have prayed so hard in the first heaven that he was raised to the second, and this continued in this process until he arrived at the seventh heaven.

716   Muslim, vol. 4, book 2, no. 2924.

717   Ibid., no. 2925.

718   Abu Al-Qayyim, *Hadith*, vol. 1. no. 33. Al-Qayyim Al-Jawziyya (1292–1350) was a Syrian, Sunni Muslim scholar, born in Harran and never married. He was known for his expertise in Islamic law, theology and science of the prophets and devoted his life to learning. He was also a student of Ibn Taymiyyah (1263–1328).

719   Ismail Haqqat (1652–1725) was a Turkish scholar of the Qur'an and Hadith literature.

720   Ibn Taymiyyah's discussion of this matter may be found in Shabal Ahmed, *Ibn Taymiyyah* (Oxford: Oxford University Press, 2015), pp. 253–255.

721   The Holy Qur'an 18:50 (author's translation).

722   Ibid.

723   Rashas Khalifa (1935–1990) was an Egyptian-American biochemist and Qur'an scholar and translator. He was assassinated in Tucson, Arizona.

724   Ibid.

725   Ali Pasha Al-Mubarak (1823–1893), as an Egyptian, Sunni scholar, he studied in Paris. Later, he was an influential thinker in the reconstruction of Cairo after World War II. Ibn Harun Al-Hamadani (893–945), was an Arab geographer, chemist, poet and scholar.

726   Muhammad Asad (1900–1992) was a Jewish-born Austro-Hungarian, linguist and scholar of Al-Qur'an. He converted to Islam in 1926. His translation of Al-Qur'an was published in 1980.

727   Ibn Abbas, *Hadith*, vol. 2, no. 141.

728   Muslim, vol. 4, book 2, no. 2869.

729 Hasan Al-Basri, no. 39.

730 Ibn Kathir, *Tafsir*, ten volumes (Lahore: Dar-Us-Salam Publications, 2000), vol. 2, p. 199. Ibn Kathir (1300–1373) was an expert on interpreting Al-Qur'an. He also was a historian and expert on Islamic law.

731 Ibn Arabi (1165–1240) was a Muslim spiritual leader from Moorish Spain.

732 Al-Hallaj (858–922) was born in the Fars province of Persia. He was a Muslim teacher, writer and Sufi poet.

733 Ibid.

734 Ibid.

735 Abdalluh, "Hallaj, the Devil, and the Proximity of Distance," www. muslimforjesus.org.

736 Ab Al-Karim Al-Jili (1365–?) was an Indian, Muslim scholar born near Calcutta. His family moved to Yemen when he was young. Later, he became a Muslim scholar and mystic. His most famous work is *The Universal Man*. It is said that Al-Jili was a descendant of Sait Gilani, the founder of an order of Sufi dervishes.

737 Al-Hallaj, *Tafsir Iblis*.

738 Al Ghazali, "Shaytan's Ways to the Heart." Ghazali (1056–1111) was one of the great Medieval, Muslim philosophers.

739 Jalaj Al-Din Muhammad Rumi, *Mathnawi*, book 2, sections 2706–2743. Rumi (1207–1273) was born in Afghanistan and was the greatest of Muslim poets.

740 Ibid., section 2730.

741 Ibid., sections 2740–2743.

742 Al-Tabari, *Al-Hilyah*, vol. 3, p. 188. Al-Tabari (839–923) was a great Persian historian and exegete of Al-Qur'an.

743 The Holy Qur'an, Surah 1:1–7.

744 Ibn Taymiyyah, *Essay on the Jinn* (Baghdad: LIPH, 2010).

745 Ibid., p. 31.

746 Ibn Taymiyyah, *The Devil's Deceptions*. This text is also called *The Criterion Between the Allies of the Most Merciful and the Allies of the Devil* (Birmingham: Idara Books, 1993), p. 26.

747 Ibid.

748 Ibid., p. 31.

749 Ibid.

750 Al-Hallaj, p. 88.

751 Ibid.

752 Ibid.

753 Javad Nurbakhsh, *Hadith*, no. 37.

754   Al-Hallaj, p. 92.

755   The forbidden fruit narrative in the Hebrew Bible is found at Genesis 2:16–17. The Hebrew word for the fruit is *pari*. In the history of Judaism, it has been identified as a grape, apple, pear, mushroom, quince, wheat and pomegranate. The forbidden tree in Al-Qur'an at Surah seven, ayat 19, is called the "Tree of *Zulimun*" or "Wrong-doers." Surah 14:26 describes the forbidden tree as "being unfit for eating or guidance."

756   Al-Hallaj, p. 100.

757   Abu Ishaq Al-Israfahinni (949–1027) was a Medieval Sunni scholar and commentator of Al-Qur'an.

758   For more on the figure of Al-Dajjal, see: Stephen Vicchio, "The Antichrist in Islamic Thought," in *The Legend of the Antichrist* (Eugene: Wipf and Stock, 2009).

759   For more on Job in Islam, see: Stephen Vicchio, "The Image of Ayyub/Job in the Qur'an and later Islam," *Bible Interpretation* (August, 2005), pp. 1–8.

760   Ibn Asakir, *Hadith*, no. 17. Asakir (1106–1175) was a Syrian-born Sunni historian and mystic; one of the greatest Muslim teachers of the Middle Ages.

761   Asakir, *Hadith*, no. 18.

762   Ibid., no. 19.

763   "Six Articles of Faith," *www.religionfacts.com/six-articles-faith*. These six articles of faith include belief in: The Oneness of Allah, the angels, the Holy Books of Allah, the Prophets, the Day of Judgment, and the Supremacy of Allah's Will.

764   The Arabic words *Malak*, *Mala'ika* and *Malakayn* appear in the following places in Al-Qur'an: Surah 2:30, 31, 34, 98, 102, 161, 177, 210, 248 and 285; Surah 3:18, 39, 42, 45, 80, 87, 124 and 125; Surah 4:97, 136, 166 and 172; Surah 6:8, 9, 50, 111 and 158; Surah 7:11 and 20; Surah 8:9, 12 and 50; Surah 11:12 and 31; Surah 12:31; Surah 13:13 and 23; Surah 15:7, 8, 28 and 30; Surah 16:2, 28, 32,33 and 49; Surah 17:40, 61, 90, 91 and 95; Surah 18:50; Surah 20:116; Surah 21:103; Surah 22:75; Surah 23:24; Surah 25:7, 21, 22 and 25; Surah 32:11; Surah 33:43 and 56; Surah 34:40; Surah 35:1; Surah 37:8 and 150; Surah 38:69, 71 and 73; Surah 39:75; 41:14 and 30; Surah 42:5; Surah 43:19, 53 and 60; Surah 47:27; Surah 53:26 and 27; Surah 66:4; Surah 69:17; Surah 70:4; Surah 74:31; Surah 78:38; Surah 89:22; and Surah 97:4. Of these references, the plural *Mala'ika* is used ninety times; the dual form, *Mala'kayn* is used twice; and the singular, *Malak* is employed eight times in the Holy Book.

765   The Holy Qur'an, 42:5. The same wording also appears at the Holy Book's Surah 40, ayat seven.

766   The Holy Qur'an 4:171.

767   The Holy Qur'an 5:116.

768   Al-Kisai (737–809) was an Al-Qur'an and Hadith scholar born in the city of Kufa.

769   In Arabic, the "Lote Tree" is called *Sidtat Al-Muntaha*. It marks the end of the Seventh Heaven. Discussed at the Holy Book's Surah 53:10–18.

770   Ibid., 53:10–18.

771   The classical Hebrew term *Qodesh* means "Holy," so the *Qodesim* means the "Holy Ones." These words are employed at Exodus 3:5; 12:16; 15:11 and 13; 16:23; 22:31; and the noun form at Psalm 34:9; Leviticus 4:3, and vv. 13–14.

772   For more on the *Kiraman Katibin*, see *The Koran* (50th anniversary edition) (London: Penguin Books, 2007), pp. 455–457.

773   For more on *Munkar* and *Nakir* in Islam, see: Shaykh Abdul-Hamid Kishk, *Munkar and Nakir*, http://www.kalamullah.com/books.html; and Ulrike Al-Khamis, "The Iconography of Early Islamic Lusterware From Mesopotamia: New Considerations," *Muqarnas*, vol. 7 (1990), pp. 109–118.

774   Ibid. Mufti Muhammad Ibn Adam al-Kawthari, in an essay called, "When Does the Soul Enter the Fetus?" suggests that the soul enters the fetus at about 120 days, or four months after conception. He also speaks of the angels responsible for conception in Islam. See: https://bit.ly/2yCAYC1.

775   The *Al-Karubiyyin* are not mentioned by name in either Al-Qur'an or in Hadith. Surah 40:8 does, however, speak of the "angels who carry the Throne." The Holy Book's Surah 69:17–18 also speaks of the "*Mala'ika* who will bear the Throne" on the Day of Judgment. According to Hadith literature, the seven levels of Paradise are *Al-Firdaws, Dar al-Maqama, Dar as-Salam, Dar Al-Akhirai, Al-Jannah, Al-Jannat Al-And* and *Al-Jannat Al-Khuld.*

776   Mufti Waseem Khan, "Stages and Gates of Paradise," http://www.theislamicnetwork.org/.

777   Whitney Hopler, "archangels Seraphiel," https://bit.ly/2Vb6RJu.

778   Henry Corbin, *Spiritual Body and Celestial Earth* (Princeton: Princeton University Press, 1977), pp. 3–16.

779   Ibid. In a fatwa written by Jumaadaa Al-Aakhit, he describes the seven levels of Paradise. *Al-Firdaws* is the highest of those levels. Anas Ibn Malik, Abu Bukhari, and Muhammad's wife, Aisha, all agree that *Al-Firdaws* is the highest level of *Jannah*, or "Paradise." But Abu Hurayra and Ibn Tabarani both contend it is a place called *Al-Waseelah*. At any rate, two Arabic words are employed to speak of one's station or status in Paradise. The first is *manaazil* that means "status" or "position." The other term is *Darajaat*, which means "degree" or "level" of Paradise.

780 See Surah 40:8 and 69:17–18.

781 Thomas Aquinas, *Summa Theologica* (Westminster: Christian Classics, 1981), vol. 1, question 51, articles 1, 2, and 3. Also see: questions 52 to 64 and 106 to 114, particularly question 108. For example, the Hebrew *Mot* and the Syriac and Aramaic, *mata*, the verb "to die." This MWT root is used 51 times in the Book of Ezekiel alone, particularly chapter 37.

782 Also see, for examples, Second Samuel 24:15, Second Kings 19:35, Exodus 12:23 and 29, and the ninth chapter of the Book of Revelation.

783 See, for example, Ned. 49a, Ber. 4b, and Hul. 7b.

784 Anwar Awlaki (1971–2011) was an American-Yemini scholar killed in a drone strike by the American forces.

785 Dov Noy (1920–2013) was a Ukrainian Jew who converted to Islam and became a prominent Hadith scholar.

786 Sulayman Al-Tabarani (873–971) was one of the greatest Hadith scholars of his age. See the article on him by Maribel Fierro, *Encyclopedia of Islam* (Leiden: Brill, 2000), vol. 10, p. 10.

787 For more in Malik and Ridwan, see: Miguel Asin Palacios, *The Mystical Philosophy of Ibn Masarra* (Leiden: Brill, 1978), pp. 78–80.

788 Ibn Al-Qayyim Al-Jawziyya (691–751) was a Sunni Hadith scholar, born in a small farming village near Damascus.

789 The Arabic word *Barzakh* was originally a Persian word meaning "barrier" or "partition." In Muslim eschatology, it is viewed as a barrier between the physical world and the spiritual world. Al-Ghazali, Al-Zamakhshari and Abdullah Yusuf Ali all comment on the state of Barzakh. Al-Ghazali calls in an "intermediary state." Al-Zamakhshari comments on Barzakh in relation to explicating the Holy Book's Surah 25:53; Abdullah Yusul Ali calls Barzakh as a "quiescent state" where the soul rests until the Day of the Resurrection, or *Yawm al-Qiyamah*.

790 Jane Smith and Y. Y. Haddad, *Muslim Understanding of Death and Resurrection* (Oxford: Oxford University Press, 2002), p. 139.

791 Also see: The Holy Book's: 30:21–27, 40:8, 44:54, 52:20, 55:72 and 56:22.

792 The Arabic expression *Ahl Al-Kitab* means "People of the Book." It is employed in Islam to refer to religious traditions in the Middle East who have written scriptures including Judaism, Christianity, Islam and Zoroastrianism.

793 Although Muhammad Abu Wardeh frequently has been quoted as someone "who recruited terrorist bombers in Israel," there is no independent proof of the fact. In fact, some Muslim scholars quote him in that regard, while having doubts that it is true. See: N. C. Asthane, *Urban Terrorism: Myth and Reality* (Jaipur: Pointer Publishers, 2009), pp. 33–35.

794   Daniel Butler, *The First Jihad: The Battle of Khartoum and the Dawn of Militant Islam* (Philadelphia: Casemate Publishers, 2007).

795   Ibn Kathir, "Wives of the Prophet Muhammad," www.islamawareness.net.

796   For more on Ephrem the Syrian, see: Sebastian Brock, *Ephrem the Syrian* (Yonkers, New York: Saint Vladimir's Press, 1997). Also see: Sebatian Brock, *The Luminous Eye* (Collegeville, Minnesota: Cistercian Publications, 1992).

797   Many of these discussions in historical, as well as contemporary Islam, is whether we should interpret Hadith literature by the aid of the concept known as *Qiyas*, a word that means "Allegory" or "metaphor."

798   Ibid.

799   For more on *Moakibat*, see: Matthew Bunson, *Angels: A to Z* (New York: Three Rivers Press, 1996), p. 247 under "recording angels."

800   The *Siyer-i-Nebi* is a Turkish "Life of the Prophet Muhammad." It was completed by Mustafa Ibn Yusuf of Erzurum, known as Al-Darir, a Mevlevi Dervish. The text is based on a thirteenth-century work by Muhammad Al-Barri.

801   For more on Islamic carpets, see: Walter Denny, *How to Read Islamic Carpets* (New York: Metropolitan Museum of Art, 2015); and Joseph V. McMullan, *Islamic Carpets* (London: Near-Eastern Arts and Recreation Center, 1965).

802   Javier Teixidor, *The Pantheon of Palmyra* (Leiden: Brill, 1979), pp. 77–78.

803   Ibid., p. 78.

804   For more on the *Marid*, see: Hans Weir, *A Dictionary on Modern Arabic* (Ithica: Spoken Language Press, 1999), p. 903.

805   The *Eumenides*, when used as a plural in classical Greek, it is employed as a euphemism to stand for the "Furies." In Greek, the term means the "Kindly Ones," or the "Gracious Ones."

806   The version of Ibn Taymiyyah's "Essay on the Jinn" used in this study can be found at www.islamicawareness.net.

807   The version of the *Stories of Awliya* we have used in this chapter comes from www.Ummah.com/forum/.

808   Jalal Al-Din Rumi, *The Masnawi* (Oxford: Oxford Classics, 2008).

809   For more on general book about Iblis, see Whitney S, Bodman, *The Poetics of Iblis* (Cambridge: Harvard Divinity School Press, 2011), and Iman Ibn Jawzi, *The Devil's Deceptions* (Karachi: Dar Us Sunnah, 2014).

810   Muhammad Al-Tabari (839–923) was a Persian scholar, historian and exegete of Al-Qur'an and Hadith. He was born in the town of Amal in contemporary Iran.

811   Abd Al-Karim Al-Jill (1365–1403) was an Iraqi-born Muslim Sufi mystic and philosopher.

About the Author

Before his retirement in 2016, Stephen Vicchio taught for more than forty years at the University of Maryland, Johns Hopkins, St. Mary's Seminary in Baltimore, and other universities in Britain and the United States. He has authored over two dozen books, as well as essays and plays, mostly about the Bible, philosophy and theology. Among his books since 2000 is his interpretation of the Book of Job, *The Antichrist: A History*; *Biblical Figures in the Islamic Faith*, and books about the religions of American presidents George Washington, Thomas Jefferson, Abraham Lincoln, and the forthcoming *Ronald Reagan's Religious Beliefs*.

Printed in Great Britain
by Amazon